The Innovator's Field Guide

The Innovator's Field Guide
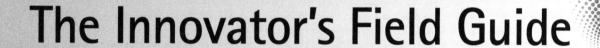

Market-Tested Methods and Frameworks to Help You Meet Your Innovation Challenges

Peter Skarzynski and David Crosswhite

JB JOSSEY-BASS™

A Wiley Brand

Published by Jossey-Bass

A Wiley Brand

One Montgomery Street, Suite 1200, San Francisco, CA 94104-4594—www.josseybass.com

Jossey-Bass books and products are available through most bookstores. To contact Jossey-Bass directly call our Customer Care Department within the U.S. at 800-956-7739, outside the U.S. at 317-572-3986, or fax 317-572-4002.

Wiley publishes in a variety of print and electronic formats and by print-on-demand. Some material included with standard print versions of this book may not be included in e-books or in print-on-demand. If this book refers to media such as a CD or DVD that is not included in the version you purchased, you may download this material at http://booksupport.wiley.com. For more information about Wiley products, visit www.wiley.com.

Library of Congress Cataloging-in-Publication Data

Skarzynski, Peter.

    The innovator's field guide : market-tested methods and frameworks to help you meet your innovation challenges / Peter Skarzynski and David Crosswhite. —First edition.

      1 online resource.

    Includes index.

      Description based on print version record and CIP data provided by publisher; resource not viewed.

    ISBN 978-1-118-64457-7 (pdf) — ISBN 978-1-118-64439-3 (epub) — ISBN 978-1-118-64430-0 (pbk.)

  1. Technological innovations—Management.   2. Creative ability in business.   3. New products.   I. Crosswhite, David, 1961- II. Title.

    HD45

    658.4′063—dc23

2013049114

Printed in the United States of America

FIRST EDITION

PB Printing   10 9 8 7 6 5 4 3 2 1

Contents

Contents

*To the clients we served over the past two decades, thank you
for your trust, inspiration, and tireless efforts to keep each of your
organizations vital through strategic innovation.*

*And to our families, thank you for your support through it all.
Your patient support helps us create the future with
others—thank you for creating it for us.*

The Innovator's Field Guide

Setting Context

You know that innovation is a top priority. Chances are that you are or have been on an innovation team or leading one within your organization.

You have a difficult job. We know this from over twenty-five years of helping others design, implement, and capture value from innovation. We've done this as consultants and practitioners in large, globally dispersed organizations and in small and midsize companies, B2B and B2C settings, and in both for-profit and nonprofit environments.

We are passionate about innovation because we have seen how it keeps organizations vital and resilient. We want your organization to stay vital and resilient: resilient to the tremendously powerful market forces of globalization, rapid shifts in technology, and an increasingly powerful customer base.

About This Field Guide

There is no lack of innovation books. Many focus on an overarching theory of innovation or focus more deeply on a particular aspect of innovation, such as rapid-cycle experimentation, design thinking, or business model innovation. At the same time, more and more organizations are following the pioneering efforts of companies like Whirlpool Corporation, General Electric, and Proctor & Gamble in viewing innovation as a discipline and process that can be taught, learned, and applied.

As we meet and work with these and other innovation leaders and practitioners globally, we hear consistently that there is not yet a comprehensive, practical, how-to guide detailing market-tested techniques, tools, and frameworks through which you can address the most pressing innovation challenges in your organization. This field guide addresses those challenges in an end-to-end fashion, helping you take action, whether you seek a specific solution, such as de-risking a promising but new-to-the-industry business concept, or you have an ambition to make innovation an enterprise-wide capability.

We write this field guide for innovation leaders and practitioners in organizations large and small who seek step-change improvement in their organization's, teams', or individual innovation efforts. Each of you faces different innovation challenges. Our goal is to provide practical techniques, guidance, and examples to help you navigate your unique situation. We hope that whether you are a novice or a master, you will find The Guide indispensable in helping you achieve your innovation goals.

There is great value in having a shared set of tools within your organization. Common tools, techniques, and frameworks help ensure consistency and can serve as a foundation for an enterprise-wide process for innovation. Yet it is important to understand that innovation is not about tools per se. You will not succeed by simply filling in a given tool. Rather, we see tools as scaffolding; they provide structure to achieve the appropriate organizational learning and dialogue about a particular issue or challenge.

Our approach to the topic of innovation is that of business managers and strategists. For over two decades, we have worked with Global 1000 companies to shape and act on their strategic growth agenda. You will see in The Guide that, rather than focusing on technology or a particular product, our innovation work features the business model and its elements as the unit of analysis. We also place enormous emphasis on both fact-based analysis and frame-breaking perspectives.

You will also see we consistently emphasize the importance of creating time and space for innovation inside your organization. By this we mean more than the notion "spend X percent of your time on anything you want" as *the means* by which to innovate at scale. In most organizations, declaring that all engineers should take X percent of their time to think of new things and innovate is simply a nonstarter, and rightfully so.

Instead we recommend that you free up time and space to pursue thoughtful and disciplined approaches and make organizing actions to allow your organization to create and drive innovation. You should, for example, build a point of view that informs your innovation. You must take time to stretch, elaborate, and iterate a given new concept. Leadership should make time to take on the roles of cocreator, sponsor, and visible advocate for innovation. And, together with leadership, you and your innovation colleagues should organize to sustainably pursue your innovation ambition. In this context, creating space to drive innovation is more than freeing up time to think great thoughts and experiment on them. It is a critical enabler to pursuing innovation in a disciplined fashion, leveraging innovation activities, approaches, and organizing elements such as those addressed in this guide.

Each chapter of this field guide focuses on an innovation challenge that consistently emerges as difficult and important within organizations across industries and geographies. In each chapter, we

Set context for the challenge and share the core design principles that should guide your efforts. The principles represent leading practices that are applicable across industries, geographies, and organizations large and small. They will help you stay focused on the outcome you are trying to achieve, allowing you to sift through alternative approaches with greater clarity and purpose.

Share techniques and frameworks that help you address the specific challenge. Most are illustrated with examples from organizations that have learned and applied the principles and achieved marketplace success.

This is the heart of *Innovator's Field Guide*: to share actionable innovation tools and approaches for you to apply, illustrated with real-world examples; and, where appropriate, to identify common pitfalls to avoid and offer specific counsel on what not to do.

● The Innovation Challenges

Raising Your Innovation IQ Through Insight-Driven Innovation (Chapter 2)

We begin by sharing techniques and frameworks you can use to develop new perspectives and new thinking about the market, your organization, and your stakeholders. The chapter offers concrete actions for developing frame-breaking insights that are foundational to success throughout a generalized front-end innovation process.

Breaking frame is so important to innovation. Gifted entrepreneurs break frame naturally. The rest of us need a bit of help. We need new perspectives and fresh insights to think and see differently. Most organizations struggle to develop rich, compelling insights, but they are critical to innovating successfully. Without new perspectives, efforts tend toward the incremental or, worse, stall completely. This chapter will help you, your team, and your organization develop the types of insights you will need to raise your innovation IQ.[1]

Enabling Breakthrough Innovation (Chapter 3)

In this chapter, we continue sharing leading practices to apply within a generalized front end of the innovation process in order to drive breakthrough innovation. We start by illustrating some of our favorite techniques for developing new ideas. We also suggest an approach that will help you focus your innovation efforts on your most important strategic challenges, and you will learn techniques to help bring greater coherence to current

and future innovation efforts across your organization. All of this will help you stay away from the business of "one-off" innovation. You will see how Crayola, Royal Dutch Shell, UnitedHealth Group, and others identify and act on new white space opportunities, sustainably and profitably guided by dynamic innovation architecture.[2]

From Nascent Idea to Business Concept (Chapter 4)

Chapter Four focuses on the work of moving from a nascent idea to a business concept, helping you advance your thinking to create a more fully fleshed-out business concept and game plan for getting started. Without this work, you may never get beyond a pile of Post-it notes. We share a generalized process to illustrate key techniques, while emphasizing that each organization will need to develop its own tailored process.

Sometimes opportunities stall. So we suggest specific techniques to help you stretch, elaborate, and iterate your thinking about and framing of the opportunity so that you can unstick that opportunity. We also provide guidelines to help you decide why you may wish to kill it off entirely.

These and other techniques will help you jump-start innovation in your organization, regardless of where the idea came from. The chapter takes you up to the "commercialization" step of a given innovation process, an area that most innovation efforts too often ignore or take for granted. Taken together, Chapters Two through Four serve as a blueprint for breakthrough innovation across the front-end innovation process, enabling you to jump to the next S-curve and propel growth for your organization.

Propelling Fast Innovation (Chapter 5)

We understand that you may not always have the time to build the types of rich insights described in Chapter Two or to pursue breakthrough innovation as we describe in Chapter Three. Sometimes you are asked to "get innovation fast." In this chapter, we share a series of case examples which illustrate how you can improve the quality of your innovation portfolio for the near term—twelve to twenty-four months out. Through the examples we share ways in which you can combine techniques already described in The Guide to achieve "innovation fast"—whether infusing innovative thinking into your annual planning

process or in a workshop-based format. We touch on collaborative idea management, open innovation, innovation accelerators, and supplier and customer collaborations.

Experimentation and De-Risking (Chapter 6)

The kind of breakthrough innovation we discuss in Chapter Three is often new to an organization and sometimes new to its industry. When you surface something that is new with respect to your past experiences, an individual, a team, or management is likely to perceive a high degree of uncertainty and risk in the new concept or business model. In this chapter, we share market-tested techniques that help you separate risk from uncertainty. The approaches help you de-risk promising but uncertain opportunities and guide you in moving your efforts forward in smart and risk-managed ways.

Innovating While in Market (Chapter 7)

In this chapter, we extend current experimentation practice, describing ways in which you can turbocharge opportunities that are already in market and reshape them for greater success. For in-market opportunities that are falling short of their ambition, we describe techniques through which you can iteratively test, learn, and refine efforts so that you can get the new product or service heading in the right direction, and optimize the "upside." For opportunities that are performing as planned, you will learn how to infuse more innovation. You might think of this as "innovating while flying the plane."

Organizing for Innovation (Chapter 8)

We opened this book with the declaration that innovation is now a top priority across organizations globally. Yet despite innovation's higher profile, we find that many organizations struggle with how to best organize for innovation. Chapter Eight guides you through ways to think about organizing for innovation within the context of your objectives and culture. We speak to specific ways in which you can strengthen innovation muscle, improve processes, and dramatically improve your chances that innovation will happen "because of the system" rather than in spite of it. We hope that this chapter guides your efforts in making innovation an enterprise discipline, process, and capability within your organization.

Leading Innovation (Chapter 9)

Much of this field guide speaks to leading innovation efforts as a lead designer and practitioner, and assumes that you have some level of organizational permission for driving systematic innovation. In Chapter Nine, we speak specifically to the leader's role in innovation. We start at the point of leadership's recognition that innovation will provide the means to achieve a particular growth goal and, when desired, to help enable cultural change. We describe the leader's role in making innovation a reality both commercially and as a process and system within the organization. We also speak to how a practitioner with little or no formal accountability for innovation can lead innovation from within—an important topic when you do not have the full set of permissions or sponsorship necessary for success.

Getting Started (Chapter 10)

Chapter Ten helps you structure and begin your innovation efforts in ways that ensure success. We provide examples of program designs that you can use to tackle the challenges described in this guide, and conclude by sharing suggested profiles of skills and mind-sets you will want to include in your efforts as you get going.

Conclusion and Looking Ahead (Chapter 11)

We conclude by sharing a few general thoughts and suggestions on driving success in your innovation efforts and systems and posit a view on the next frontiers for innovation in large organizations.

● Principles of Innovation

Over the years, we've seen what works and what does not. In looking across these successes and failures, one can tease out a set of principles of successful innovation that hold true regardless of industry, constraints, or circumstance—principles that organizations apply to help them innovate and to do so systematically over time.

You will see that the principles advocate driving *strategic* innovation. In this context, we recommend that you enter the innovation room through the strategy door, so to speak. Aim innovation efforts at your most central growth issues and needs. Drive holistic, business-concept-level thinking and iteration.

Develop a shared point of view on what qualifies as innovation and what is most important to drive toward. Develop multi-level points of view of innovation targeting priority growth spaces and concepts within the spaces. Engage in strategic dialogue and decision making to ensure that there is shared and aligned leadership understanding and commitment. Each of these actions follows from the principles guiding strategic innovation and is central to your success.

Of course, in translating principles to action, your specific designs and approach will vary greatly. But the principles are centrally important. Therefore, we make them explicit here and throughout The Guide so that you will keep them top of mind. You should think of these principles as "why you are doing what you are doing."

+ *Articulate a clear definition of innovation for your organization* by defining what you are trying to achieve. Do you seek transformative, disruptive innovation? Is your goal to create profitable incremental and sustaining innovation? Might you have an ambition to shift mind-sets or change the culture incrementally or in a more substantial way?

Don't start with new ideas. Start with new insights.

Whatever your objective, you need to have a definition that you and your colleagues can use as a compass to guide your work and keep you focused on the outcomes you seek. We speak to this issue throughout the book, and most specifically in Chapter Eight.

+ ***Aim your efforts at the business concept*** so that you focus not just on the "what" of products but also the "who and how." A singular focus on "what" constrains you to the default thinking of "what" new product or service or "what" new technology you can commercialize into a new product or service. It's an appropriate focus, of course. However, you can expand your innovation potential greatly by also including "who and how."

By "who" we mean, Who is your target customer, and what is the value proposition you offer to him or her? "How" refers to how you go to market, your value proposition to the distribution channel(s), how you create and capture value, and how you create and sustain advantage. Chapter Four speaks most directly to the application of business concept techniques and frameworks.

+ ***Understand that innovation equals new learning.*** This is a big one. Think of it this way: if you have little to no new learning, then you have little to no chance of finding truly new innovation. You can gain this new learning in many ways, as described throughout this guide. We urge you to create the space to attain new learning and then to synthesize and process it for all the potential that it holds. Give yourself sufficient space to diverge in your learning, thinking, and ideation. Also ensure that you create sufficient space again to converge and synthesize down to the best learning and actions *for your organization*. In nearly all chapters, you will see techniques, approaches, and examples illustrating how to act on the principle of making space for acquiring and then processing new learning.

+ ***Earn the right to ideate through insight-driven innovation.*** Don't start with new ideas. Start with new insights, which help you develop new and different perspectives about your particular innovation challenge. New perspectives lead you to ask a different set of questions. New ideas should derive from new, relevant, frame-breaking insights—however you attain them. All leading practice demonstrates that when concepts are created in this way, they are much more likely to be breakthrough and compelling in the marketplace and for your organization. When they are not new insights, they are likely to be regenerations of the same old ideas—one reason that the work of innovation gets a bad rap. As Drucker, Hamel, and others suggest, new questions lead to new answers. Before trying to create new ideas, work on new perspectives. This principle is inherent in all the techniques described in The Guide, and is most directly addressed in Chapter Two.

+ *Focus on strategic innovation to avoid one-off efforts.* Too many innovation processes and work efforts look for silver-bullet insights and ideas. We suggest another path: strategic innovation through which you develop specific product and service concepts within the context of a coherent, compelling, longer-term view of a market space you will pursue over time. The longer-term view enables you to fill your pipeline with a related set of product and/or service concepts that you can bring to market over time. It gets you out of the business of having to restart your innovation efforts from scratch whenever you wish to refresh the pipeline. In Chapter Three we suggest such techniques to move beyond one-off innovation.

+ *Make the work of innovation not merely the generating of new ideas but an end-to-end process through to successful commercialization.* We like to define the work of innovation as that which ultimately enables a new idea to be successfully commercialized. Thinking of innovation in this end-to-end way drives the discipline of viewing innovation as more than just new idea generation. Indeed, the work of innovation spans from gaining new insights to generating new ideas to engaging in business planning and strategic planning to conducting in-market experimentation and garnering continuous learning for constant improvement of in-market offerings. This end-to-end definition enables you to achieve better results because it doesn't partition innovation off as an

We define innovation as a new idea, successfully commercialized.

ideas-only notion or a "front end of the process" concept. The chapters throughout The Guide describe all phases of innovation from insights to commercialization and even postlaunch actions that continue to work the innovation agenda.

+ ***Build innovation capability through a learn-by-doing approach.*** At all levels of the organization, learning new innovation techniques and approaches is best facilitated by applying the techniques to real problems or challenges. Classroom training and practice sessions have their purpose, but these alone will not create or embed skills and capability. You may want this to be a guided experience from the beginning. It is hard to learn to ride a bike when you are in a classroom talking about it; the same is true of learning to drive innovation within organizations that are geared to efficiently churn out their existing offerings. We share learning-by-doing techniques throughout The Guide.

+ ***Be systematic and systemic in your approach.*** Too many leaders and practitioners believe that one can either have a creative, innovative approach *or* have a planned and disciplined approach. The reality: disciplined, systematic innovation is not an oxymoron. You can enable and manage disciplined processes that drive innovation and provide the flexibility you need to make alterations as new learning dictates.

The key is to view the techniques and approaches as infinitely flexible—like LEGO blocks you can piece together in ways that are most productive for your objectives and constraints. You will need to develop design skills so that you can configure these LEGO blocks according to each circumstance, using the principles of innovation as guideposts.

Similarly, you can make appropriate organizational changes to enable innovation through adjustments to process, skills, and metrics so that your organization innovates because of the system rather than despite it, as we mentioned earlier. Organizing actions need to be thought through holistically and in an internally consistent and systemic manner if you seek to develop sustainable innovation capabilities. Systematic and systemic are two different things: you need both. Throughout the book, we offer techniques for systematic innovation. Systemic design of organizing levers is addressed in particular in Chapter Eight.

- ◆ **Embrace and apply open innovation** (OI), keeping in mind Henry Chesbrough's dictum that "to be open externally one must first be open internally."[3] Throughout The Guide, we suggest techniques through which you and your colleagues can become more open internally by exploring new perspectives, new opportunity spaces, and ways in which to structure and organize your innovation efforts. Extend the principle of "innovation equals new learning" beyond the water's edge of your organization's boundaries. Learn to access outside sources—for learning, for ideas, for technologies, and for commercialization resources. Chesbrough and others write extensively and well about OI, so we do not delve deeply into the topic in The Guide. However, Chapter Five speaks directly to useful OI techniques.

● As You Read The Guide

The Guide speaks to the "how-to" of all these principles of innovation and a few others as well. Before we dive in, a few notes:

- ◆ You will see examples throughout that illustrate the points and the successful execution of the approaches and techniques we recommend. We have deliberately drawn examples from a diverse set of companies, industries, and geographies: from Shell to Whirlpool Corporation to Mondelēz to Crayola to UnitedHealth Group to the U.S. Special Operations Command, and others. Some organizations are good examples of systematic and systemic innovators, and thus are used repeatedly; others are good illustrations of specific techniques in The Guide.

- ◆ We use both business-to-business (B2B) and business-to-consumer (B2C) references and examples throughout. Robust innovation techniques are applicable across both worlds, although particulars of how to investigate insights, develop and elaborate ideas, and commercialize vary from one to the other. In the context of speaking to both circumstances, you will see references to both consumers and customers. In referring to consumers, we are typically referring to the end user of a particular product or service. In referring to customers, we are typically referring to the next-level buyer in the value delivery system, which can include (but is not limited to) retailers. We will identify each (consumers versus customers) as we refer to them.

- We provide key take-aways at the end of each chapter. If you think you would find it helpful to first read a quick summary of each chapter in a page or less, please skip to the back of the chapter to do so.
- We refer to the teachings of others from whom we've learned over the years of working in the field. For a small slice of further reference materials (which are vast in quantity), refer to the Notes section of the book, where we reference sources of information and inspiration we've learned from and pulled from as we constructed *Innovator's Field Guide*.

Last but not least, have fun with your innovation work! Innovation is hard, but it is one of the greatest challenges and professional privileges you will take on. Recognize the opportunity and enjoy the ride.

Raising Your Innovation IQ Through Insight-Driven Innovation

2

How do I make sense of the changes in our market?

How might I use our existing know-how (competencies) to enter and flourish in new markets?

How can I surprise and delight my customers with products and services "they have to have"?

Where and why might I be "blind" to new opportunities?

"Thinking different" is essential to innovation.

"Think different." Apple's iconic marketing campaign was highly innovative, with complimentary winks both to its customers—**You** *are different in ways that matter*—and to its development teams—**We** *are different (and better) than any other company.*[1]

Apple's cofounder Steve Jobs was perhaps the best example of a great entrepreneur who succeeded by *thinking different.* "Thinking different" is essential to innovation. But most companies don't have a Steve Jobs with naturally reflexive innovation instincts. What to do?

You can think like an entrepreneur. Each of us can. Most of us will not achieve the same success as Steve Jobs. But we can all raise our innovation IQs by learning how to use the same perspectives and mind-sets. As British historian Paul Johnson says, "There is creativity in all of us, and the only [challenge] is how to bring it out."[2]

If you seek innovation—especially breakthrough innovation—you have to think differently. Here's why: You will not get to breakthrough by asking the same questions. Instead you need to break frame through new insights. New insights help you develop new perspectives: new perspectives on your customers, your market, and your company. New perspectives give you the foundation on which to develop new thinking. New perspectives give you the right to ideate.

What Is a "Great Insight"?

WPP's Jeremy Bullmore famously quipped, "Why is a good insight like a refrigerator? *Because the moment you look into it, a light comes on.*" Bullmore suggests that "high-potency insights, because of their immediacy—because they evoke as well as inform—behave like the best viral ads on the Internet. They are infectious; we only have to hear them once to remember them, to apply them, to pass them on to others. By contrast, the low-potency insight sits there sullenly on its PowerPoint slide, moving absolutely nobody to enlightenment, let alone action."[3]

You should be able to describe a good insight crisply, often in a brief sentence. The insight should do two or more of the following:

+ Reveal deep and previously unrevealed behavior
+ Suggest the potential for disruption—a discontinuous shift

- Point you toward a customer compromise or trade-off that, given the choice, the customer would rather prefer not to make
- Challenge current conventions in the market or industry
- Make some people uncomfortable while inspiring others
- Create an "oh yes" moment through which you *think different*

Earning the Right to Ideate Through New Frame-Breaking Perspectives

We describe five specific types of insights in the next section. Developing new perspectives within any of the five types will help you develop new and interesting ideas.

As you will see, however, you are more likely to develop compelling ideas by looking at the intersection of multiple insights. As Gary Hamel remarks, the combinatory power of multiple types of insights will significantly enhance your ability to develop truly breakthrough concepts and to identify and capture "white space" opportunities.[4]

Why these five types? Reflect for a moment on what makes a great entrepreneur like Apple's cofounder. Sure, great entrepreneurs take risks. But how do they *think?*

How do they approach their business and markets?

Great entrepreneurs are more naturally empathetic to consumers' frustrations. They sense unarticulated needs of customers, so they can conceive of products or services that don't yet exist, and solve problems that customers may not be able to describe. Think about Apple's iPad; social media businesses like Instagram, Pinterest, Twitter, Facebook, and LinkedIn; Bruce Johnson's Breathe Right nasal strips; or the broad product portfolio of Sarah Blakely's Spanx fashion empire.

Great entrepreneurs experience more of "the fringe" of a market. They make sense of the early signs of change. They anticipate disruption and discontinuous change.

They also are not bound by a current set of products or services. Rather than defining their business as what they make or sell, they view growth potential from the standpoint of their current and evolving know-how: their competencies.

Great entrepreneurs are contrarians. They do not accept the dominant logic of a given industry or market. They intuitively, naturally, and instinctively challenge and overturn core assumptions about what drives success, and create new business models that perform differently in ways that matter to customers. By challenging the core assumptions of their business model and industry, they are able to see new opportunities. Consider the success of Virgin Air, easyJet, GOL Air Transport, Netflix, Zipcar, Tata Motors, and IKEA.

Five Insight Types

We will now look at each of these five insight types:

+ Type 1: Customer insight
+ Type 2: Market discontinuities
+ Type 3: Competencies and strategic assets
+ Type 4: Industry orthodoxies
+ Type 5: Seeing and mapping white space

For each insight type, we will first share a definition and set the context. We will then describe how you can quickly get started in developing the insights and using them in the context of your specific innovation challenge. Finally, we will suggest a few pointers for applying them to your own organization.

Getting Started: Identifying Customers' Unmet Needs

Surfacing unarticulated needs is a two-step process. First, gather information on customer behavior using direct observation and related techniques. Then step back and analyze this information using methods to extract and infer potential unstated needs. Separating the information-gathering and analysis steps allows you to shift focus from identifying the visible "what the customer is doing" to surfacing the underlying and vitally important "why they are doing it." Even experts use this two-step process, although they may move between the steps so quickly as to make them appear to be a single step.

Obtaining Data

"You can observe a lot by watching."[5] So says American baseball great Yogi Berra, and so say successful innovators, and so say proponents of design thinking. High-impact observational research techniques integrate design thinking and human-centered design principles to help you "get into the skin of the customer." It helps you understand the customer's context, desires and aspirations, and fears and frustrations, so that you can

● ● ● Insight Type 1: Customer Insight

Several successful entrepreneurs and innovators have described some forms of traditional market research as "like driving while looking in the rear view mirror."[6] We agree.

To be clear, we do recognize that traditional research methods are critically helpful in many contexts, particularly in the later stages of innovation. But traditional methods—focus groups, quantitative surveys, concept testing, and the like—are less helpful at the early stages of innovation. Even worse, the traditional approach may mislead you.

The companies and organizations we study and work with who have brought compelling, disruptive new products and services to market did so, in part, through other research techniques. Their fresh way of thinking allowed them to identify unmet or unarticulated needs of their customers or their customer's customers. They did so by looking for "problems" and unmet needs both up and down their value chain.

Take the "fridge pack" for a twelve-pack of beer or soda. The Coca-Cola Company described it as one of the most innovative packaging developments in its history. Before the fridge pack was introduced in 2002, there was no easy way to store an entire twelve-pack in the refrigerator. But the idea for the fridge pack did not originate with the global beverage giant. It was a supplier, Alcoa, that first developed the idea.

Alcoa wanted to sell more aluminium cans. They began to think about what prevented consumers from drinking more Coca-Cola products. Through some of the **customer insight** techniques we describe here, Alcoa innovators realized that the *package* was "actually hindering the use of cans. People tended to put several cans in the refrigerator [and would] then store the remaining cans in a cabinet or closet. When all the refrigerated Coke cans were gone, they usually chose a different drink from the refrigerator instead of retrieving a can from storage."[7]

Take note that Alcoa did not ask consumers what type of packaging they wanted, nor did they ask Coca-Cola consumers when and how they consumed the beverage. Rather than focusing on stated needs, Alcoa observed consumer behavior and inferred an unmet need from a pattern of behavior that was consistent across observations of multiple individual consumers and households. Motivated by their insights, Alcoa partnered with a packaging company to develop the fridge pack. Through iterative experiments with Coca-Cola, Alcoa eventually achieved double-digit sales increases on the strength of the innovation.

Specific techniques, such as those applied by Alcoa, can be taught and mastered. And although we don't think that learning them will make you as intuitively innovative as Steve Jobs or as contrarian as Sir Richard Branson, our experience does suggest that doing so will make you a dramatically better innovator.

identify their unmet and unarticulated needs. The tensions and trade-offs you observe in their decisions and behaviors will allow you to develop new solutions they could not have conceived of on their own.

Let's look at an example. Crayola is an iconic brand spanning product lines within a privately held consumer products company. From your childhood, you likely know it as a "crayon" company. Today it is much more. Through years of steady focus on innovation, Crayola has reimagined its business, redefining the categories in which it competes and achieving significant growth.[8]

When leadership initiated its innovation efforts in 2004, they hoped to bring value to children through positive, enjoyable learning experiences that would go well beyond crayons. Foundational to their efforts was to more viscerally understand the ways in which children, caregivers, parents, and teachers figured in multiple types of experiences. Crayola set out to learn more about these experiences, observing "in situ"—children in school and at home, teachers in the classroom, and parents (typically Mom) and caregivers interacting with children in various settings throughout the day.

Crayola engaged in direct observation of the customers in a broad range of creative play situations, paying particular attention to the broader context in which those situations occurred. They also conducted interviews subsequent to the observations that allowed for probing of specific actions or unexpected behaviors.[9]

When You Can't Observe Directly

Although direct observation is a preferred approach, it isn't always possible. In these situations, you can use other techniques to obtain observation-like data that can be evaluated just like those of an actual observation.

+ Exercises that place you in the shoes of the customer can be particularly effective. The goal is to experience and feel what the customer experiences and feels by doing it or using it yourself, in situ. These exercises can be structured around any portion of the customer experience, including both purchase and use. The important thing is to document the experience for further evaluation just as if it were an observation.

+ Another alternative to direct observation is to construct realistic customer experience scenarios. For example, anecdotes and stories from customers, customer service representatives, sales managers, channel partners, and others can easily be developed into more comprehensive scenarios. Build the anecdotes and stories into observation scenarios that can be "played back" during the analysis and insight extraction phase. Be sure to view each scenario as a discrete observation rather than as a composite or average of all experiences.

Analyzing the Data

Through the techniques we describe above, you will collect a rich and extensive set of observations for analysis. Now you can turn your attention to inferring unarticulated customer needs. We find three techniques to be particularly effective:

+ Identifying and resolving tensions
+ Customer experience mapping
+ Jobs to be done

Each of these approaches provides helpful ways of reaching beyond obvious and superficial needs to achieve a deeper understanding of unmet and unarticulated needs of customers (and noncustomers).

Identifying and Resolving Tensions

Observations often point to implicit tensions and trade-offs that might be productively resolved. These tensions can be internal to a single customer who is trading off between two things he or she cares about, or between different customers or stakeholders who have different and conflicting desires and objectives. They are rich areas to dig into to identify unarticulated needs.

Crayola noticed a number of unresolved tensions during their observations of mothers and children.[10]

+ Mom wanted her child to have a fun, engaging, and fulfilling "artistic experience"—as much as possible without limits as to where or when. At the same time, she wanted to prevent messes or damage from her child's free-flowing behavior. As a result, she was reluctantly placing restrictions on where, when, and how art, coloring, or painting work was being done.
+ The child wanted to play without interruption or rules and to be "in control and self-directed."

By understanding the tensions within and between what mother and child sought, Crayola achieved a eureka moment:

Mom wanted a mess-free, deeply immersive and rewarding artistic experience that her child could own and self-direct, without limitations as to where or when.

This insight was not previously appreciated. Crayola's new understanding of mother and child color time—immersive without the limitations and without the risk of mess—emerged after deep consideration of what they had observed.[11]

Figure 2-1 provides a framework for surfacing and addressing tensions and trade-offs

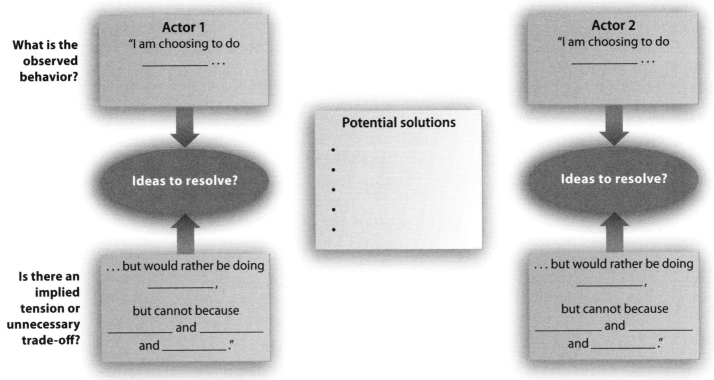

What is the observed behavior?

Actor 1
"I am choosing to do _____ . . .

Ideas to resolve?

Is there an implied tension or unnecessary trade-off?

. . . but would rather be doing _____,
but cannot because _____ and _____ and _____ ."

Potential solutions
-
-
-
-
-

Actor 2
"I am choosing to do _____ . . .

Ideas to resolve?

. . . but would rather be doing _____,
but cannot because _____ and _____ and _____ ."

Figure 2-1   Exploring Customer Tensions

once you have the basic insight building blocks gathered from observations or other techniques.

Crayola resolved the mother-child tension by providing "fun and engaging" activities with their swath of new products that placed "no limits" and caused little or no mess. The company promoted their new line of products with new names or emphasis that included "erasable," "mess-free," and "washable" on the packaging.[12]

● ● ●

Industrial gas company Praxair provides another example of surfacing and resolving unresolved tensions. The company's Grab 'n Go® all-in-one portable medical oxygen system resulted from observational research and immersive interviews during which Praxair and its suppliers surfaced the needs and frustrations of two important actors within a given hospital system[13]:

+ *Purchasing and procurement was relentlessly seeking "lowest-cost suppliers."* As a result, they would purchase (among many other things) several variants of medical oxygen cylinders and associated equipment, many of which had their own (and separate) regulators and valves that had to be managed and assembled at time of use.

+ *Nurses and other caregivers were frustrated by anything standing in the way of caring for their patients.* Helping sick people get better is, of course, why someone enters nursing. Having to assemble medical oxygen delivery systems from multiple components during care delivery (or critical care delivery) was in the way.

Using the Figure 2-1 framework, we can begin to see tension between the two primary actors. Praxair and others in the medical gas industry were making the purchase and especially the use of medical oxygen too complicated. Praxair's solution was the Grab 'n Go®, a one-piece, light, ready-to-use oxygen cylinder with an integrated regulator and valve that the caregiver could quickly and easily carry into the patient's room, connect, and use. The new medical oxygen delivery system won product design awards and acclaim (see photos).

The Grab 'n Go. Photo provided by Praxair Corporation and Praxair innovation leadership. © Praxair Corporation, 2013.

Intuitively you can see why the then director of marketing described the new product as "user-friendly, [eliminating] the time-consuming hassles and guesswork that the conventional post-valve system has caused medical staffers for the past 50 years."[14]

Stepping back from this example, you can see that through structured observations of customers (the purchasing manager) and noncustomers (nurses/caregivers), you can surface unmet and unarticulated needs of the organization. You will find that when you are using these or other techniques for gathering consumer insights, adopting specific behaviors and mind-sets—empathy, persistence, inquiry—is most helpful to ensure that you get to rich and actionable insights.

Customer Experience Mapping

Variously termed "customer experience mapping," "customer mapping," "customer experience ecosystem," and (occasionally) "value chain mapping," this technique helps you visualize the end-to-end experience of your customer (or your customer's customer).[15] By applying customer experience mapping, you will be able to surface the customer's pain points that might be relieved, aspirations or positive assumptions that can be heightened, and trade-offs that can be resolved positively for your customer.

Although the specific stages of a customer experience map may vary from organization to organization, some broad components of the experience are shown here:

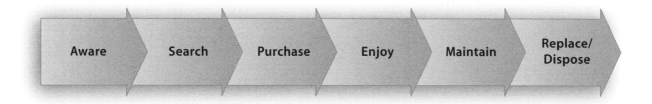

Aware: The stimulus that provokes the customer's or consumer's interest in acquiring the product or service

Search: The steps and actions he or she takes to inform the purchasing decision

Purchase: The customer's or consumer's beginning-to-end experience in executing the purchase of the service or product

Enjoy: How he or she engages with and uses the product or service after purchase

Maintain: The customer's or consumer's involvement and interactions to maintain and repair the product or service

Dispose/Replace: The steps, if any, he or she takes to dispose of and/or replace or upgrade the product

In your particular circumstance, you may find that some of the stages of the depicted framework should be combined.

Your first step in using the framework is to identify which types of potential customers or noncustomers you wish to analyze. Often it is helpful to think of different groups of customers as a specific "persona." For example, were Nestlé to consider what professional women might want from a small indulgence snack, the persona might be one or more of the following:

+ Single, well-educated woman, urban living, professional
+ Married woman with two children, juggling professional and family lives
+ Recent college graduate

Too often, we find that teams constrain the focus of the customer experience analysis to existing customers buying an existing product within the existing customer experience. Typically such efforts are ways to make a process or end-to-end experience more efficient, providing helpful but at times only incremental value in terms of surfacing substantial *new* insights. To go beyond the incremental, try to include noncustomers in your customer experience mapping efforts.

Once you have identified your customer and noncustomer personas, map each relevant observation against stages of the experience. Depending on your objectives, the number of observations required will vary, but often ten to fifteen will give you high-quality, qualitatively robust findings. Some organizations may prefer a larger number of observations, but our experience is that the results are unlikely to change.

Here are the steps you should take:

First, select a persona. As an example, let's use one of the three personas from the hypothetical Nestlé list.

Julia, a recent college graduate and working professional

Next, consider what experiences you wish to observe. The persona offers hints, as you know that she is probably in her early twenties, well educated, and likely to be working in an urban or suburban area. As the following table suggests, you can plan for your observations by thinking through who, what, and where: Who is the person, where might I find her, and in what activities do I wish to observe her? For this persona—Julia, a recent college graduate and working professional—your plan might look like this:

Whom to observe	Twenty-something females alone or with friends
Where to observe	In work environments, suburban office parks, and urban plazas; in cafes, restaurants, and bars in and around those areas On the go while on commuter lines: subway, bus, or driving alone or with friends
What to observe	What does she choose for "small indulgences," whether a snack, a small food treat, or a beverage? Is she alone? How does she interact with others? Can you sense how she feels or reacts to the snack?

To learn more about "indulgent snacks" for Julia, you need to map her behavior across the different stages of her experience as a consumer. You may be able to do so with data from a single observation. More likely, however, you will require multiple observations from which to gather data on all stages of Julia's experience. You should expect to have to aggregate the information from multiple observations to complete the end-to-end picture of the experience.

Here is a guide to what you should look for in each stage:

1. What is the customer's objective? What "job" does the customer want the product or service to perform?
2. On the positive side: What pleases or surprises her? What makes her happy?
3. On the negative side: What frustrates or annoys her? What compromises do you *infer* based on what you observe and what you know she is trying to do?
4. As possible, understand the value that is potentially created at each stage and/or across stages

The next step is to use your data to develop insights about the persona. Carefully consider any unexpected or unusual behavior, which may be an indicator of unmet needs. Focus on the underlying "whys" of the behavior and create "insight candidates" in crisp framing, summarizing the insight in a sentence or two:

In the voice of the persona, describe why:

+ I am pleased by _____ because _____.
+ I am annoyed because _____.

+ I would rather do _____, but can't because _____; so, I compromise and do _____ instead.

With these data, you now have insights about Julia and can further elaborate her persona based on your observations across the experience:

	Aware	Search	Purchase	Enjoy	Maintain	Replace/ Dispose
Objective — job to be done						
Pleased? Surprised?						
Annoyances? Points of pain?						
Trade-offs? Compromises?						

Now, in our hypothetical Nestlé context, you have a window into Julia's world.

Jobs to Be Done

"Jobs to be done" is a useful framework and technique to help you escape the confines of an existing product or service. The pioneering concept, conceived by Harvard's Clay Christensen, asserts that a given product or service is "hired" to do a specific job for the customer. For example, a commuter may "hire" Starbucks to provide her with a convenient and flavorful first cup of morning coffee, through a drive-through or in the store. In this example, what the consumer seeks is "good-tasting caffeine quickly."[16]

As Christensen writes, "with few exceptions, every job people need or want to do has a social, a functional, and an emotional dimension. If marketers understand each of these dimensions, then they can design a product that's precisely targeted to the job. In other words, the job, not the customer, is the fundamental unit of analysis for a marketer who hopes to develop products that customers will buy."[17]

Let's imagine other ways that the consumer might hire Starbucks to fulfill the job of delivering good-tasting caffeine quickly. Could the company sell good-tasting energy drinks or caffeine tablets? Offer a line of rich dark chocolates with different doses of caffeine?

The jobs-to-be-done approach helps you break down a given product or service into its customer objectives–based components. To do so, you analyze customer observation data and consider the customer's behavior, either with a specific product, a specific experience, or, in some cases, across the relevant part of her daily life. Some people can do this intuitively. For the rest of us, we've outlined some simple steps to use as a guide: The

> *With few exceptions, every job people need or want to do has a social, a functional, and an emotional dimension.*

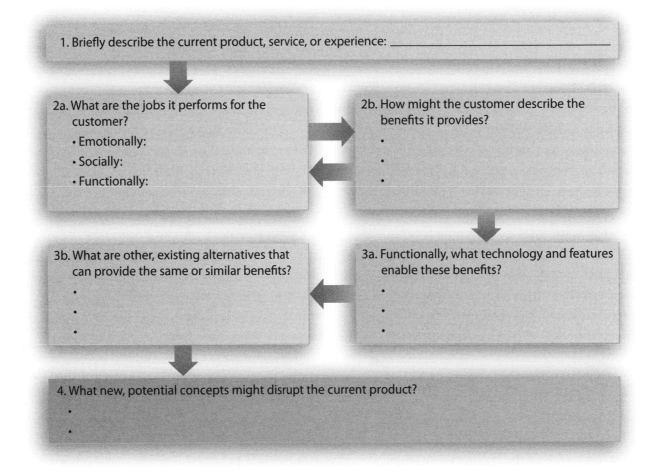

1. Briefly describe the current product, service, or experience: _____

2a. What are the jobs it performs for the customer?
- Emotionally:
- Socially:
- Functionally:

2b. How might the customer describe the benefits it provides?
-
-
-

3b. What are other, existing alternatives that can provide the same or similar benefits?
-
-
-

3a. Functionally, what technology and features enable these benefits?
-
-
-

4. What new, potential concepts might disrupt the current product?
-
-

most important part of this work is to make sure you and your colleagues give sufficient time to discuss and explore steps 1 and 2 in the framework depicted above.

1. Review the observation data for the current product and service experience. What works well? Do you see behavior(s) that are unusual—for example, is the consumer bypassing

prescribed steps or improvising in other ways? What are the points of annoyance, pain, delight, and/or satisfaction?

2. What types of jobs are being fulfilled? What is the customer trying to achieve? What do you see that meets his or her emotional needs, such as indulgence, increased productivity or efficiency, or self-reinforcement? What social interactions are involved? Is status involved? Community? Functionally, what is delivered:

Let's bring this framework to life by analyzing a familiar product: coffee purchased at a Starbucks location:

Current benefits and how they may describe it:	Good taste, aroma, a wake-up or energy boost, easy access, interaction with "personal" barista, convenient location
How benefit is enabled, functionally	Caffeine, specific beans (aroma) and higher-than-required heating, walk in or drive through

Other current products or services that may provide the same benefit or functionality	McDonald's for convenience and lower cost
	The beverage 4-Hour Energy—for an intense caffeine boost
	Chocolate

In this deliberately simplified example, each of the alternatives did in fact disrupt a portion of Starbuck's business. McDonald's grew their coffee business and captured share by outperforming on convenience and cost and achieving parity or better on taste. Caffeinated energy drinks extend the dimension of convenience by offering grab-and-go (from your home) portability.

Immersion Interviews

Immersion interviews provide a means by which to have a more detailed conversation with a customer target. The interviews can be conducted in groups or individually.

Snap-On Tools regularly uses these types of interviews to surface unmet and unarticulated needs of its core customer, the vehicle mechanic. Chief innovation officer

Ben Brenton terms this approach "customer connections" and describes it as one that involves "forming a relationship with the customer—listening to and observing the customer to better understand their needs. It's about getting the voice of the customer to create insights that lead to opportunities. It is an interaction where you listen to understand, not to educate or sell. [The goal is to] understand unarticulated needs, pain points, behaviors, attitudes and motivations."[18]

Through an immersive interview, you also want to understand the broad context in which customers and noncustomers are making purchase decisions for a specific product, service, occasion, or process. Here are some examples:

Product or Service	Occasion or Process
An investment account	Planning and saving for retirement
A mobile phone	Staying connected
A bagel	Eating breakfast on the go
A laptop battery	Managing power

Notice that "occasion or process" links closely to "the job to be done" sought by the consumer. Because doing so helps you think beyond a current product or service mindset, we recommend that you focus more on occasion or process than on product or service if your goal is to come up with newer and more "breakthrough" insights.

Once you make the customer comfortable with the dialogue, you will want to move on to questions focused on your specific objectives. For Snap-On's Ben Brenton, the questions typically focus on surfacing unmet needs. In other instances, it may be appropriate to focus on the purchase and use of a product or service:

+ How do you become aware of a need (for a product or service)?
+ What steps do you take to research and evaluate alternatives that might fit that need?
+ How do you compare the options you surface?
+ When using [this product or service], what frustrates you? What makes you comfortable, satisfied, or excited?
+ What would cause you to consider using more of it or using it more often? Or to use less of it or use it less often?
+ What would cause you to stop using it?

Example: How Saint-Gobain Used Immersion Interviews

Innovation leaders within Saint-Gobain Performance Plastics recognize the value of insight-driven idea generation. Beginning in 2012, the company deployed an insights-driven approach to develop new ideas within each of their seven business units across sixteen countries at fifty locations globally.

As part of this effort, business teams were trained in specific techniques for eliciting customer insight in thirty different market applications. Innovation director Jean Angus fully appreciates the difficulty of capturing insights in a B2B environment: "In the B2B world, we face two difficulties. First, it is hard for current customers and noncustomers to candidly share their *strategic* perspective. So we need to take the time to build trust and always approach the effort with great humility. Second, for some in B2B environments, speaking with customers is not always a natural act. So we help by building comfort, confidence, and skill among colleagues so that they can engage productively with the customer."[19]

Jean and her team trained internal teams and practiced techniques that were focused more on dialogue and exploration than on "question and answer." As Jean frames it, "Success flows from being able to ask the right question in the right way. Listening is so important, and that is a skill that must be learned and practiced."[20]

Teams engaging with customers to develop new insights spend 80 percent of their time listening and 20 percent asking questions. Their questions follow the creativity process of "focus, diverge, and converge." They start with simple background questions like "Tell me about your market space [your customers], [your value chain]." They follow up using probing questions like "Is one more important than the other?" and "Why?"

Teams start divergent thinking using questions like "What are your main challenges?" They follow with such questions as "How big a challenge is that for you? How so? I am hearing you say . . . Is this correct? Why else is this a challenge?"

Questions like "What would you like to see in your ideal world?" prompt customers to envision future needs. The team offers information about trends and asks, "Could you think of any needs that may arise from any of these trends?" which also prompts thought about future needs. If customers surface solutions during the dialogue, teams ask, "What would that do for you?"

The goal of these questions is to create comfortable customer dialogue that results in deep insight into customer needs. The process ends using converge questions, such as, "If you could have any of these needs solved today, what would they be?" Then the teams highlight top needs.

Ultimately, over three hundred colleagues were trained across locations globally. More important, the effort moved beyond a Saint-Gobain learning center and into the field, resulting in stronger relationships and new revenue from both current and new customers.[21]

Netnography

Pioneered by Richard Kozinets, netnography is an inexpensive, unobtrusive, and quick technique to develop insight into consumers on the basis of their online behavior.[22] He describes it as *"naturalistic,* following social expression to its online appearances. It is *immersive,* drawing the researcher into an engaged, deeper understanding. It is *descriptive,* seeking to convey the rich reality of contemporary consumers' lives, with all of their hidden cultural meanings as well as their colorful graphics, drawings, symbols, sounds, photos, and videos. It is *multi-method,* combining well with other methods, both online and off, such as interviews and videography."[23]

Netnography's value to the innovator as a window into the consumer's world will increase as consumer power increases through the use of social media. Some posit that the "intention economy" will ultimately drive product and service providers to respond to *actual intentions of customers,* broadening the range of economic interplay between supplier and consumer.[24]

Broadly speaking, there is a four-step netnography process, which we have adapted from Kozinets:

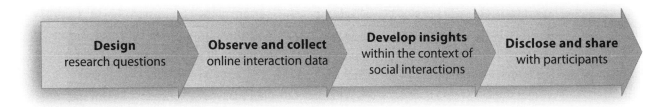

Design
research questions

Observe and collect
online interaction data

Develop insights
within the context of
social interactions

Disclose and share
with participants

As you observe and analyze the online interactions, you must focus on the "what," "how," and "why":

- What individuals are saying online
- How they are saying it
- Why they are saying it

●●● Insight Type 2: Market Discontinuities

Peter Drucker observed that "systematic innovation . . . consists in the purposeful and organized search for changes [that] . . . as a rule . . . have occurred already or are under way."[25] Changes, as Drucker notes, are the things that are already happening in the world around us—things that *you* can see, observe, and learn about.

Hamel builds on Drucker's notion, suggesting that by looking deeply within and across a wide variety of *observable trends*, you can "understand what has already changed and [can] identify the portent of those changes" for your organization. In this context, "seeing the future is not all forecasting and it is not all scenario planning. [Rather] it is imagining what you can make happen, given what is already changing."[26]

Of course, many organizations, perhaps including your own, track trends. Insight-driven innovation, however, requires more than "trend tracking" or exploring the implications of a single trend. To develop rich insight, you "must be informed by [the changes in] trends in lifestyles, technology, demographics, geopolitics," values, religion, regulations, and socioeconomics, so that you can imagine the future. You can think of these changes as **discontinuities**.[27]

Discontinuities can help you anticipate disruption. They are insights describing shifts that you can anticipate by looking at the intersections of market, industry, regulatory, technological, demographic, and other trends.[28] As Hamel frames it, identifying and understanding discontinuities allow you to develop proprietary insights (that is, the discontinuity) through publicly available data (that is, the group of trends which suggest a shift). Discontinuities help point you toward the future you create, rather than the one you "accept" by following others.

Getting Started: Discontinuities

Because you develop discontinuity insights based on observation of changes that are already happening, you need to start by gathering data about trends across relevant areas. Typically, we see organizations capture trends that reflect shifts in the broad areas we mentioned earlier, such as:

Lifestyles: shifts in fashion, living habits, popular television shows

Technology: observable decreases or increases in the cost of specific technologies, the emergence of new technologies, shifts in the

> *You develop discontinuity insights based on observation of changes that are already happening.*

consumption of digital content, shifts in specific areas of science within and outside your industry

Demographics and socioeconomics: changes in the composition of age, race, education, mortality, and quality of living within and across societies

Geopolitics: changes in power structures, influence, and economies within a country or region

Values: shifts in observed behaviors and sentiment regarding "what is important"

Regulation: changes to regulatory structures and rules

Religion: changes in formal or informal religious practices within and across societies

Industry (or market space): changes in the structure and/or basis of competition, including market share, profitability, value chain, and leadership positions

Although it is often helpful to capture "shifts" across each of these trend categories, you may find that in your specific circumstance, you need to place more or less emphasis on a given category and perhaps modify how you define your categories of interest. For example, if you are an NGO seeking to use innovation to tackle challenges of water scarcity, the **Industry** you focus on might include other NGOs with activity in "water scarcity" as well as government and for-profit organizations. At the same time, **Technology** would likely be of critical importance to you, and **Religion**, perhaps, less so. By contrast, if you are working for an automobile insurance company, you may pay particular attention to the trends that point to the unbundling and rebundling of your industry's legacy value chain.

To gather these data, you can likely turn to internal resources, such as your marketing research or strategy functions. Beyond the four walls of your organization, you can quickly find trends in general publications such as the *Financial Times*, the *New York Times*, and the *Wall Street Journal*; or, for a broader global view, you might look at the *Hindustan Times*, the *China Daily*, or the *Jornal do Brasil*. Within a given area—**Religion**, for example—you will find a plethora of online sites and publications devoted to the topic.

With sufficient trends collected, you are now able to look across the trend set to identify the themes that cut across trend categories. Those themes may portend a current or emerging disruptive shift.[29] Figure 2-2 provides one framework for synthesizing trends.

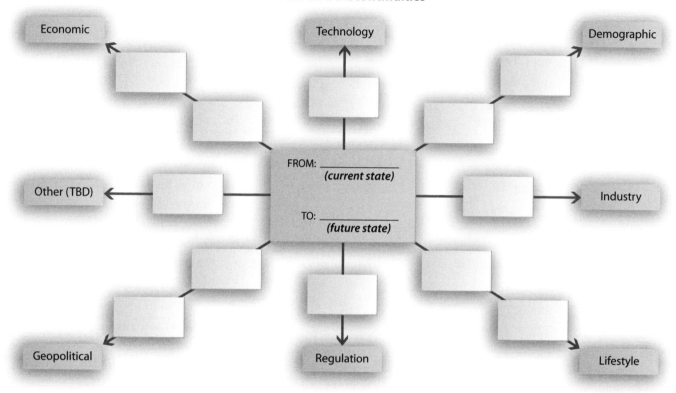

Trends and Discontinuities

Figure 2-2 Surfacing Discontinuities

Use the framework in Figure 2-2 as a guide to post related trends in each of the areas highlighted at the framework's borders. At the center, you would post "candidate discontinuities," or disruptive shifts. Subsequent to your initial efforts at synthesis, you will need to subject each candidate to more thorough discussion and subsequent vetting in the form of seeking confirmatory (or disconfirmatory) evidence.

Your ultimate goal is to identify a small set of discontinuous changes that have the potential to significantly impact your organization and its current operating model. You may identify potentially positive or negative shifts, such as:

Type of Shift	From . . .	To . . .
Technological	• The Web-based Internet • Intelligence in computers	• The Internet of things • Intelligence in all objects
Societal	• Trust in institutions • The traditional (western) family with two spouses	• Distrust in all things institutional: churches, corporations, governments • Single-parent households • Multigenerational households
Global trade and politics	• Outsourcing • BRIC (Brazil, Russia, India, and China) as the developing world	• In-sourcing • BRIC as rising regional and global centers of influence • (Parts of) Africa as an emerging, growing economy
Nature of product	• Food as source of nutrition, taste, and/or satiety	• Food for improved health

You should note that the examples in the table are not trends per se. Rather, the shifts represent your view of what a set of related trends suggest to you about relevant, potentially disruptive changes within your market and industry.

Taken together, customer insights and discontinuities provide a rich, external perspective by which you are able to conceive of new possibilities.

Now let's look at additional techniques for gaining a fresh perspective that is more

●●● Insight Type 3: Competencies and Strategic Assets

Looking at your **competencies and strategic assets**—rather than focusing solely on products, services, or businesses—provides a perspective that forces you to think of the organization itself as deep, leverageable, and differentiated "know-how." This view allows you to think more broadly about potential growth and provides one criterion by which to select and act on strategy. It provides the logic of "why you can win" in a market or business in which you may not compete today.

The notion of competing on competencies was far from mainstream when Gary Hamel and C. K. Prahalad published their seminal article "The Core Competence of the Organization."[30] Like other enduring management concepts, competence-based thinking has its roots in Peter Drucker's writings.[31] And, like many management concepts, the term, concept, and framework are often misused.

Growth-minded practitioners have used this type of analysis to see new opportunities, reinvent their core business, and enter entirely new markets. For example, Philadelphia-based utility PECO concluded that it could prosper by becoming a hyperefficient, safe operator of nuclear generation. "Working to examine its hidden assumptions, PECO uncovered a core competency in operating large, mission-critical infrastructure—a competency honed in time of crisis a decade earlier when PECO grappled with bringing its own Peach Bottom nuclear plant into regulatory compliance. PECO emerged from the Peach Bottom process with a proven ability to bring 'problem plants' to high capacity performance with low operating costs."[32] The strategy that resulted from those insights into their core competency propelled PECO to an industry-leading position starting with the acquisition of the troubled Three Mile Island reactor for just $23 million, a bargain in the world of nuclear generation assets. Eventually PECO merged with Chicago-based Commonwealth Edison to become the largest producer of nuclear energy in the United States.[33]

internal to your organization, starting with core competencies.

As Hamel asserts, you can identify your organization's core competencies by examining its most significant successes within, say, the last five-year period. In essence, what you are doing is deconstructing your successes into the specific elements and actions which enabled them.[34] Figure 2-3 provides a framework you can use to surface your organization's core competencies. Use it to guide a dialogue:

1. **Benefit:** What made the "significant success" possible? What value did we create? What benefits did we provide?

2. **Enabling actions:** What did we assemble and integrate to achieve success? An enabling technology or technologies? a particular skill? Did we leverage a unique physical or intangible asset?

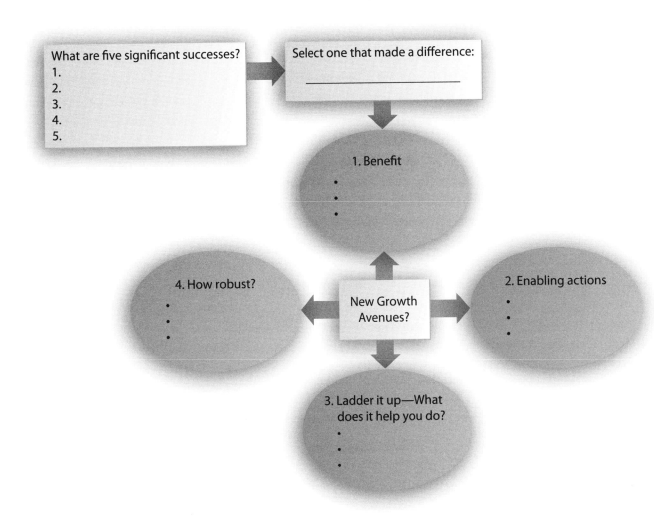

Figure 2-3 Unpacking Your Core Competencies

What you are doing in this part of the dialogue is, as Hamel frames it, looking for "a bundle of constituent skills and technologies" that are fundamental to delivering the benefit. "A core competence represents the integration of a variety of skills and it is this integration that is the distinguishing hallmark of a core competence."[35]

3. **Ladder it up—What does it help you do?** Looking across the enabling actions, how would you characterize this potential competency? What significant company- or organization-wide ability do the enabling actions add up to?

4. **How robust?** Did our potential competency provide a clear and compelling benefit to an end user or customer? Will it still provide benefit to the marketplace in the future? Does our potential competency appear to be relatively unique, or can it be replicated easily?

Once you identify a candidate core competency, you should, as Hamel suggests, objectively assess it against three criteria[36]:

+ *Customer value:* Does it make a "disproportionate contribution to perceived value"?

+ *Better than direct and competence competitors:* Does the competency make us competitively unique? In what way(s)?

+ *A gateway to new markets:* To what extent might the competency enable entry to new markets and/or help us disrupt the existing market(s) in which we compete?

You will find that your assessment will not result in a yes-or-no conclusion. Rather you will likely find relative degrees of strength. A core competency provides an important strategic rationale for competing or entering markets in a competitively defensible way. So when you are confident that you understand the competency, you should be asking yourself:

What else might we do with this capability? How would we use it to reinvent or improve our core business? How might it help us move to an adjacent market or a new business model?

● ● ●

Saint-Gobain's president, Tom Kinisky, recognized early on that competencies are enormously helpful as a screen and filter to select specific ideas to pursue. In practice, as training efforts unfolded, the innovation team quickly recognized that a deep understanding of their competencies was a prerequisite for success in engaging customers in strategic dialogue. He found that an understanding of the company's competencies enabled productive dialogue within each of his business teams and ultimately led to much more attractive opportunities. For example, one of the significant successes in the business is that they make over one billion bearings for customers, and every single one is custom engineered.

Saint-Gobain teams began to detail a specific competency (confidential to the company) tied to this success—one supported by a "bundle of constituent skills and technologies." When they assessed it against Hamel's suggested criteria listed above, they understood that it was a strong and defensible competency that would enable success for a set of new products. Armed with the competency perspective, teams could speak credibly to ways in which Saint-Gobain could address specific unsolved problems, resolve trade-offs, and eliminate tensions.[37]

●●● Insight Type 4: Industry Orthodoxies

Industry orthodoxies are industry conventions or paradigms that represent potentially ignored "rocks worth overturning" to explore growth spaces or opportunities. To investigate industry orthodoxies is to take the notion of "industry best practices" and turn it on its head, enabling you to see "white space" opportunities with objectivity and clarity.

In the context of developing frame-breaking insights, we believe that employing a holistic business model framework is especially useful in challenging existing industry orthodoxies to identify new, compelling opportunities. In essence, the business model "describes the rationale of how an organization creates, delivers and captures value."[38] When you look holistically across the business model, it is easy to spot the specific choices your organization makes to enable success. You can think of these choices as orthodoxies—that is, their beliefs about what drives success.

We find it most beneficial to identify orthodoxies related to specific elements of the business model. Alexander Osterwalder and Yves Pigneur describe the nine building blocks of a business model, which we summarize next.[39]

Who are your customers, and what benefits do you offer?

* What is your customer value proposition (CVP) and "benefit" offered?
* Which segment(s) do you serve, and what is your customer relationship with each segment?

How do you go to market?

* What is your value proposition to your channel partner(s)?
* What is the set of activities you perform?
* What activities are performed by your channel partner(s) to deliver your CVP?
* What are your key partnerships, beyond channel, that enable your success?

How do you capture value sustainably?

* What are the revenue streams that result from successfully delivering on your CVP and channel value propositions?
* What is the cost structure you require to capture the revenue streams?
* What is your source of sustainable advantage?

The next table summarizes business model choices of two highly successful educational organizations. We are all familiar with the Harvard Business School (HBS), which enjoys a sterling reputation, has a sizeable endowment of nearly $3 billion, and, in 2013, charged approximately $50,000 in tuition.[40] You may be less familiar with Apollo, the parent company of the University of Phoenix and the largest private education provider in the world. As of this writing, the for-profit school has a total market capitalization of $2 billion and a thirty-two-thousand-member faculty who deliver online and classroom courses.[41]

	Harvard Business School (HBS)	**Apollo–University of Phoenix**
Who is the customer, and what benefits do you offer?	Individuals seeking the Harvard educational experience and "brand" on their diploma and the contacts and network it provides. HBS turns away customers.	Business professionals (and their companies) seeking to advance their careers through education. The school accepts most applicants who can pay. Fits around their work schedule—students take classes after work. Includes "lifelong learner" customers.
How do you go to market?	Customers come to HBS at a fixed location.	Offers both online classes and classroom teaching through multilocation "campuses" including traditional office buildings. Presence in the United States, India, Chile, Mexico, and the United Kingdom.
How do you capture value sustainably?	Tuition, continuing education courses, and publishing revenue models. Corporate and alumni donations create and sustain the largest endowment among other private, nonprofit institutions. "Star" professors publish and actively consult to major corporations globally.	Fee-for-courses model. Primarily utilizes high-quality but unknown instructors, some with only undergraduate degrees. Makes extensive use of federal education grants and loans to individuals.

Often organizations are so conditioned to "the way things work around here" that they are blind to other potential avenues of growth."

As you can see, each organization has achieved success by operating under a set of specific and differing business model choices.

Your organization also made choices about its business model. By explicitly surfacing those choices, you can identify orthodoxies for you and other organizations operating in your market space.

Getting Started: Developing High-Impact Orthodoxy Insights

It is easy to see orthodoxies in organizations with which you do not compete or regularly interact. We have found, however, that teams tend to struggle to identify orthodoxies inside their own industries. Often they are so conditioned to "the way things work around here" that they are blind to other potential avenues of growth. Several techniques can help you unpack your orthodoxies.

Ask yourself, "What would our organization choose *not* to do?"

Recall that orthodoxies represent business model choices. HBS chooses to emphasize the reputation of its professors as one means to promote its brand and, separately, to limit its physical campus to Cambridge, Massachusetts. HBS would not do any of the following:

- Admit everyone who applies and can pay for a course
- Allow students to attend classes virtually as a regular practice
- Teach students in suburban office buildings scattered throughout the United States
- Declare that it is a "for-profit" institution.

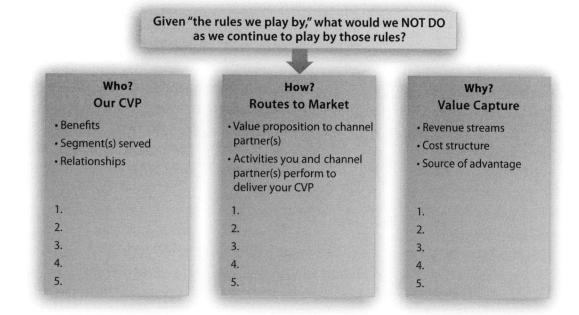

Given "the rules we play by," what would we NOT DO as we continue to play by those rules?

Who? Our CVP	How? Routes to Market	Why? Value Capture
• Benefits • Segment(s) served • Relationships	• Value proposition to channel partner(s) • Activities you and channel partner(s) perform to deliver your CVP	• Revenue streams • Cost structure • Source of advantage
1. 2. 3. 4. 5.	1. 2. 3. 4. 5.	1. 2. 3. 4. 5.

Once you have surfaced underlying orthodoxies, you can select a particular practice (something you would not do) and explore it further, explicitly identifying new opportunities you might potentially pursue:

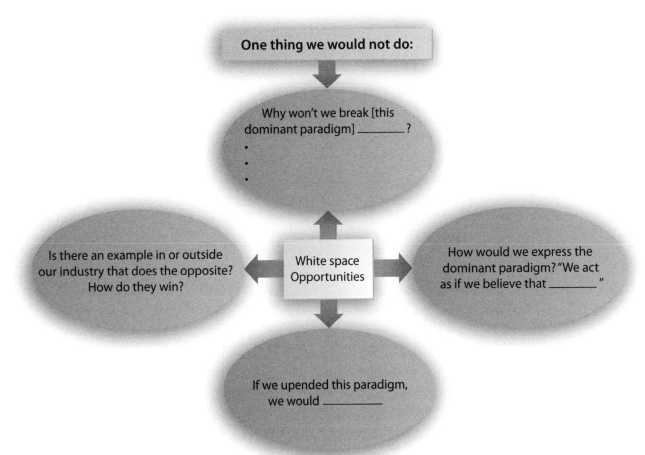

You can use such a set of frameworks in an internal discussion or meeting with colleagues or in an external discussion or working session with trusted suppliers or even customers.

Identifying orthodoxies through desk research or internal dialogue:

+ **Review analyst reports on the industry, your company, and competitors.** Take note of the implicit and explicit assumptions being made about the industry and organization.

+ **Review mission statement and vision.** Look at how your company and its competitors are portrayed (for a public company, refer to the 10K or annual report). Understand the relative emphasis of technology, channels to market, and customer segments served. Review the relative importance of alliances and partnerships.

+ **Interview employees, both longer term and those new to the organization.** These discussions can point you toward orthodoxies. You may find some of the following questions helpful in the discussions:

Newcomers:

+ What approach to our [markets, customers, or business] surprises you?

+ Which practices are holding us back?

+ In your (short) time here, have you encountered any "sensitive topics" that lead you to conclude that it is an "undiscussable" subject? Why?

+ What would you do differently?

Longer-term employees:

+ Why do you think that our approaches to our [markets, customers, or business] are sources of strength?

+ Why and how do they help us win?

+ What is the underlying belief or key success factor implied by those approaches?

Identifying orthodoxies through analysis of analog competitors:

+ We define "analog competitors" as organizations that have business model elements that may serve as helpful pointers to productively overturn one

> *Orthodoxies are beliefs about what drives success in your industry. They are the rules by which you compete and (try to) win. Potentially, these rules are also "blinders" to alternative ways of competing.*

or more of your industry's orthodoxies. Analog competitors may not compete with you directly or compete with you at all. In fact, by definition, analog competitors play by a different set of rules, relative to the orthodoxies in your own industry.

A brief reminder:

Orthodoxies are beliefs about what drives success in your industry. They are the rules by which you compete and (try to) win. Potentially, these rules are also "blinders" to alternative ways of competing.

A thorough orthodoxy analysis surfaces the industry rules or dogma that your organization and others follow. If your orthodoxy insights suggest that your organization may be blind to a particular way of operating, looking at one or more analog competitors may be helpful to stimulate and reframe your thinking.

Let's look at a few examples in this table:

Surfacing Orthodoxies via Alternative Models

Industry and Company	Orthodoxy Insight	Alternative to the Orthodoxy
Consumer electronics—Samsung, LG, Lenovo, Dell	We sell a product enabled by (often parity) technology to provide specific functionality.	**Apple:** We sell an experience enabled by technology to delight and engage.
Automobile insurance—Allstate, Allianz, State Farm	We sell a product that the consumer is required to buy by law but that is not one for which consumers have a strong emotional desire.	**Progressive:** We offer you a "smart choice" that saves you money while bundling additional protection into the product.
Banking or finance—Chase, Standard Charter, Citibank	We provide the funding and financial services to help grow medium-size and small business.	**GE Capital:** We provide the basics (like Chase) and also help customers improve their business operations through our world-class capabilities in Six Sigma, quality, and operational improvement.

As the table suggests, you identify analog competitors by thinking about companies in and outside your industry that play by a different set of rules. In the following table, we offer a starter list of examples of distinct "rules" and suggest a few analog organizations for each. Although not all of these examples will be relevant to your particular circumstance, we have found that several among them fit many situations. Using these examples, you can work in a small group or by yourself to select the appropriate analogs and then ask, "What would [analog competitor] do differently if they were attempting to enter our markets? How would they serve current or new customers differently?

Using Analogs to Challenge Orthodoxies

Business Model Habits: Winning Through . . .	Analog Examples
Great consumer experience	Ritz-Carlton Hotels, Four Seasons Hotels, Disney World, Coast Capital Savings, Apple Stores
Web retailing	Amazon, eBay, Progressive, Alibaba.com
Hyperefficiency	McDonald's, Wal-Mart, Apple*
Information and Big Data	American Express, Capital One, IBM, Accenture
Natural, organic	Aveda, Whole Foods, Natura
Integration of services with products	GE Medical, Siemens Medical, IBM Global services and consulting, UPS delivery services and logistics expertise
Risk management and mitigation	State Farm, Allstate

*Apple is consistently rated as having the most efficient end-to-end supply chain, outperforming Dell, among others. For example, see the Gartner Group, "The Supply Chain Top 25," 2012, http://www.gartner.com/technology/supply-chain/top25.jsp.

These examples are intended to illustrate the concept and application of analogs as a technique to guide you in challenging and overturning business model orthodoxies. Obviously, there are many types of business models with additional, different elements. You will need to identify the analogs best suited to the customer problems or issues you are looking to address.

●●● Insight Type 5: Seeing and Mapping White Space

We define **white space** as new growth spaces (not yet specific opportunities) within the core business, adjacent to it, or entirely outside of it. Success in any of these new possible growth spaces requires meeting an unmet or unarticulated need and/or resolving a significant customer trade-off or tension. Further, capturing white space within the core is typically enabled through overturning established orthodoxies.

Think of it as playing by a new set of rules. Adjacent and noncore white spaces are almost always opened up by pivoting to new areas based on a core competency and/or a strategic asset.

You can begin to identify potential white space by using the four insight areas we've already discussed: customer insights, market discontinuities, competencies and strategic assets, and industry orthodoxies.

Using the Jobs-to-Be-Done Framework to Identify White Spaces

Recall that the jobs-to-be-done framework helps you escape the confines of an existing product or service. By focusing not on your existing product or service but on the job the customer is hiring you to do, you escape the mind-set of served markets and existing products. You focus on the *outcome* the customer seeks. As you develop alternative jobs you or others could perform for the customer, you can map them:

	Our Choices	Traditional Competitors and Peers	Nontraditional Competitors	Potential White Space
Who is our customer?	• • • •	• • • •	• • • •	• • • •
How do we go to market?	• • • •	• • • •	• • • •	• • • •
How do we capture value?	• • • •	• • • •	• • • •	• • • •

Your objective using this framework is to explicitly depict the business model choices (that is, orthodoxies) for your organization, its traditional competitors, and, as possible, competitive newcomers who may be entering or adjacent to your market space. You can then explore new ways you might compete by breaking with one or more current industry practices in order to solve a customer problem in a new,

value-adding way—the question being posed in the fourth column of the framework in the figure.

For example, consider the financial services market for small and medium-size businesses. Mainstream players like Chase, Bank of Montreal, and Deutsche Bank provide funding and financial services to help grow and sustain their customers' business. So does GE Capital.

Recently, GE Capital has moved into an adjacent white space—helping "take on their toughest challenges" and improve their customers' operations through their world-class capabilities in Six Sigma, quality, and operational improvement.[42] GE innovators knew from their own experience that these operational disciplines can unlock significant value in any organization. They could see an unmet need to do so in the small and medium-size business market. And they knew that they had the core competencies in operational improvement within and across the broader GE organization to deliver.

Starting with the logic framed in the figure just presented, they were able to see the opportunity to deliver more value to the core market in competitively advantaged ways. Implicitly if not explicitly, they must have asked these kinds of questions:

- What are the broader set of customer problems and challenges in growing the business beyond financing?
- Are there additional services we can offer that our competitors cannot?

Using Customer Insights to Identify White Spaces

Sometime back, a B2B company conducted observations, immersive interviews, and experience mapping within one of their segment customer groups, heavy manufacturing. Historically, their existing customers were purchasing component products from competitors and from the B2B company and integrating the products into a particular solution. As the insight team went further into their work, two critical insights emerged:

- The customer's tendency to purchase components from several suppliers was, in some cases, driving unneeded complexity and higher costs for the customer's operations.
- The customer's customer was increasingly searching for solutions with built-in intelligence and smarts. That is, they wanted their products to offer ever-increasing self-diagnosis and self-management with regard to maintenance and upkeep.

These two insights led the B2B insight team to create this white space map:

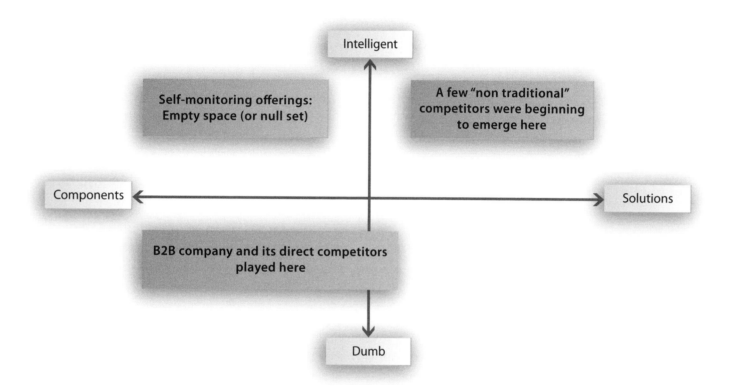

The map makes it clear that none of the major competitors were competing in the top portion—the "space" in which customers appeared to have the most pain. The B2B team was then ready to develop specific ideas regarding how it might capture white space opportunities.

Key Take-Aways

- Keep the principle of Innovation = New Learning central to your efforts. Structure your efforts to acquire new learning through new insights relevant to your particular innovation objective.

- Unpack orthodoxies and look at "jobs to be done" as ways to gain new insights, although there are many others at your disposal.

- Aim your insight efforts within boundaries shaped by a particular challenge, ideally one of strategic importance. As you do so, maintain a holistic view of the business model (or individual business concept) as a central focus of your work. In particular, understand how the new insights you develop may lead you to concepts that target different "who, what, and how" elements of the business model.

- Earn the right to ideate by developing frame-breaking new learning (new insights) first, before you develop ideas. You can develop ideas based on a single type of new insight or based on combinations of multiple, relevant, frame-breaking insights.

- Use frameworks to guide your efforts and to frame dialogue. Think of them as scaffolding to support the hard work of stretching the imagination—yours and your organization's. Avoid thinking of them (or using them) as "templates to be filled out to get to the innovation answer." One of the keys to good innovation outcomes is to translate new learning into new ideas and opportunities. The frameworks are a means to an end rather than an end in themselves.

Enabling Breakthrough Innovation

3

I need strategic innovation—innovation that is coherent and hangs together.

My (CEO or leader) says he/she wants to disrupt the competition . . . How do I do that?

What are the opportunities for me to lead disruption in my market(s)?

I want to identify, capture, and defend new "white space" opportunities.

Use the intersections of insights to stimulate substantially new thinking and ideas.

Insights are foundational to innovation. They help you "think different" in three important ways. You can use your insights to

+ Generate initial ideas. You know from Chapter Two that insights give you the right to ideate by helping you develop new perspectives about your customers, market, and company. In this type of ideation, you use insight intersections—combinations of insights to stimulate thinking and generate substantially new ideas.

+ Identify specific, breakthrough white space opportunities and build an associated pipeline of new product and service concepts that enable you to capture and competitively defend your white space. We refer to this technique as **domaining**.

+ Develop a strategic logic that brings coherence and focus to your innovation efforts over time, allowing you to aim them at the most promising opportunities. We and others describe this technique as creating an **innovation architecture**.[1]

Enabling Breakthrough Innovations Through Insight Combinations

Combinatorial Power of Insights: Identifying White Space Opportunities at Ericsson

Global telecom giant Ericsson deploys a multifaceted, strategic innovation process to identify and act on breakthrough white space opportunities. Their approach has the goal of "using innovation to empower people, business, and society within an envisaged 'networked society' that is sustainable and where everything and everyone that can benefit from a connection will have one."[2]

Ericsson's M-Commerce services portfolio, a next-generation mobile commerce solution, was launched in 2013 after a period of under-the-radar, in-market experiments. Through the service, consumers with access to a mobile device but without direct access to a financial institution can conduct Web-based financial transactions safely and securely. The business also serves Ericsson's operating customers, helping them capture additional wireless revenue.

Here is a closer look at the foundational insights for this breakthrough opportunity.

Industry Discontinuities

Innovators looked at several trends that, taken together, signaled potential disruption.

- Industry forecasts projected that there would be *fifty billion* connected devices by the year 2020.
- Global consumer data showed that whereas 1.5 billion people have a bank account, there are an additional 1.7 billion consumers who have phones but are not customers of any financial institution.
- A substantial number of consumers are using services from the telecom operators whose charging and billing systems are provided by Ericsson.

Realizing that there might be a substantial segment of underserved, underappreciated consumers seeking help with basic financial services, Ericsson explored further, focusing more intently on these consumers.

Consumer Insights—Unmet Needs and Jobs to Be Done

As the team dug deeper, they discovered a global pattern of migration of unskilled workers to the developed world. This workforce regularly wired money back home.

Ericsson surfaced several pain points in the current way money was sent: Mail was unreliable and far from secure. Wire transfers were expensive, and users were too often not treated with respect and dignity. The consumer was not fully in control of the process.

There had to be a better way: a business model that would remove consumer frustration and help operators provide new and better features, one that was a good fit with Ericsson's competencies and strategic assets, one that challenged both Ericsson's and the money transfer industry's orthodoxies.

Core Competencies and Strategic Assets

The company worked with many different telecom providers—companies like Vodafone, China Telecom, and others—with which they had strategic relationships and underlying technologies and know-how specific to the interoperability of disparate telecom systems and infrastructure globally. Although Ericsson was not the market-facing entity providing wire transfers and other M-commerce services, their technology and enabling support was and is critical to the secure and speedy delivery of those services.

Industry Orthodoxies

Historically Ericsson sold equipment and enabling software. In this context, their industry orthodoxy might suggest that "we are not in services." Yet, in many of their strategic relationships, Ericsson adds tremendous value in services to its telecom customers. More recently, the company has been offering strategic innovation consulting to companies inside and outside of its core industry.[3] This experience led the team to consider other ways in which they could add value through services in this domain.

The M-Commerce opportunity started with the initial findings that shaped the discontinuity insight. As the team dove deeper, they reached the "oh yes" moment in which they began to "think different" about what the opportunity could be. We see the opportunity as emerging from the intersection of the insights—the combinatory power of insights—as depicted here:

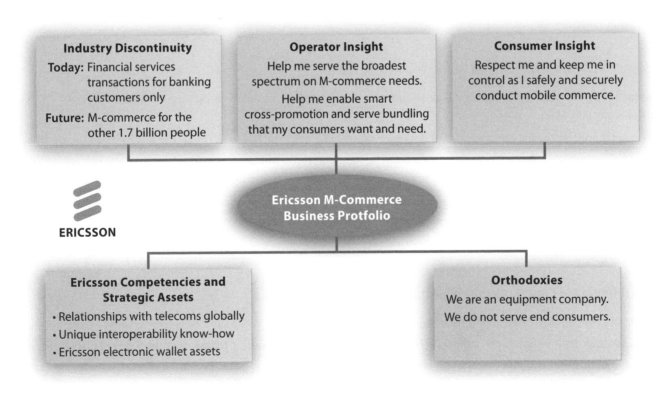

Industry Discontinuity
Today: Financial services transactions for banking customers only
Future: M-commerce for the other 1.7 billion people

Operator Insight
Help me serve the broadest spectrum on M-commerce needs.
Help me enable smart cross-promotion and serve bundling that my consumers want and need.

Consumer Insight
Respect me and keep me in control as I safely and securely conduct mobile commerce.

ERICSSON

Ericsson M-Commerce Business Protfolio

Ericsson Competencies and Strategic Assets
• Relationships with telecoms globally
• Unique interoperability know-how
• Ericsson electronic wallet assets

Orthodoxies
We are an equipment company.
We do not serve end consumers.

● Domaining: Building a Pipeline of Related Concepts

We define a domain as **a portfolio of specific product and/or service concepts, each of which provides the same customer (or consumer) benefit**. A well-crafted and well-executed domain carries with it a cumulative logic, encompassing specific opportunities and specific enabling actions required to win.

Note that you need not engage in "domaining" to develop an interesting opportunity and bring it to market. Domaining helps you pivot off of the one-off innovations that too frequently flow from many new product development (NPD) processes in both B2B and B2C settings. Whether or not you want or need domain development as a part of your innovation work will be situationally specific.

Use the domaining technique if you would like your new product or service efforts to

+ Tell a growth story, based on an insight-driven point of view regarding how and why you are going to occupy and defend the white space over time.
+ Ensure that your growth efforts integrate a top-down, strategic view and a bottom-up view that details both the

specific opportunities you will pursue *and* the actions you will initiate to realize those opportunities.

+ Place importance on creating and dynamically managing an integrated set of actions that support your NPD efforts, explicitly connecting short-term and long-term actions.

> *A well-crafted and well-executed domain carries with it a cumulative logic, encompassing specific opportunities and specific enabling actions required to win.*

Domains help you tell a growth story to build coherence in your NPD efforts.

Recall that a well-crafted and well-executed domain carries with it a cumulative logic, encompassing specific opportunities and specific enabling actions required to win. The leaders guiding Shell's GameChanger process cite three reasons for using domains to target breakthrough growth across their organization:[4]

+ To connect the shorter term with the longer term, implicitly bringing logic and coherence to a set of related opportunities.
+ To link strategy and technology. Most Shell GameChanger projects have a proprietary technology within them.

♦ To connect bottom-up with top-down innovation efforts, each of which are initiated by different teams, sometimes without explicit awareness of each other.

UnitedHealth Group (UHG) also uses a domain-centered approach to guide their development of breakthrough innovation, aiming their efforts at the most important strategic challenges. They do so by applying insight techniques to shape a point of view about the most compelling customer problems they might solve, the orthodoxies they could productively overturn, and the competencies and strategic assets that would enable new growth. For example, their consumer-based domain is exploring ways to "help people live healthier lives."[5]

Unlike the more traditional approach to product road mapping, domaining requires you to ensure that each opportunity within a given portfolio is helping you advance toward the same destination, your North Star. We often find that an NPD pipeline for a given business unit contains decent and sometimes quite compelling opportunities. Too often, however, these opportunities are not strategically connected. By contrast, domains drive you to tell a strategic growth story rather than merely providing a set of opportunities that are only somewhat related.

Let's look at an example of a successful domain and then describe the steps you can follow to create a domain (or domains) relevant to your context.

Crayola uses the domaining technique to fill its pipeline with new growth opportunities. They began by developing foundational insights that helped them greatly expand their notion of the potential products, markets, and even industry in which they competed. As you read in Chapter Two, among their new learning was the tension felt by the child's caregiver between, on the one hand, her desire for the child to have a fun, immersive, self-directed experience and, on the other hand, her (understandable) worry about the situations in which the child can do this. Such experiences were achievable if she could attend to the work with her child, but were more problematic when she could not (for example, when driving, or preparing a family meal).[6] These and other insights led to new growth domains, including the "No Limits" domain depicted here:

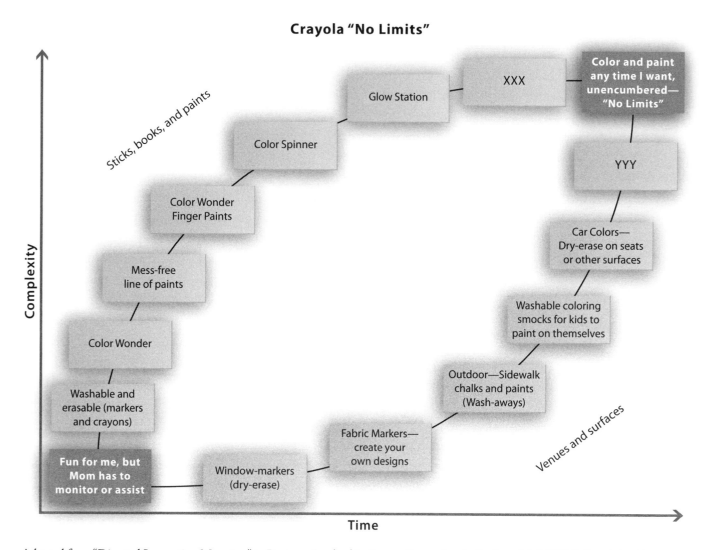

Crayola "No Limits"

Adapted from "Directed Innovation Mapping," in Business Leadership Forum, *Innovating the Business Model While Sustaining Core Performance* (Arlington, VA: Corporate Executive Board, 2008), 65–98, and interviews with Crayola innovation leadership, June–August 2013

Let's take a closer look at the construct.

For Crayola and other organizations, the domaining framework is enormously helpful in conceiving of and acting on breakthrough opportunities. The two dimensions of time (x-axis) and complexity (y-axis) guide teams to think about the appropriate sequence of each concept, providing a longer-term view of specific, discrete product concepts that can be brought to market over time.

At the upper right, the innovation team frames a longer-term, benefit-based destination for the domain—an aspiration or dream space. The dream space acts as a North Star, guiding development efforts.

Note that the domain can have more than one "path" in its migration description. Multiple paths can work "future back" from the North Star aspiration. These paths represent domain-specific dimensions of innovation and competitive advantage that the teams are trying to develop. Each path is populated with specific product and service concepts.

A Corporate Executive Board study documents the Crayola story, correctly noting that the platforms represent dream spaces that "will often require stepping outside of the product categories and business model to which the company is accustomed."[7] Using the domaining technique, the company is able to deploy staff to those opportunities that are ready for execution, while simultaneously looking ahead to capabilities that they will need to develop to enable the fulfillment of future potential opportunities that are more of a stretch. The technique also allows Crayola to manage the development of technologies to enable it to migrate toward the targeted dream space.[8]

Ericsson's M-Commerce opportunity enables the company to bring a benefit-based portfolio of products and services to the market over time, as depicted in the Ericsson M-Commerce Business Portfolio image.

Insight-Driven Domain Development

You can develop a domain with inputs from different types of sources: insights and/or areas of strategic importance.

- **Insight-driven** domains are developed from a subset of the ideas generated through the combinatory power of insights—insight collisions—as we saw in the Crayola and Ericsson examples.

> *Domain development allows you to proactively drive new offerings AND their underlying technology and capability development agenda.*

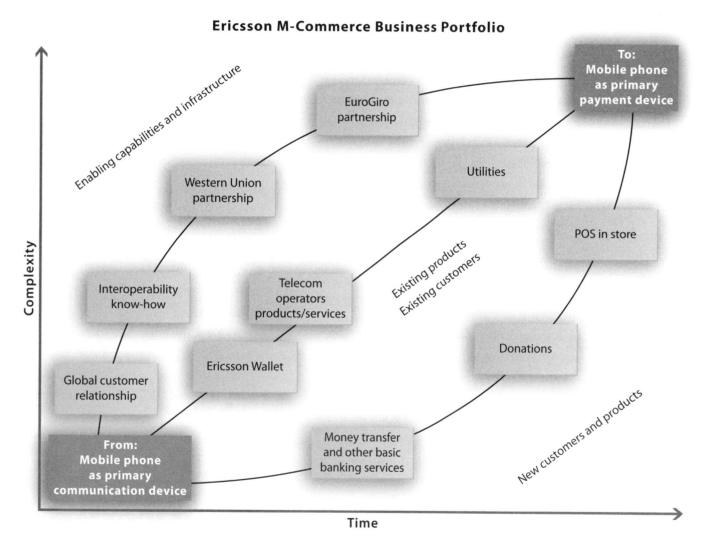

Ericsson M-Commerce Business Portfolio

Note: Ericsson's migration map reflects those products, services, and enabling actions that are visible now in the marketplace. For reasons of confidentiality, we have not described details on planned and funded actions that will be rolled out in the following years.

+ **Areas of strategic importance** can point you toward potential domains—or, at least, focus your insight efforts.

The most effective way to create domains is to build on a strong foundation of insights. As we've said elsewhere, insights give you the right to ideate. Why? Because the insights are developed in the context of a broad objective focused on a particular challenge, such as UHG's strategic focus on "helping people live healthier lives."

Sharing Insights and Sketching Out Possible Domains

In practice, this type of insight-based ideation process is structured as a set of steps, the first of which is to share the insights prior to generating ideas and creating domains. Include the insight team and, as possible, other internal colleagues with relevant expertise, skills, and passion.

Look at useful collisions of individual insights to stimulate thinking about new growth opportunities. You can capture the ideas resulting from the collision on a simple Excel spreadsheet or with other such software.

The initial idea sets will not be fully detailed business concepts. Rather, they are likely to be fragments of detailed concepts based on the inspiration of a particular set of insights. Transforming the fragments into candidate domains is a creative exercise executed with these steps:

1. Review all the idea fragments to look for themes and threads that represent interesting growth spaces (potential domains).

2. Once you have candidate domains in mind, for any given domain of interest, begin to detail your view, asking yourself these questions:

   + **Who is the customer or consumer target?** What is the problem the domain addresses? What tensions are resolved? What benefit or value is delivered?

   + **How does the customer solve the problem today?** What do they do? What benefit or value do they receive from this choice?

   + **Why might we be a better solution or alternative?** Why might we be able to provide or deliver a step-change improvement over what happens today? What will be better from the customer's perspective? What is our source of advantage?

+ **How big might this domain white space be?** What is our rationale for our view on size of the space?

3. Select a smaller number of domains on which you will elaborate more rigorously. The appropriate number of priority domains for further investigation will vary by organization and circumstance. Also, you may find that some domains warrant combination due to similarities in benefit or because combining related propositions yields an enhanced single proposition.

Once you have developed your candidate domains you will be ready to select the most promising domains for further elaboration.

Elaborating and Assessing Your Domain

After you select one or more domains that appear to offer high potential, bring them to life through more detailed elaboration. As you detail the new domain, you will find that there is much you do not know about the opportunity space it represents. Therefore, you may need a few weeks to fully describe and investigate the domain with clear and strong business logic.

You can use the domain elaboration framework shown in the next image as a guide for considering or discussing your initial views and examining unknowns and uncertainties that may surface. Begin by describing the domain from the customers' perspective: specify the target customers, consider the problem they are facing and how they solve the problem today, and form your view regarding why your solution will be different enough for customers to care.

Assessing Capabilities and Competitive Context

With an initial view of the customer problems and tensions you address and the value you might provide, you should next deepen your understanding of how you and both traditional and nontraditional competitors would attempt to win in the domain. The

Domain Elaboration

Domain Title:	
Elevator Description:	

Value Proposition	**Differentiation**
Who is the target customer?	How will this be better than currently available solutions?
What is the problem we solve for the customer? What unmet needs does the customer currently have?	
What are we providing with this domain? What is it about?	How will we win with this domain? What is our source of advantage?
What benefits will this provide? Why will target customers care?	

next table lists helpful questions to frame your dialogue.

Take note of the questions on unknowns and risks:

Unknown refers to a knowledge gap—an issue that may be unclear in regard to the extent of internal capabilities and/or the availability of technology and IP you might license from the outside.

Risks are issues you see clearly, such as an economic shock beyond your control, and other risks that can be mitigated (for example, by learning more about the potential for customer acceptance).

"What must be true" for your domain to succeed means, "What must go right for us to win?" instead of the more typical mind-set of "What could go wrong?"

Domain Assessment Questions–I: Differentiation and Advantage

Competition	• Who are the current players in the space?
	• What are the current available offerings to customers?
	• Where do current offerings fall short of customer needs?
	• Who are the possible future entrants, and what might they bring to the space?
Differentiation	• How, specifically, will we differentiate ourselves in the space? What will we bring that others do not?
	• What are our short-run advantages over existing solutions?
	• How will we maintain differentiation over the long run and sustain advantage?
Capabilities	• What capabilities and assets do we bring that are valuable to the space? What gives us permission to play?
	• Which capabilities and assets are unique? Why will we win over time?
	• What capabilities that are required to win do we lack? How can we fill those gaps?
	• What internal challenges will we have to overcome to pursue this domain?
Risks and Unknowns	• What must be true for us to succeed in this space?
	• What are the most central unknowns for us in successfully pursuing the domain?
	• What next steps would help close the knowledge gaps with regard to those key unknowns?

You may find that as you explore your domain by discussing the nature of the competition, sources of advantage, and both existing and new capabilities, you are iteratively refining your initial take on the target customer and potential value proposition.

Understanding the Economic Physics of Your Domain

At this point, you are trying to get a sense of "how big is big" relative to your domain, with particular emphasis on determining that the domain is big enough to matter for your particular context. You are not aiming for "audit-ready" financials in any way. You only want to focus on the physics of the economic model (the important drivers of revenue, growth, cost and profit) for the domain and understand its overall market potential. This table offers a few important questions to guide your team's discussion:

Domain Assessment Questions–II: Economic Attractiveness

Our Economic Model	• What is the likely (or most attractive) business model we will use to drive economic value for ourselves in the space? Are there multiple models? • How, specifically, will we realize economic rents for value provided in the model? • What assumptions are we making that have to be true for this to be realized?
Market Potential	• What is the evidence or case that the space is large? • How large is the market we are looking to address? • How or why is the benefit we are offering to that market substantial? Can we capture a sufficient portion of the addressable market? • How can we make the space bigger and even more attractive for customers and for ourselves? • How high is up for us? What is the underlying logic to our view?

Building on Osterwalder and Pigneur's conception of the business model, these questions on economic model and market potential are intended to guide you in advancing your framing and your dialogue about the domain space. As we will assert repeatedly, the tools and frameworks described throughout the book are intended to help you focus your learning process and dialogue effectively. This is not an exercise in template filling!

Migration Maps: Sequencing Your Efforts Smartly

Recall the definition of a domain: **a portfolio of specific product and/or service concepts, each of which provides the same customer (or consumer) benefit**. Of course, you will not act on all opportunities within the portfolio simultaneously. Rather the opportunities will be time sequenced, based on such interdependencies as customer acceptance, evolution of technology, development of a given distribution channel, and scale of investment.

It is important to be thoughtful about the sequence of migration, so it can be helpful to use a framework such as the one in Figure 3-1.

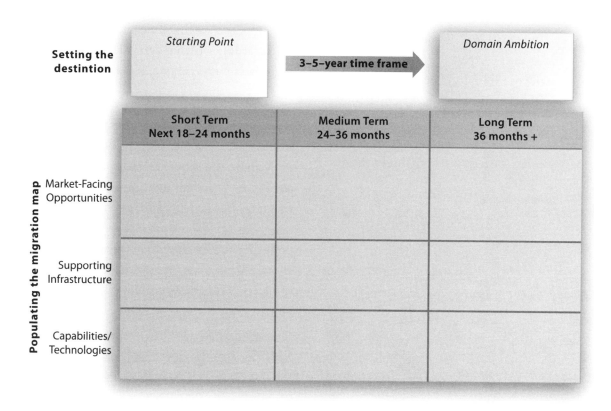

Figure 3-1 Developing Migration Paths

To construct the migration map, work from the "future back," starting with your North Star ambition. Of course, the time frames shown on the map are illustrative and highly dependent on your innovation objectives and company context. In the energy industry, for example, the migration map might depict a ten- or even a twenty-year migration. In consumer products and high tech, the time frames are no longer than three to five years and, in some instances, could even be shorter.

With your initial ambition declared, you should consider the specific opportunities that belong on the map. The ideas you used to create the domain are a great place to start. Review each opportunity and consider whether it

+ Is delivered to a target segment you already serve
+ Requires an existing or new channel to market
+ Uses existing technology or requires new technology
+ Requires a partner to develop the product and/or bring it to market
+ Depends on another concept within the domain to be commercialized first

As you develop greater clarity regarding the time sequence of opportunities, you will start to surface other enabling actions, such as the

+ **Supporting infrastructure** required, including information systems, channel distribution support, and training for your (direct or indirect) sales force
+ **Capabilities and technologies** that support a specific concept(s) and a view regarding whether you will rely on new or existing internal or external technology

As you iterate and identify "enabling actions," your understanding of the domain will mature. As a result, you will modify and evolve both the sequence and specifics of actions and opportunities on your migration map. You may find that additional ideas either emerge from your discussions or are pulled from your initial idea generation efforts. These changes are a natural outcome of rich discussions and should be welcomed.

Selecting Early Opportunities for Opportunity-Level Elaboration

Once you create the domain and populate your first version of the migration map with notional product and/or service concepts, you may then want to move to focusing on one or more early opportunities as your starting point for making the domain even more tangible and actionable.

Assess several opportunities or potential actions qualitatively. Use specific criteria such as these:

+ **Customer benefit and problem:** How well does the opportunity or action deliver on the core benefit of the domain? How well does it address the customer problem or resolve a significant customer tension?
+ **Competitive advantage:** What are the sustainably defensive advantages you bring to this opportunity? Examples might include brand, channel, customer relationship, or proprietary technology.
+ **Size of prize:** How big do you think the specific opportunity could be? Typically, you would base your estimate on a view of how the target customers for your opportunity solve the problem today through other means.
+ **Timing:** How soon might you be in market? What is the time to value?

+ **Gateway:** Is this a logical first step as a gateway to developing additional opportunities within the domain? Does it provide valuable learning and experience toward another (larger) opportunity on the migration path? Are the prerequisites in place? Is this opportunity dependent on other capabilities or opportunities? Why is it logical to start here?
+ **Barriers to success:** What gives you pause? What might make this opportunity difficult?

Of course, further elaboration and assessment of any individual opportunity will be required. The criteria here are simply guides for assessing which of those opportunities you might want to frame and assess first or "next" as the case may be.

Bringing Strategic Focus to Your Efforts: Innovation Architecture

United Health Group aims its innovation efforts broadly through its strategic aiming point of "helping people live healthier lives." As we mentioned at the beginning of the chapter, there is another technique you can

> Innovation architecture represents your proprietary point of view regarding how you want to innovate to win.

use to bring strategic focus to your innovation efforts: innovation architecture.[9] The architecture provides a blueprint of sorts to guide your efforts. It informs broad boundaries within which to focus. It also speaks to particular dimensions on which you believe you can compete and win.

Your innovation architecture represents your *proprietary point of view* regarding the future you wish to create. You base the architecture on a shared view of the underlying insights and a view of your most promising new growth domains. A good architecture implicitly or explicitly speaks to the benefits you are delivering and the unique competencies, know-how, and assets that help you compete and win sustainably.[10]

Example: Apple

As context, let's remind ourselves of Apple's portfolio, circa 2013:

- Over one billion TV show downloads and 380 million movie downloads[11]
- A *profit pool* share of 45 percent[12] for personal computers and 69 percent for mobile phones[13]
- Nearly six hundred million unique iTunes accounts with an average *profitability* of $40 each[14] and over twenty-five billion unique downloads—ten billion since 2010.[15]

Impressive to say the least.

If you look closely at Apple's success from the launch of the iPod to its current product and services portfolio, you can infer the few, select dimensions on which it uniquely competes and wins.[16] Of course, much credit for Apple's success is given to Steve Jobs. And certainly his leadership, passion, and considerable creativity are significant reasons for the success. Yet Apple's success is not based solely on the contributions of a single individual, however uniquely talented. Rather, it is built on a point of view, passionately held and shared within the company, regarding the few dimensions on which the company will compete and win. Jobs shaped the view and held all to exceed its standard. But the point of view was also shaped and promulgated by others.

Apple's innovation is represented by three reinforcing and complementary dimensions we use to describe its innovation architecture:

- **Reducing and/or removing complexity** of the consumer's digital life experience by ensuring that Apple maintains control of each stage of development: design and development of material, hardware, and software; content procurement and distribution; online and brick-and-mortar retail and warranty; and service and repair.

  In this respect, Apple is the most successful vertically integrated retailer on the planet. All efforts—from the early stages of its supply chain to the consumer's experience with purchasing and use—are aimed at integration. Across products, the ease of use and interoperability make it simple and easy for the consumers to experience and enjoy their digital lives.

- **Focusing obsessively on understanding and improving on the consumer's digital life**—and doing so at the individually discrete pixel level within that experience—in ways that holistically enhance the experience.

  This obsession is manifested in small details that cumulatively enable a distinctive user experience across all Apple devices. It is why the user can employ TrueType fonts, retina display, rubber band scrolling patents, and scalable calculator numbers. The value is not focused on one feature or another. Rather the value has to do with creating an experience that continues to reveal itself over time through exposure and increased familiarity with the products. It is about an experience that feels natural by comparison to that offered by other competitors.

- **Making it personal** by building a smaller number of products that magnificently address individual human indignities and fulfill deeply felt desires—rather than "needs or use cases."

Apple makes beautiful products because they *believe* it is what we desire. We *want* these products rather than need them. Apple consumers understand that the products cost more to be made beautiful, but believe that beautiful things work better and are more valuable. This context makes clear why Apple focused on music, movies, and personal creation rather than on spreadsheets and enterprise applications. They made a bet that *personal passion* was going to be a growth industry that would be served by personal digital devices. In this regard, they put the personal back into the personal computer.

For Apple, a consistent and relentless focus in three complementary and reinforcing areas brought clarity of purpose and cumulative impact to their efforts over time. *Think different.*

Key Take-Aways

- You can create compelling ideas by looking at the interactions and combinations of a subset of your insights. The combinatory power of insights enables breakthrough innovation.

- Individual ideas can be laddered up to bigger, bolder ideas through the technique of building domains. Domaining is an excellent way to identify, act on, and capture white space opportunities within, adjacent to, and outside your current business.

- Like other aspects of innovation, domaining is an iterative, interactive learning process. Iteration helps you refine and clarify your thinking, enabling you to persuasively articulate the business logic of the domain.

- Leading organizations advance their vision even further by holding a shared aspiration that represents the sum of their opportunities, domains, and growth actions. This summary view represents their innovation architecture. It is an explicit, shared view that is proactively managed and relentlessly driven.

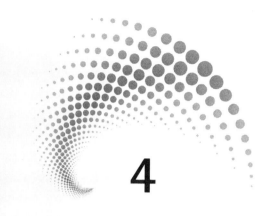

From Nascent Idea
to Business Concept

4

I have a nascent idea; now what? How do I turn this into something I can evaluate and act on?

I have a promising idea that is stalled in my development pipeline—how do I get it "unstuck"?

My team (or a team) is overly focused on technology . . . How can I "unstick" their thinking?

My team is focused only on product or brand—how can I broaden their thinking?

Suppose you have landed on an interesting idea. You may have captured it on a sticky note, detailed it in short form in a concept brief, or characterized its essence with a customer value proposition (CVP). Although the new idea is energizing, you nonetheless know there is much more to do in order to determine if it might become a new avenue of growth. You need to take your idea and turn it into a full-fledged, well-thought-through business concept. Think of it as advancing that thought on the sticky note to the point where it is an actionable, vetted, and compelling opportunity.

You may also need to know how to get an idea "unstuck" by breaking out of an all too common singular focus on the "what" of product, brand, or technology and broaden your thinking to the "who and how" elements of the business model. You need to productively challenge the conventional (and rigid) wisdom of your organization and industry. And you need to know how to broaden thinking even further through market-proven business concept elaboration techniques: **stretch, elaborate, and iterate (SEI).**

You may have colleagues in your organization who move from nascent idea to compelling concept naturally and instinctively—like maestros, so to speak. But the "maestro model" is not scalable. And without scalability, the organization will remain stuck. You need a way to approach the challenge systematically, and that is what the SEI method provides. SEI applies the discipline of iterative divergence and convergence—a scalable and enduring process that will yield much greater impact over time. It is an innovative, disciplined way to systematically drive an idea or concept from sticky note to action.

● Changing Your Mind-Set About the Innovation Process

The best path to interesting concepts is through insights generated at the initial stages of your innovation process. The next challenge is to focus on developing an actionable and compelling innovation concept.

The next graphic depicts a generalized innovation process. The specifics will differ significantly across organizations, but this generalized process describes the critical activities on which you should focus.

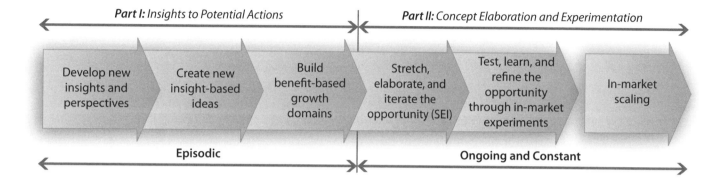

The foundation for good ideas lies in part I of the generalized process: rich external and internal insights leading to interesting ideas, which may ladder up to distinct opportunity domains (depending on your process and use of chosen steps within that process).

If yours is like most organizations, part I is viewed as difficult and challenging, with its activities conducted episodically to replenish the pipeline or to respond to an unanticipated market development.

Many organizations view part II rather differently. Typically, the second part of the process is managed as ongoing and continuous work, with ideas progressing through various stages of increasing coherence as you move to go/no-go commercialization decisions. Many organizations view their experience in executing part II as sufficient if not robust and thus believe that succeeding in part II "is just an execution issue." In our experience, this type of assessment is off the mark—and significantly so.

Why? Well, let's first set context. As noted elsewhere, we define innovation as **an idea, successfully commercialized**. One important implication of this definition is the imperative that you focus innovation principles and efforts on both part I and part II of the process. We often hear or read self-assessments proclaiming, "We have plenty of ideas; our issue is execution. We are not effective at getting the ideas to market." In practice, these voices are speaking to part II of the generalized process depicted above, implicitly declaring that "we know how to do part II with our typical techniques."

We typically find that shortcomings in part II of the process are not due to execution alone. Rather, we too often find that the concepts progressing through the back end undershoot their potential. The most common root causes have to do with concepts that

> *Commercializing distinctive concepts requires more than using existing or "assumed" business model constructs and levers.*

+ Become diluted as teams hand off the idea through the back-end stages leading to commercialization. Compromises are made, and, often unintentionally, the initial distinctiveness of the CVP is weakened.
  + Reflect that the team has failed to fully explore all aspects of the potential business model, most commonly by focusing only on the "what" of products or offerings without equal exploration of the "who and how."
+ Are more appropriately suited for experimentation rather than for full-scale launch.

+ The team did not continue to stretch, elaborate, and iterate the concept, implicitly assuming that all necessary learning has already been attained or captured in the front-end innovation work performed up to the point of idea development.

We believe that a high-performing innovation process must include all aspects of innovation, from insights to in-market realization. That is the best path to delivering "an idea successfully commercialized."

The SEI Approach

Commercializing and scaling distinctive concepts demands that innovation remain inherent within your nascent concept through to the back end (part II) of your innovation work (or process). It requires much more than just taking the concept and executing it using "assumed" existing business model constructs or levers. You must **stretch, elaborate, and iterate** (SEI) the ideas through disciplined and structured thought processes that bring continued new learning on the "what, who, and how(s)" of the business concept. It is through this nuanced discipline that ideas turn into actionable products, ventures, or business opportunities without dying on the vine or losing the original gestalt of the idea and its inherent innovation.

Underpinning the SEI approach are several principles to keep front and center in your work efforts:

+ **Elaborate all elements of the business concept.** In addition to the **What** of products, technology, and brand, you should also focus on the **Who** of benefit and target and the **How** of go-to-market, value capture, and defensibility. Elaborating around all elements of the business concept widens the aperture for innovation significantly.
+ **Start with the CVP, and let the rest follow.** Keep in mind that if there is no compelling CVP, there is no opportunity. Start your elaboration here and let technology, routes to market, and all the other elements of the business model follow.
+ **Surface explicit, critical assumptions as you iterate.** Track those assumptions so that you can prioritize and proactively manage risk (unknowns) later.
+ **Iterate and refine.** You rarely get it right with only your first pass through the framing of the business concept. More typically, as you elaborate certain elements of the business concept, you will reconsider and revise other elements. Iterative elaboration is of great value and helps ensure that you are thinking systemically.

With these principles in mind, we'll describe select techniques for SEI which you and your organization can learn, apply, and use repeatedly. As we do so, we will speak to different circumstances where these techniques are most helpful.

Developing the CVP

Let's start with the most important aspect of elaborating an opportunity: understanding the value of your opportunity to the customer. The next chart depicts a technique and thought process through which to stretch, elaborate, and iterate the customer or consumer value proposition for a particular concept.

Remember, no compelling value proposition, no opportunity. So start your elaboration efforts there.

Unpacking and Repacking the Value Proposition

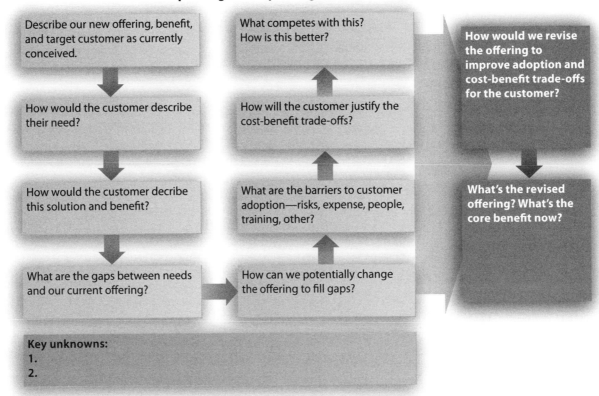

Describe our new offering, benefit, and target customer as currently conceived.

↓

How would the customer describe their need?

↓

How would the customer decribe this solution and benefit?

↓

What are the gaps between needs and our current offering?

→

What competes with this? How is this better?

↑

How will the customer justify the cost-benefit trade-offs?

↑

What are the barriers to customer adoption—risks, expense, people, training, other?

↑

How can we potentially change the offering to fill gaps?

How would we revise the offering to improve adoption and cost-benefit trade-offs for the customer?

↓

What's the revised offering? What's the core benefit now?

Key unknowns:
1.
2.

Note that each question within the framework requires you to think from different perspectives about the potential value provided to the customer. The purpose in doing so is to guide you and your colleagues to pull apart and then piece back together your view of the customer benefit.

The framework forces you to discuss the benefit from many different angles to help you articulate a more compelling benefit. Through your unpacking-and-repacking dialogue, you will more likely create an expanded, improved, and much better vetted proposition right from the start.

There are additional benefits to the approach:

+ It inherently challenges orthodoxies by asking how the concept will be better than current alternatives in meaningful and distinct ways.
+ It forces you to iterate the CVP (benefit) and offering as you and your colleagues debate the questions.
+ It helps you surface the critical assumptions that underpin your concept, enabling you to explicitly test and validate those assumptions.

Global telecom giant Ericsson applied this type of thinking in its approach to its M-commerce business portfolio (discussed in Chapter Three). The company's initial sense of opportunity emerged from its awareness of the 1.7 billion consumers who have access to a mobile device but do not have a bank account. From there they began to consider the consumer's context: her frustrations, the trade-offs being forced upon her by her current solution, and, as possible, her unarticulated needs. And because Ericsson is a B2B company, the team of course also explored the same context for its potential B2B customers, telecom operators like Deutche Telecom and Verizon.[1]

Unsticking a Nascent Concept

Sometimes a team becomes overly enamored with a particular technology or feature that they believe is central to the new concept. But their obsession with a technology or feature that they sense has inherent value blocks them from clearly articulating the value for the customer. As a result, the opportunity may be killed, or, worse, it may linger for months or more in the early or middle stages of the development pipeline.

A simple framework to unstick a team's thinking in this type of situation is outlined here:

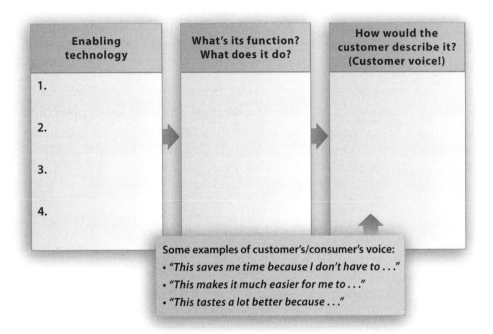

Enabling technology	What's its function? What does it do?	How would the customer describe it? (Customer voice!)
1.		
2.		
3.		
4.		

Some examples of customer's/consumer's voice:
• *"This saves me time because I don't have to . . ."*
• *"This makes it much easier for me to . . ."*
• *"This tastes a lot better because . . ."*

This approach is straightforward.

+ First, focus on the technologies that you instinctively believe have enormous value. Ask yourself: What does the technology do? What functionality does it enable?
+ Second, ask yourself: Why would the consumer or customer care? How would *they* articulate the value *in their own voice?* Note that the cause for the concept's being "stuck" is **not** one of execution or a commercialization hand-off. Rather, it is insufficient clarity on the customer benefits and the CVP.

Working through this simple process will help you unstick your thinking by guiding you to the aspects of the technology about which a customer may care. In this way, you move from "technology-speak" to "customer-speak," allowing you to move on to elaborate the business model elements of your concept.

Developing the Supporting Business Model

Once you have a clear sense of the benefit and value to the customer, you can shift your focus to other elements of the business model.

The framework in this chart guides the iterative dialogue you and your team should have about your nascent concept's potential business model. It compels you to consider ways in which your concept will be distinct from the options and experiences

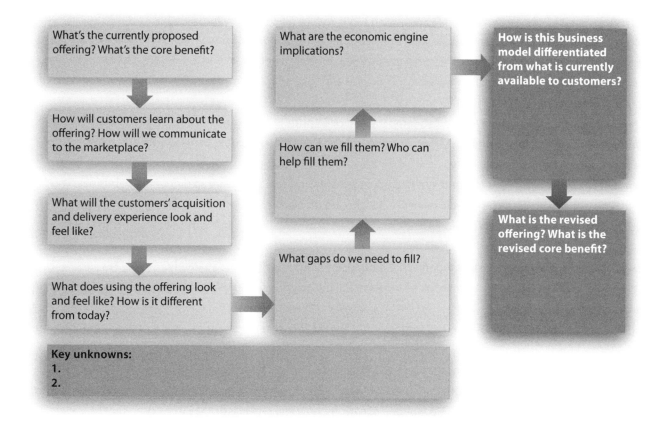

What's the currently proposed offering? What's the core benefit?

How will customers learn about the offering? How will we communicate to the marketplace?

What will the customers' acquisition and delivery experience look and feel like?

What does using the offering look and feel like? How is it different from today?

What are the economic engine implications?

How can we fill them? Who can help fill them?

What gaps do we need to fill?

How is this business model differentiated from what is currently available to customers?

What is the revised offering? What is the revised core benefit?

Key unknowns:
1.
2.

currently available. Also important, it sheds a bright light on the feasibility of delivering on the concept's promise by forcing you to address the specific capabilities required for commercial success. It also helps you surface unknowns about which you must learn more, and assumptions fundamental to success that may require in-market experimentation.

Business Model Iteration: Crayola

To make this process more concrete, let's turn again to Crayola. Imagine how you might answer the business model elaboration questions regarding Crayola Color Wonder. Crayola introduced Color Wonder in 1999. The product offers a "mess-free" solution in that the coloring book and the markers produce color only when used together, thus eliminating the problem of young, unsupervised children drawing on walls, tables, or other surfaces you prefer to keep clean and "mark-free." The product (and subsequent product developments as well) provided a new benefit and experience of "no mess," "no limits" on where and when the child could use it, and surprise and delight for the user as well.[2]

When Crayola first introduced Color Wonder, the company had been putting high-quality 16-, 32-, and 64-count boxes of crayons on the shelves of retailers for decades. Their crayons and children's markers could be used with any coloring book or paper. The new Color Wonder concept offered new benefits ("no limits") through a new delivery model (books and markers interdependent with one another). Because the new product benefits and solutions were so different, the business model questions were different as well. Thus the Crayola team probably found themselves asking:

- What does the overall business model look like?
- Should we sell the markers and the books together? Should we continue to sell them separately?
- What is the best route to market? Do we want all channels to sell the coloring books as well? Should we create an open or proprietary "system"?
- What happens when the child finishes using a coloring book? Should she or he purchase a new package altogether, or just a new book?
- How about pricing? The Color Wonder concept presents a different and very compelling value proposition—what's it worth? What about merchandising and communication? At retail, how can we convey this new thing and its advantages? Given how different this product is from a 32-count box of crayons, how will retailers display it?[3]

You get the point: if it's truly new and innovative, the business concept has new-to-the-company and new-to-the-industry—perhaps even new-to-the-world—elements and aspects to it. Therefore, you need to apply new and iterative thinking in a structured and disciplined manner. This iterative and expansive thought process greatly improves your chances of landing on a differentiated value proposition within a business model that is optimized with reinforcing elements of "who, what, and how."

Continuing Your Learning Through In-the-Room and Out-of-the-Room Exploration

Not all new learning is facilitated by tools and frameworks. You should think of the work of innovation as that of converting new learning into new actions.

As we have said elsewhere in The Guide, the frameworks we share are simply scaffolding to help structure your dialogue and learning. You will need to get out of the conference room and into the market to fill knowledge gaps, learn about new analogs, and develop new perspectives. We find that innovation teams understand this for the front end of their innovation work

(perspectives and ideation). However, as they progress to the back half of the work (part II), they too often fail to continue learning. In this respect, they fail to engage in SEI—to stretch, elaborate, and iterate.

You must continue building and integrating new learning and new perspectives across the end-to-end process if you are to be successful. This learning is best facilitated by a mix of "in the room" and "out of the room" exploration that allows the organization to create truly new and innovative insights and business concepts and models—concepts and models that have expansive and innovative logic, along with the type of "stickiness" that allows for the sustained pursuit necessary for successful realization.

Using Analogs to Stretch the Business Concept

Even after you've explored the CVP and the delivery business model (both "in and out of the room"), you can further expand the model if you wish to do so. Although there are many techniques available, we find that using analogs can quickly help you stretch, elaborate, and iterate further. Here is a framework that enables exploration of the concept from multiple angles, including the basis

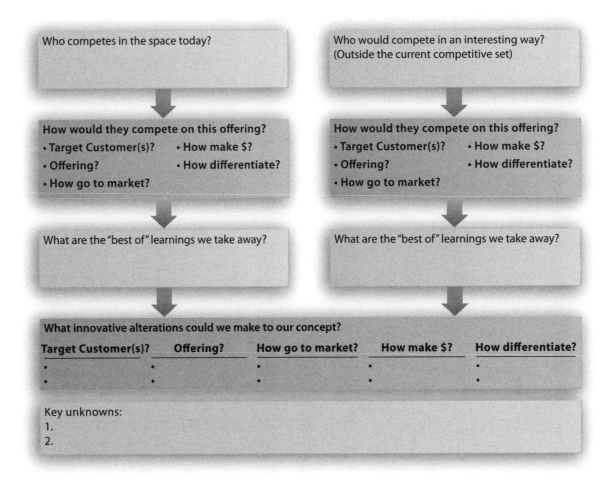

Who competes in the space today?

Who would compete in an interesting way?
(Outside the current competitive set)

How would they compete on this offering?
- Target Customer(s)?   • How make $?
- Offering?   • How differentiate?
- How go to market?

How would they compete on this offering?
- Target Customer(s)?   • How make $?
- Offering?   • How differentiate?
- How go to market?

What are the "best of" learnings we take away?

What are the "best of" learnings we take away?

What innovative alterations could we make to our concept?

Target Customer(s)?	Offering?	How go to market?	How make $?	How differentiate?
•	•	•	•	•
•	•	•	•	•

Key unknowns:
1.
2.

of competition, an explicit articulation of relevant internal and external insights, unknowns, and key assumptions. It places you in the mind-set of a different organization, asking you to consider:

+ What if Company X or Y were to pursue this idea? How would they do it? What would they do differently? What new expansions of the opportunity would they think of? What new riffs would they play?

- How would they communicate it to the market? How would they merchandise it?
- How would they price it and why?
- How would they think differently about the economic engine (and extracting economic rents)?
- Which of these ideas or learnings might we apply to our concept, and how?

A few other considerations will help you benefit from this framework:

- When thinking about nontraditional competitors, think broadly about your market space and your framing of that space. Returning to Crayola as an example, if they were stretching a concept, they might want to think broadly about the many companies competing for Mom's and child's time, attention, and share of wallet. In this broader frame, Crayola is also competing with game makers, toy marketers, and motion picture studios.
- To gain richer insights, you should broaden your competitive frame to include direct competitors and other, nontraditional competitors who may be hired by the consumer to do a similar job.
- When thinking of companies "outside your industry," it is best to consider organizations that are both interesting and in some way relevant to your specific situation. But regardless of the analog you choose to apply, ensure that you are generating ideas that are relevant to your context. Your challenge is not to mimic the actions the analog would specifically take if acting on its own. Rather you should consider how your organization would design and execute the concept if it were to apply the mind-set of the analog, coupled with your organization's strengths, needs, and propensities.
- The in-the-room and out-of-the-room learning concept applies here as well. You may not know as much as you think you know about how the analog actually operates or works in market. If you don't, you can and should take the opportunity to go learn before you apply the SEI techniques. Doing so will pay dividends in multiple ways: accurate information and more new learning infused into your innovation efforts, both of which add up to a higher-efficacy application of the technique.

When elaborating your opportunity, broaden your competitive frame to include traditional and nontraditional competitors the consumer may hire to do a similar job.

Framing and Elaborating the Economic Model

Finally, think through the economic model of your new concepts. We suggest that you make this the last step in the elaboration process. Too often, teams start with—or are asked to start with—detailed descriptions of the economics of a given concept without first developing a clear understanding of the customer target, the problem they hope to solve, the potential route(s) to market, and the source(s) of differentiation and advantage. By first stretching, elaborating, and iterating the concept, you will be best positioned to thoughtfully address the way(s) in which your concept will help you create and capture value. And you are more likely to avoid the mistake of simply assuming "old" or traditional delivery models or concepts, of which you then model the economics. Here is a framework and thought process helpful to this exploration:

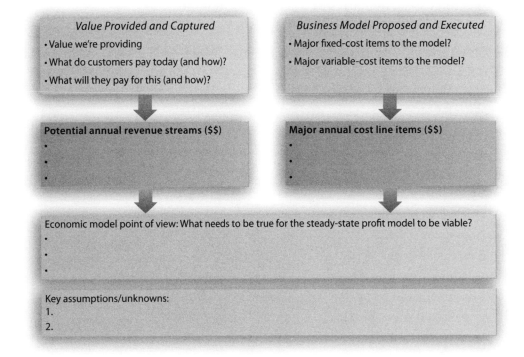

Value Provided and Captured
- Value we're providing
- What do customers pay today (and how)?
- What will they pay for this (and how)?

Potential annual revenue streams ($$)
-
-
-

Business Model Proposed and Executed
- Major fixed-cost items to the model?
- Major variable-cost items to the model?

Major annual cost line items ($$)
-
-
-

Economic model point of view: What needs to be true for the steady-state profit model to be viable?
-
-
-

Key assumptions/unknowns:
1.
2.

Although this framework features framing and quantification of the opportunity, its central purpose is to frame and expand on the economic physics of the model—that is, to articulate the drivers of revenue, cost, and profit.

There are two equally important steps in this conversation:

+ Consider and detail the physics of the economic model. How will the economic model work? What are the underlying beliefs and point of view that lead us to conclude we will be successful? For which of these are we most confident? Least confident? What critical things do we not know and ought to go investigate further? How does any of that thought process or new learning alter or expand our view of the economic engine of the opportunity?
+ Focus on the numbers and build the business case.

Note that the framework focuses on the first of the two steps. Organizations know how to build business cases. The framework focuses on the economic logic part of the process.

Also note that the framework does not start with a default assumption that the organization's current business model and economic engine are the right fit for your concept. As we mentioned earlier, if you start with that default assumption, the sheer force of habit will lead you to your typical commercial execution, pulling what you imagined as new and novel back to the mean of "business as usual." By avoiding the default assumption that the current economic engine is the best fit, the two-part thought process represents a departure from many that we often encounter.

Additional frameworks exist to assist you in the work of SEI on your business concept: stretching through application of additional customer (or consumer) needs, mapping the concept against the entire customer experience, and others. While acknowledging there are other techniques suited for particular circumstances, we share this SEI approach because it can assist you in a very large majority of business concept framing scenarios.

Using an Iterative Learning Process

Innovation is an iterative learning process that is not confined to a room, a tool set, or a specific technique. As you think through a new

High-impact innovation always results from new learning through iteration. Embrace it!

business concept, you will often find yourself returning to one or more of its "who, what, and how" elements, and you will find that a more nuanced view of the economics may affect your initial framing of how you go to market. For example, a clearer view of the "who" and "what" might lead you to refine the CVP.

You will and should find yourself iterating within a given framework and across the frameworks you employ to detail your specific concept. The iterative learning process is inherent in innovation. Significant, high-impact innovation always results from new learning. Embrace it. It will help you tremendously.

This iterative process also surfaces critical unknowns—aspects of the opportunity that are central to its success but about which you know little or nothing, or at least "not enough." Typically the most important unknowns relate to specifics about the customer, demand, routes to market, operational capabilities, technology gaps, and unfamiliar competitors or competitive responses.

Unknowns like these represent uncertainty and risk. Think in terms of managing and even mitigating risk rather than just living with it. Risk mitigation and management through experimentation and iteration represents a critical discipline that should

be learned and utilized often in the world of innovation. In Chapter Six, we speak to this in much greater detail, sharing additional frameworks and examples.

Don't Take Opportunity Elaboration and Framing for Granted

When the ongoing activities of the back end of innovation (part II of the generalized innovation process depicted earlier in this chapter) are taken for granted, innovation can be squeezed out of the concept. Why? Because too often when organizations run their back end of innovation work, they're not engaging in SEI. Success demands that you continue to advance and refine your concept through new learning in the back end of the process as well as the front end, if your goal is to move beyond the incremental.

You can apply these back-end (part II) techniques in many different situations and contexts. The situations you may frequently encounter include

+ **An end-to-end run of your innovation process.** You will develop insights and convert them to sets of ideas and, perhaps, growth domains. Then you need to do the work of harvesting ideas and getting them to implementation-level opportunities by employing sound back-end techniques for learning and iterating on the concept.

+ **An opportunity emerging outside your "normal process."** Often an idea or nascent concept has not come out of a formal innovation process, but instead has emerged serendipitously or out of some other source or process. The techniques are fully modular and applicable to nascent ideas, regardless of source.

+ **A stalled but promising idea that needs to get "unstuck."** You may believe that your nascent concept is a diamond in the rough, but others in the organization do not recognize its value. You can use these techniques to expand and reframe the idea in a more compelling fashion. SEI is a powerful technique to employ in this circumstance.

+ **Product, brand, or technology myopia.** You may have a sense that the team is overly focused on a single element: a particular product manifestation of an idea that is not compelling enough to move on, or a technology that you can't seem to frame into a "commercialize-able" concept, or a brand-based idea. The

back-end techniques will help you get unstuck in circumstances such as these when an idea or specific concept could really use some more innovation "juice."

● Fast-Tracking Opportunities When You Believe Speed to Market Is Critical

The SEI techniques we have described in this chapter can also be tremendously helpful when you want to move fast. Specifically, if you have a product or service concept for which you believe there is a limited "time-to-market window," the concentrated application of these techniques will help you move faster than your traditional stage-gate process typically allows—and/or can help you unstick the opportunity from within your current stage-gate process. You would likely not do this for every opportunity, as the techniques can be resource intensive to execute. But for those opportunities that warrant the attention and resources in service of speed, the techniques can be quite helpful.

The next graphic depicts one example, executed by a consumer goods

> *The concentrated application of SEI techniques can help you move faster than a traditional stage-gate might allow.*

organization when they had an extraordinary opportunity that required fast-track attention and needed to be addressed outside the normal process.

Fast-Tracking a Priority Business Opportunity for Go-To-Market

Days, not weeks	Weeks, not months	Days, not weeks	Weeks, not months
Initial opportunity plan development (workshop)	**Field learning, secondary research, constituent input, analogs**	**Opportunity development and refinement (workshop)**	**Business concept finalization and go-to-market plan**
• Initial hypotheses and opportunity structure • Unknowns and assumptions • Learning plan	• Structured learning plan taking on multiple aspects of business concept, in parallel	• Revised opportunity and go-to-market specifics • Remaining unknowns	• Implementation plan • Residual in-market risk management plan • Resources for launch

As the process indicates, the approach requires resources and concentrated time, and the learning on multiple aspects of the business concept is moved toward conclusions in parallel, rather than sequentially. The approach is punctuated by two workshops in which in-market learning is surfaced, discussed, and used to refine the business concept using approaches similar to what we have described. They include

+ Articulating your hypotheses about the holistic business concept up-front
+ Using those hypotheses to articulate your key assumptions and unknowns

and your learning agenda to close those knowledge gaps
+ Designing and managing parallel learning processes to close or narrow your knowledge gaps regarding customer, competitors, technology, and the economics drivers of your concept

You should draw on the appropriate perspectives and resources as early as possible in this "parallel learning process," for the benefit of both the learning and the business concept synthesis exercises. And be sure to use parallel learning processes and workshop-based synthesis sessions to accelerate your business concept development cycle.

Key Take-Aways

- Keep SEI—stretch, elaborate, and iterate—in mind throughout the back end of innovation. Recognize that successful back-end innovation requires much more than just creating new ideas through front-end techniques. Success demands that you transform nascent new ideas into assessable, actionable business concepts through every step in the back-end innovation process. It is a critical part of any innovation work effort or process and is taken for granted all too often.

- Start with the benefits. The first step in the back-end process should be to unpack and stretch the benefits and value proposition. You want to ensure that the benefits and value delivered are clear and distinctive relative to current choices.

- Consider all aspects of the "who, what, and how" of the business model as you explore ways in which to create distinct, differentiated high-value concepts. Do not assume that your organization's current business model is best for the new concept. Instead, work "market back," starting with customer insights and the CVP.

- Develop a robust point of view about the economic model through a two-step process: first develop the "physics of the model" (that is, the drivers of revenue, cost, and profit), *then* run the numbers. Running the business case first leads to defaulting to current models, which may or may not serve the opportunity well.

- Fast-track application of SEI techniques is a powerful way to accelerate the development of high-priority and high-potential opportunities that need to get to market quickly.

Propelling Fast Innovation

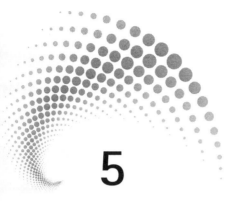

5

I need to fill my pipeline for next year and get some new concepts into market quickly.

I'd like to infuse more innovation and innovative thinking into our upcoming meeting, or planning cycle.

I need innovation, but we are short on resources.

I want "quick" innovation, from as many places and people as possible (even though it may be "small-i" innovation).

I'd like to leverage outside resources for innovation—not internal resources only.

We live in times of greatly accelerating change. Here are some quick facts to illustrate what you no doubt feel already:

+ As much as 50 percent of annual revenues globally come from products launched in the last three years across a number of industries—not just high tech—making time to market a critical challenge to replenishing decaying revenue streams.[1]
+ Apple's iPad reached $1 billion in sales in under 120 days in 2010.[2]
+ The average CEO tenure declined to 7.5 years in 2012 from 10 years in 2000.[3] Some studies show tenure falling to only 5 years in the United States.[4]

> You need to understand clearly the trade-offs of using "fast innovation" techniques, and be certain that your key stakeholders understand the same.

What does the pace of change have to do with your innovation efforts inside the organization? A lot! You no doubt appreciate that the external pace of change places time pressure on every aspect of your organization, including, of course, innovation efforts. The hard reality is that you are often pressured to "get ideas really fast," whether you need them for the annual planning round, in response to surprising competitive actions, or because there is a new leader with an urgent initiative in your organization.

In an ideal world, you would have the time to develop foundational insights and then proceed to domaining and/or innovation architecture techniques. As a leading practice, you should do so. If you keep your insight foundation fresh and you are able to manage and migrate within a chosen domain, you will position yourself well to move fast while still applying the rigor you would optimally desire in your innovation efforts.

Of course, we don't live in an ideal world. Your organization may not keep refreshing your insight foundation. Or you may not have a rich insight foundation at all. You may not have the organizational support to create space and time to develop domains. In those situations, you need techniques that help you move fast when you have to. You need to understand clearly the trade-offs in moving fast and be certain that you and your key stakeholders have a shared understanding of what can and cannot be delivered "fast."

● Engaging the Organization Through Focused Innovation Challenges

Fast Innovation in U.S. Special Operations Command

One of the most interesting fast innovation examples we know comes from the procurement function of the U.S. Special Operations Command (USSOC). The unit—Special Operations Research, Development, & Acquisition Center (SORDAC)—provides "rapid and focused acquisition, technology and logistics to U.S. Special Operations Forces."[5] SORDAC acquisition executive James "Hondo" Geurts and his team relentlessly ensure that the unit operates in an agile and lean way similar to the operations of its internal "customers"—special operations forces in the field. These customers operate within tight constraints, operating in small teams, often far from "the larger organization."

In many instances, SORDAC receives a request for equipment that does not yet exist with a requirement that it must be in field ASAP, so Geurts uses these constraints to enable innovation.

When innovating fast, the organization responds to a "customer need" as described in a single-page "commander's intent" detailing the specific goal(s) and the constraints within which the goal(s) must be achieved. Constraints detail the operating environment and degree of time urgency regarding the objective. In one operation, SORDAC modified combat aircraft to meet a particular goal at one-sixth the normal cost within three months rather than three years. Two additional examples of fast innovation include

- Project HI-BEAM, a specialized lighting device that enables U.S. aircraft to signal partner-nation forces on the ground while on separate patrols, so as to avoid friendly fire casualties. The initial prototype device was fashioned from existing technology in seventeen days, and a prototype was deployed in less than fifty days for initial use.

The authors are grateful to USSOC and SORDAC for providing and granting permission to use the Project High Beam photo and images depicting the MTRC modules.

- A Mobile Technology and Repair Center (MTRC) enabling "in-situ" capabilities to develop, modify, adapt, and repair equipment and material to maintain or enhance Special Operations Forces (SOF)—including Civil (civilian) Affairs at SOF forward-operating bases. The MTRC has several modules that can be deployed individually or as a system, including a tool room, a vehicle repair center, a communications hub, and a micro power unit with solar panels and wind generator arrays.[6]

Beyond these examples, there are many other illustrations of fast innovation within SORDAC. As one indicator of success, SORDAC personnel represent approximately 0.025 percent of U.S. Department of Defense (DOD) acquisition personnel, but they have received over 25 percent of all relevant DOD-level awards in the last five years.[7]

The authors are grateful to USSOC and SORDAC for providing and granting permission to use these images depicting MTRC modules.

SORDAC enables fast innovation through process and culture. A cross-functional, cross-hierarchical team dubbed the Crazy 8's has the official charter of "destroying the organization and recreating with step change improvement in performance." This team took a page out of Apple's retail playbook and initiated a monthly "idea bar" at which colleagues come forward with ideas they wish to make more clear and actionable. The Crazy 8's goal: to help shape thinking so that the idea can either move ahead quickly or be cast aside.

SORDAC leadership also relies on a "young guns" team to act in an advisory role, constructively challenging the organization's core operating processes.

Leadership enables innovation in a fit-for-purpose way within SORDAC, working with the grain of the culture of the organization. As one reminder for the staff, successfully implemented "bureaucracy buster" awards are displayed on the panel of an old airplane that hangs prominently in SORDAC's offices. This communication tactic, of course, is adapted from a fighter pilot's practice of personalizing his or her fighter jet by name and accomplishment.

Fast Ideas Fast: IBM's IdeaJam

Initiated in 2001, IBM's IdeaJam is a selective crowdsourcing process through which the company quickly (in two to three days) captures ideas from across the organization on a specific question or topic of interest. Its efforts in 2006 and 2008 surfaced ideas that ultimately led to new businesses, such as smart health care payment systems, simplified business engines (a prepackaged set of Web 2.0 services for small and medium businesses), and intelligent utility networks (the smart grid).[8] IBM even focused an IdeaJam (ValueJam) on an internal discussion of its values. The Jams are created out of IBM's internal communications function, with detailed planning and post-Jam follow-up.

Collaborative Idea Management: UnitedHealth Group

Since 2010, innovation leaders at UnitedHealth Group (UHG) have been engaging their associates on focused innovation challenges through a process similar to IBM's IdeaJam. UHG's experience is typical of those organizations that do this well, enabling leaders to efficiently capture ideas from within the organization or across the entire enterprise.

Brandon Rowberry, vice president of innovation, leads UHG's enterprise innovation efforts and continues to refine the company's approach to "focused innovation challenges."[9] Most recently, he teamed up with UHG's CEO Stephen Hemsley and colleagues Greg Hicks and Todd Nielson to invite ideas from anyone in the organization within four specific strategic areas:

- How can we create consumer "stickiness" for our brands, products, and services?
- What products, services, information, or customer care that we provide at low costs today could we provide for FREE (or almost free) that our key stakeholders will find valuable?
- How could we reimagine "supported technology" for the Physicians office that would also significantly reduce the administrative and cost burden?
- How can we drive rapid and deeper adoption of innovations we have already developed?

Asking people to respond to four specific challenges is helpful in two ways. First and most obvious, the challenges set broad boundaries for the types of ideas people will submit. Second, by framing the challenge areas, UHG's CEO, in essence, translated enterprise strategy into framing questions so that even those at the most junior levels in the organization could contribute to shaping and evolving company strategy.

The end-to-end process that runs from "idea to proposal" is elegantly simple, integrating both virtual and physical interventions, a bit of gaming through an idea tournament, and hands-on support for the most promising few ideas. The following graphic illustrates the process and includes dates as an example of timing.

UnitedHealth Group Innovation Challenge Process

Ideation (complete) → Pairwise: All (Ends 4/5) → Pairwise: Top 64 (4/15 – 4/19) → Top 16 Prepare → Top 4 Selected: Innovation Day

Graphic provided by UnitedHealth Group innovation leaders, July 2013.

Within each of these steps, there is quite a bit of detail that animates and sustains the process. During the first three weeks, all employees are invited to submit their ideas. Colleagues can offer comments and post "likes" to an idea, and authors can improve their submissions.

After three weeks, any employee can vote for a given idea through pairwise comparisons that are automatically generated by UHG's idea management system. The pairwise technique ensures that all ideas are evaluated: the total set is narrowed first to sixty-four ideas; then, through additional pairwise voting, that set is narrowed to the top sixteen. Of course, all votes count equally regardless of one's hierarchical position.

The top sixteen, representing four ideas within each challenge, are selected to proceed to an "idea workout." This two-day session led by internal UHG innovation experts helps the idea author stretch and elaborate his or her idea through UHG-tested tools and frameworks. In 2013, over one hundred volunteers—selected for their skills and passion—joined the innovation team, playing the role of coach in portions of the two-day idea workout.

During the idea workout, UHG places great emphasis on the customer value proposition, design thinking, and explicit statements of potential competitive advantage. The UHG innovation team also brings in additional internal subject-matter experts at appropriate points during the two-day session so that the team can benefit from the best thinking within UHG. As you can quickly infer, collaboration is a central behavioral goal for the effort.

The sixteen ideas are featured at UHG's annual company-wide Innovation Day, which begins with a casual breakfast meeting attended by the sixteen idea teams, innovation leadership, and UHG's CEO and leadership team. During the day, each of the ideas is showcased in a trade-show-style format with separate booths manned by each team. The booths allow for interactive discussions and displays. Every senior executive attends the event.

Each idea is presented by its author(s) in a three-minute "power pitch." The pitch has several elements that describe the elements of the concept:

+ Customer target and problem addressed
+ Value proposition

+ Rationale for why UHG can be successful, including what strengths UHG brings
+ High-level description of how revenue would flow, cost elements, and a rough sense of the potential "size of the prize"

A single winning entry in each of the four categories is selected based on attendee voting. In addition, many of the remaining twelve ideas are "pulled" into a business unit or function for further elaboration. In this sense, every idea brought to the session has a reasonably high probability of being taken forward.

Broadly speaking, votes are cast based on the voter's assessment of the ideas against a few criteria:

+ Potential extent of positive impact on the health care system
+ Potential consumer impact
+ Extent to which the team has creatively addressed the core innovation challenge and provided a workable solution

As you can see, UHG does not over-complicate the evaluation. Rather, they use and apply qualitative criteria that guide a dialogue among the decision makers.

UHG's approach to its innovation challenge process reflects implicit design principles that guide the structure and management of the process from start to finish:

+ Structure the process so that it is open and inclusive
+ Focus the idea generation on a significant strategic or operational challenge
+ Keep the time frame for idea submission short—in this case, three weeks
+ Infuse a bit of fun in the process to keep things interesting
+ Integrate "market mechanisms" to guide idea selection
+ Support a few promising ideas with additional tools and hands-on coaching
+ Encourage the right amount of collaboration to improve the concepts and advance them within the organization

UHG sets it mission as "helping people live healthier lives and helping make the health system work better for everyone."[10] From the perspective of executive leadership, the positive impact on culture enabled through their innovation process is one of several ways that this mission is made more tangible. In fact, the mind-set shift and culture change this process represents— ideas from anywhere, with a constant focus on strategic challenges—are at least as important as the result, which sees ideas carried forward through further funding and support.

UHG advances a good number of incremental ideas through these efforts. In addition, though early in its development, the UHG process does yield some bigger, bolder concepts—both through the process we described here and through more deliberately structured transformative innovation efforts—and these are working their way through the company's development funnel. The bigger, bolder concepts that emerge from the challenge process cannot do so without the deliberate intervention of the two-day idea workout with the sixteen finalists. UHG innovation leaders understood that if they wanted to increase the potential for breakthrough ideas, they needed to augment efforts by providing some fairly intensive hands-on coaching to idea contributors—hence the workout.

● ● ●

It can often be the case that an "innovation challenge" yields incremental

Fast innovation designs vary by organization and objective—fit-for-purpose design is the key.

ideas. Incremental innovation is not necessarily a bad thing. For example, Portuguese Telecom (PT) boasts that their innovation process is based on incremental ideas that capture "contributions of all employees [focused on] continuous improvement of processes and services." The process has drawn participation from over two-thirds of the company. PT estimates that efforts since 2009 have produced benefits in excess of €30M.[11]

Supermajor Shell Oil also values collaboration and openness, recognizing that the "innovation capabilities of every employee to make things that are different [is present in] every day [work throughout the company]." One simple idea from an associate in Thailand—to shift from selling single containers of lubricants for motor bikes from 1-liter to .75-liter cans—increased lubricant market share by 80 percent. The simple insight: match the volume of the can to the volume required by the motor bike. It is, after all, what the customer really needs.[12]

UHG, Shell, and PT used different approaches to achieve different objectives and get innovation fast. For UHG, an explicit strategic focus, coupled with more intensive support, led to bigger-impact ideas. For PT, a disciplined process with a more hands-off approach yielded good results. Shell's approach yields simple improvements, some of which impact the business substantially.

Collaborative Idea Management at Ericsson

Ericsson is another of many companies that use "frontline innovation" to draw ideas from anyone, anywhere within the organization—and sometimes from outside it. Magnus Karlsson, director of new business development and innovation, reports that the collaborative approach, called the IdeaBoxes™, "is unique in the way that it is deployed [across the enterprise]. It has been growing internally since 2008, with over 25,000 users who have submitted 35,000 ideas [for which colleagues have provided] over 70,000 comments. One out of every thirty ideas is implemented. The Ericsson system is a self-organizing, distributed-accountability, virally spread, pull-demand-driven system."[13]

The self-organizing aspect of the IdeaBoxes process is critical, ensuring that there is both demand for and supply of ideas helpful to the organization. Demand is set by sponsors, who are called "box managers." It is up to each unit to decide to open an

IdeaBox, appoint a box manager, and start gathering ideas. Every function, region, and business unit within the company may have multiple active IdeaBoxes in the system at any given time. Once an initiative emerges from the process, the innovation manager, who is often the same person as the box manager, manages the maturation of the idea from conception to execution.

At the enterprise level, Magnus and his team manage a strategic innovation funnel with IdeaBoxes focused on strategic challenges that by their nature require breakthrough ideas. The team meets regularly to review the most recently submitted ideas. There is a dedicated budget to fund early exploration of the ideas, and Magnus's team meets at least monthly with the CEO and his leadership team to discuss progress on an idea or to share a new proposal.

The success of Ericsson's IdeaBoxes centers on ensuring that three key roles are played well:

+ **Employees** from anywhere in the organization can submit an idea. Prompts that help employees frame the idea more clearly are set individually for each box by the box manager. Prompts might include "What is the problem you are solving?" "How does your proposed solution help a customer?" "What are the unknowns?" "What might be the rough scale of impact?"
+ **Innovation coaches** help idea authors or teams enrich their ideas and guide them through the innovation process. This assistance is critical, as the initial idea typically needs further elaboration and refinement.

The coach works with the idea author to refine the concept, using the appropriate tools from Ericsson's innovation tool kit as a guide. There is a dedicated internal training program for innovation coaches to build competence and create a network for learning and sharing practices. These coaches also support enterprise training, acting as stewards of an evolving innovation tool kit, and nurture and strengthen their own innovation coach community.

+ **Box managers and innovation managers**—and there are hundreds within Ericsson—are part of the self-organizing, self-sustaining innovation management system. Within the units and functions, the innovation manager typically plays the role of box manager as well. The box manager can create a challenge or theme for which he or she wants ideas. He or she is the screener for the ideas, with accountability either to resource a given submission or to reject it. The innovation manager is responsible for a specific initiative that emerges from the process, ensuring oversight and managing the maturation of the idea from conception to execution.

Innovation manager and innovation coach are formal job roles in Ericsson's HR system, intended to increase the visibility of innovation activities and build a community that is practicing systematic innovation. Taken together, these distinct roles ensure that there is reinforcing activity on both the demand and supply sides of innovation, as shown here:

IdeaBoxes as Innovation Marketplace

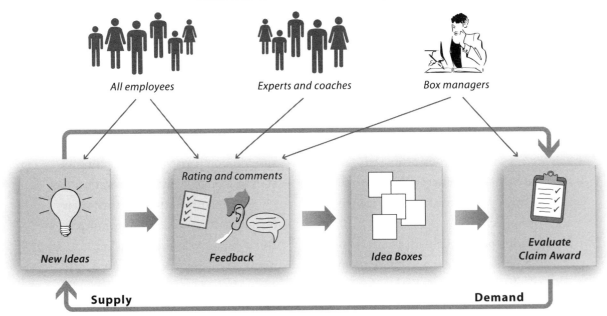

More specifically, here are the steps one takes to set up an IdeaBox:

1. Unit leadership considers the question, "Given our stated strategy and goal, given the 'job(s) to be done' by my unit, do we need an innovation initiative, or will current and planned activities enable us to realize our goal?"
2. If leadership determines that innovation is required, an innovation manager (formal full- or part-time role) is appointed to set up and drive the innovation initiative.
3. The innovation manager may decide to engage one or more innovation coaches (formal role, typically secondary and part-time) to help develop ideas into robust opportunities.
4. If the innovation manager wants ideas from employees for the initiative, he or she can decide to use IdeaBoxes and then also become box manager. To start a box, one must
   - Define and detail the scope clearly—for example, the type of ideas sought
   - Articulate the submission process—timing, boundaries, and criteria
   - Provide resource people who can assist with taking the select ideas forward
   - Be willing to display authentic passion for listening and discussing ideas from employees

The result of the IdeaBoxes process is a dynamic "ecosystem" of innovation initiatives inside the organization, emerging from the strategic needs of units at different levels. These initiatives are all connected and visible to everyone, accessible via one online tool—a one-stop shop for any idea to find the best place to be implemented. All boxes are "one click away" from any employee.

Like UHG, Ericsson employs a fit-for-purpose approach. When Hans Vestberg became Ericsson's CEO, he established the principle that all should have a chance to be involved and engaged in innovation. Magnus and his team recognized that if the company were to tap into the collective imagination of the entire organization, there would need to be both healthy demand for and supply of ideas of all stripes. The IdeaBoxes within the system emerge on the demand side, as they are by definition created by a person with an innovation need and the budget and resources to follow through. The supply side: ideas that emerge through a bottom-up self-organizing system. As a whole, the approach ensures that efforts are focused on supporting the strategic and operational priorities of the business. No wonder, then, that it is the longest-sustaining innovation process within the company.

Innovation Accelerators

Another technique to get to "innovation fast" is through a process and structure often described as an innovation accelerator (sometimes called an incubator). Shell's GameChanger is one type of virtual accelerator, matching an internal or external idea creator with additional support resources to elaborate and refine his or her idea. There are also aspects of acceleration in UHG's idea workout session, as described earlier in this chapter.

Companies (and consultants) operate physical and virtual "accelerators" to meet several distinct types of innovation challenges. Among the most common of these challenges are a need to

+ Create concepts to fill a new product or service pipeline
+ Set or affirm the broad strategic direction for a business unit or function
+ Surface potential ways to disrupt one's business—or a competitor's

+ Develop response(s) to a disruptive market development by a traditional or nontraditional competitor
+ Jump-start a promising but stalled opportunity

For example, in Argentina, global snacks giant Mondelēz[14] created a physical innovation space that they brand as the Fly Garage. And although they term it an "incubator," it in fact acts as an accelerator. As they describe it, Fly Garage is "about allowing ourselves the freedom to explore and learn by doing . . . It's about leaving the roles and hierarchies behind . . . [It] is a place where everyone brings and everyone takes out. This is much more than an innovation incubator, for us it's a social experiment."[15] Time in the Fly Garage varies from a few days to a week. More generally, the typical time required for a specific accelerator session ranges from a day to a week, depending on scope, with pre- and post-session work by a smaller group in addition.

Preparing for the Accelerator Session

Speed and success in a one- to five-day intervention is wholly dependent on the quality of your preparation. We find it best to start with your objectives: What are you trying to achieve? What perspectives might be helpful in meeting those objectives? What are the implications for your session design?

Think through your design iteratively, determining first what you want to achieve and then what can you achieve practically. As you iterate, you will sometimes conclude that the initial objectives cannot be achieved, given particular practical constraints. In such cases, it will be most critical for you to ensure that all key stakeholders understand the necessary trade-offs you may need to make.

This table shows the frameworks and approaches you might use as you think through your design:

If You Have This Objective . . .	. . . Consider These Design Elements
It is important to challenge our basic assumptions about product, market, and industry. We need to challenge all assumptions about our business model.	• Unpacking industry orthodoxies • An analog tool—thinking like someone from outside your industry
We want to find new ways to surprise and delight the customer. We want improve or transform the customer experience.	• Customer experience mapping and other human-centered design approaches • Jobs to be done
We seek to disrupt our competitors—and, perhaps, ourselves.	• Jobs to be done • Unpacking industry and company orthodoxies • Industry and market discontinuities
We wish to revisit our strategy.	• All insight areas
We have a promising but stalled opportunity.	• Customer experience mapping and other human-centered design approaches • Jobs to be done

Some of these design elements can be completed or, at minimum, begun before the actual session. For example, if you thought it helpful to develop

+ **Orthodoxy insights**, you could capture input efficiently through an internal survey or by holding a few orthodoxy workshops prior to the session
+ **Discontinuity insights**, you could create a set of insights by applying the techniques described in Chapter Two of The Guide
+ **Customer insights**, you could consider including a lead customer in your session and/or conducting a few immersive interviews beforehand

Open Innovation: Moving Faster Than Your Internal Development

Henry Chesbrough, the intellectual god-father of the open innovation (OI) movement, appropriately reminds us that one's own organization does not have a monopoly on the best thinking and best technology in a given market.[16] If you don't already have a well-established OI process in your organization, using OI to move fast is not an option. Indeed, enabling OI within a large organization often requires significant changes in mind-set, process, and incentives and only begins to take hold after several years. The organization must be comfortable working across internal silos and hierarchy; it must be moving toward collaborative behavior as a daily routine. As Chesbrough frames it, "to be open externally, you must first be open internally."

If your organization has an established or even a nascent OI process and infrastructure, you can and should look to it as one means by which to move faster. Most studies analyzing OI efforts share the conclusion that OI saves time and creates a competitive advantage.[17]

Moving Faster: Collaboration with Suppliers

One way to move faster on existing priorities is to engage your suppliers in a focused way. For example, Mondelēz operates a supplier challenge process that is enabled by marketing leaders in each business unit and managed by the R&D organization.[18] In brief, it works like this:

> "To be open externally, you must first be open internally."
> —Henry Chesbrough

1. Marketing provides a brief that describes a particular consumer problem or need that the company would like to address. This step is critical, as it engages the businesses from the start, clearly defining Mondelēz's internal demand.

2. The supplier community is invited to respond to the brief, which typically would be seeking ideas about packaging or an enabling technology. The suppliers are given a defined time frame (based on the complexity of the program) to prepare their response.

3. Mondelēz hosts a daylong event at which suppliers pitch their ideas to business unit and R&D leaders. For its part, Mondelēz promises a "nay/yea" decision in thirty days or less.

Winners proceed to development with Mondelēz; those who are not selected are then free to pursue their idea with any other company, including Mondelēz's direct competitors. The compressed time frame heightens supplier commitment to the effort, ensuring focus and speed.

To date, Mondelēz has conducted well over a hundred supplier challenges. And although the efforts are typically incremental in nature, they have shortened product development times while increasing supplier commitments to the company.

If your organization has an established or even a nascent OI process and infrastructure, you can and should look to it as one means by which to move faster.

"If Only I Could": Reducing Cycle Times on Breakthrough Products

Todd Abraham has been shaping the OI approach with Mondelēz (and, previously, Kraft) since 2005. He offers clear and pragmatic advice for moving faster when focused on breakthrough new product development, encouraging teams to stimulate their creative thinking beyond the current product mind-set by asking "If only I could" questions.

That's what happened a few years back when a Mondelēz (then Kraft) development team began to stretch their thinking about the coffee experience at home and at work. They knew that after a development cycle of several decades, Nestlé's single-serve Nespresso coffee machine was scaling successfully. So the team was searching for a disruptive response of its own.

Starting with "If only I could . . .," they began to consider how the at-home or at-office coffee experience could be as good as or better than that of the best coffeehouse. The question began stretching their thinking to solve consumer problems and address trade-offs or tensions: "If only I could . . ."

+ Provide single-serve coffee that tasted as fresh as a just-roasted bean . . .
    + . . . and deliver that experience across several taste profiles
    + . . . and ensure a "real dairy" experience to consumers

Within this frame, the team began asking three other important questions:

+ What do we know already about creating such an experience?
+ What don't we know?
+ Who else outside the company might know more or have different information?

The team quickly realized that they would need outside partners. They used specific criteria to consider and select a partner, including, of course, a match of specific technological capabilities. Of equal importance to the team were criteria related to culture fit, R&D investments, and the partner's philosophy toward brands.

As the list of potential partners narrowed, the team focused on three evaluation criteria[19]:

+ Do the companies have a shared vision?
+ Do their overall missions aim for the same goal?
+ Will their fundamental principles make for a strong partnership?

The final result: the Tassimo beverage system, which delivers single-serve coffee, with or without dairy. Today, revenues for the product line are about $500 million globally. The system has two main components: the Tassimo brewing machine and the proprietary Tassimo discs (T DISCS) with barcodes on each. The microprocessor reads the T DISC barcode and perfectly calculates the water quantity, temperature, and brew time to make the beverage you want. "All of the brewing happens inside the T DISC. An inverse flow of filtered water guarantees optimal flavor with virtually no clean up or residue from previously made beverages. Most beverages are ready in under a minute."[20]

Mondelēz's success represents the combined efforts of Kraft Foods and the Bosch and Siemens Home Appliance Group.[21] The team's OI efforts did not stop with the first iterations of the product. More recently, the team drew on outside expertise and technologies to improve the flow of water through its Tassimo coffee capsules.[22]

Within the Mondelēz global R&D unit of three thousand colleagues, there is an OI framework that guides developers to meet the enterprise mission: "Inventing delicious." The diagram here depicts the framework:

- **Knowledge management** focuses on the capture and reuse of information. As Todd says, "The thing about knowledge is, it grows as you share it. We need to make sure we do so."
- **Intellectual property management** speaks to IP strategy, pointing toward those technologies that Mondelēz wishes to patent, keep as trade secrets, and/or monetize through licensing or sale.
- **Open innovation** focuses on those technologies that should be accessed externally through OI partnering.

Taken together, Mondelēz's "inventing delicious" framework reflects the leading practices the company integrates to advance the enterprise mission. As we saw in the Tassimo example, leading OI practice starts with the "what"—a customer or consumer problem you are trying to solve. The following diagram outlines this process, starting with Todd's "If only . . ." question.

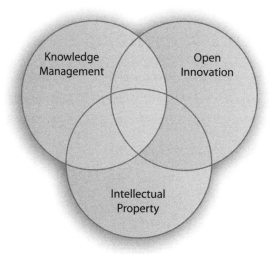

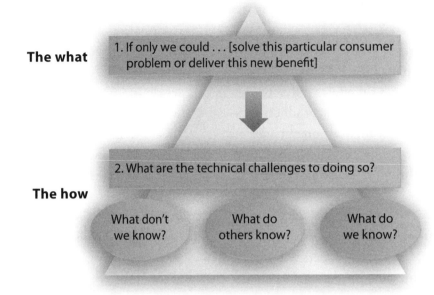

The what

1. If only we could . . . [solve this particular consumer problem or deliver this new benefit]

2. What are the technical challenges to doing so?

The how

What don't we know?

What do others know?

What do we know?

The "how" is enabled by a shared understanding, mind-set, and culture within Mondelēz that, though not perfect, is focused on moving fast through OI-enabled processes.

Moving Faster: Customer Collaboration

Avery Dennison is a global B2B materials company providing packaging and labeling solutions to end-use customers across a broad variety of industries, including consumer products, durables, pharmaceuticals, and apparel. Most typically, their product—pressure-sensitive material—is sold to "converters," who print and die-cut Avery Dennison's packaging material and affix it to a given product. Although the company had been successful for over seventy-five years supporting its customer base and current go-to-market model, the structure did not allow for any day-to-day interaction with the ultimate consumer. Indeed, the company is even one step removed from a given product marketer, such as Nestlé or Bayer.

In late 2011, the company's innovation leadership realized that they risked missing shifts in consumer behavior and preferences related to packaging materials, given their go-to-market model and distance from the consumer. Moreover, they feared that a lack of deep consumer understanding hindered productive collaborative relationships with end-use customers—Nestlé, Proctor & Gamble, Ambev Budweiser, and others. To be clear, Avery Dennison did not see a need to change their business or go-to-market model. Rather, they wanted to work with their current customers and at the same time find a way to build and manage an innovation agenda rooted in a deep and rich understanding of *consumer's needs* as the means by which to grow their business and that of their direct customers.

Innovation leadership began an intensive effort to develop proprietary insights into the unmet and unarticulated needs of consumers across each of its major business segments. Initially, it used these insights as one means by which to identify and detail new growth opportunities. Soon after, they began to expand innovation efforts to include end-use customer collaborations. They termed their process Brandfire.[23]

Brandfire took much work to create, though it is now implemented on a per-customer basis in only a day's time— innovation fast! The goal is to develop specific new packaging concepts through a consumer-centric approach in a highly engaging, interactive face-to-face dialogue with an end-use customer. As the following graphic depicts, the one-day session uses three inputs to stimulate ideas, and concludes with a prioritized list of opportunities.

Brandfire Process

brandfire |

Trends

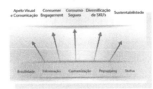

Consumer Insights

Materials

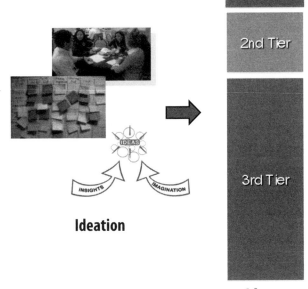

Ideation

Ideas

Avery Dennison develops the three inputs, describing significant and potentially disruptive trends, consumer attitudes, frustrations, and unmet needs regarding packaging and technology developments specific to packaging. The insights are specific to the customer's business. For example, a Brandfire focused on personal care and beauty products would speak to consumer needs for that market, whereas a session focused on over-the-counter medicines would speak to different consumer attitudes and needs.

Success requires trust and collaboration. Prior to the one-day session, the Avery Dennison team and their customer agree on a set of problems around which to focus the discussion. The customer shares their strategic plan and current new product development pipeline. Avery Dennison, in turn, shares proprietary information regarding their technology and R&D agenda. So far, every Brandfire session has led to shared development efforts for near- and longer-term products—all in a single day's work.

• • •

UHG, Ericsson, IBM, Shell, Mondelēz, and Avery Dennison operate in very different industries, competing and creating value through very distinct business models. Each shares an ambition to enable fast innovation. And although their specific business objectives and fast innovation designs differ, each succeeds by applying similar principles.

Key Take-Aways

- "Innovation fast" requires trade-offs relative to other, more time-consuming efforts. If you pursue innovation fast, you must ensure that your business owner understands and supports your approach and understands what your effort will and will not deliver.

- Success in fast innovation requires a disciplined approach: fit-for-purpose, rigorous processes that are structured with explicit design rules and clear governance. Efforts succeed or fail because of it.

- Collaborative idea management is a productive technique to yield innovation fast. When done well, it will stimulate employee engagement, enabling a more open culture and mind-set over time. Efforts are especially productive in surfacing incremental ideas that can be acted on in the near term. If you seek bigger, bolder ideas addressing critical strategic challenges, you must provide additional coaching and expertise to develop the ideas into clear and compelling business concepts.

- OI efforts will help you move faster if you have an established or nascent OI process in place. OI is more than just accessing technologies; it is a fundamental shift in culture and mind-set. To be open externally, the organization must first be open internally.

- Suppliers and customers are a great source of ideas to help you move fast, if you structure your collaboration with clear objectives and discipline.

Experimentation and De-Risking

6

I have an idea, but it has risks—how do I move it forward in a smart and risk-managed fashion?

How do I do smart experimentation that helps me with proof of concept or with iteration and improvement of the concept?

I have a business concept, but it has many unknowns. They are slowing up the commercialization efforts (or drawing them to a halt). How can I move it forward?

Let's say you reach the point where your new concept is fully developed—on paper. You are excited. You want to move forward into execution. You see a plausible path forward. You also see uncertainties. You also see risks.

Most organizations identify risks in very general terms, including

+ **Customer** risks, such as the newness of the value proposition, potential switching costs, and stickiness
+ **Channel** risks, such as fear of alienating existing channel and customer relationships through changes in marketing mix; shifts in other channel support; uncertainty regarding the channel's willingness to take on a new product or service and/or create new routes to market
+ **Marketing** risks related to building awareness, trial, and repurchase
+ **Operational** risks in developing the required capabilities, managing supply chain complexity, and the need to work with existing or new partners
+ **Competitive** risks arising from concerns regarding the defensibility of the concept or competitive retaliation in another market

+ **Regulatory and legal** risks of all types—within and across geographies—such as patent protections, environmental issues, and industry-specific regulations
+ **Financial** risks reflecting concerns about the size and scale of investment to succeed, the ability to hold pricing levels, and potential cannibalization of existing products
+ **Technology** risks relating to feasibility, development lead time, and the extent to which a given technology will provide sustainable advantage

What to do about so many types of perceived risk? If you are like many others facing this situation, you quickly conduct a risk assessment, identifying broadly the types of risk you perceive and their relative severity. Then you might take a next step, such as one of these:

+ **Roll the dice and say**, "This is innovation—it carries risk, but let's be courageous and move forward."
+ **Stop in your tracks**, because you see too much risk in the proposition. It seems overwhelming. You have other things to do. You move on.

+ **Drag your feet** by doing more opportunity-specific analysis, which leads to . . . more dragging of feet.
+ **Do even more risk assessment** by conducting even deeper analyses on financial, operational, customer, channel, technology, and others risks.

Rolling the dice is brave but stupid. Stopping in your tracks won't get you anywhere. Dragging your feet or doing deeper risk assessment defines the term "analysis paralysis"!

Leading innovators avoid each of these four tactics and instead not only assess but also proactively manage and mitigate risk. They do so by applying techniques that explicitly identify the critical assumptions that they believe must be "true" for their concept to succeed. With these assumptions clearly articulated, they then design and manage learning paths through which they can efficiently increase their understanding and certainty regarding the concept's viability, and subsequently make adjustments to iterate the opportunity based on their learning.

Stefan H. Thomke first suggested deploying experimentation as an innovation discipline.[1] More recently, Eric Ries advocated testing assumptions rigorously on a minimal viable product (MVP).[2] He suggests that testing the MVP "is the scientific method: the business equivalent of clinical trials. Assumptions must be tested rigorously."[3] Ries's advice focuses on start-up ventures. "Lean," he explains, "does not mean cheap; it means eliminating waste by testing ideas first . . . Companies shouldn't ramp up personnel and facilities until they've validated their business model . . . Reacting to customer behavior is not incompatible with creating breakthrough products like the iPhone," Ries says, "which in the popular imagination [wrongly assume that it] sprang fully formed from the mind of Steve Jobs."[4]

● Framing Risk to Manage It

Your best approach to dealing with uncertainty and risk is to manage it proactively and in a disciplined way. As a starting point, you may need to reframe the way in which you define risk. First, let's acknowledge that there are some risks you cannot manage or mitigate from your position as an innovation team—or even as a large multinational. Examples include risks related to geopolitical disruptions, macroeconomic shocks, or natural disasters that have far-reaching societal or economic effects.

But you can manage and mitigate most other risks. Successful innovators who bring and scale new-to-the-company and new-to-the-industry concepts define risk as the central and specific assumptions you believe must be true for your concept to win in the market. Assumptions are by their nature unknowns. You believe them to be true, but you don't yet know if they are valid and true.

In some cases, what's unknown to you may be something that some other company knows—you just need to learn it from them. For example, if your new concept's success rests in part at being exceptional at integrating services into products, you might learn more from such organizations as GE, Siemens, and IBM, which know quite a bit about integrating data and services in product bundles. However, if your concept is so new or novel that no one has yet had market success with that type of concept, you cannot rely on desk research alone to learn more.

Once you identify the critical unknowns, you must increase your understanding and knowledge quickly and cheaply, and you need to define your learning path to do so.

> *Successful innovators who bring and scale new-to-the-company and new-to-the-industry concepts define risk as the central and specific assumptions you believe must be true for your concept to win in the market.*

Defining Your Learning Path

Let us say that you have described the critical assumptions that must hold true for your concept to win in the marketplace. You hope your assumptions are true, but you lack information and/or experience to support them. You have a knowledge gap that you need to close.

To close your knowledge gap, you can think of your specific opportunity with respect to its relative "newness" to your organization, markets, and industry. Is the concept similar to something else in your industry? Might there be an analogous concept outside your industry? Or do you believe that it is "new to the world"? Is it something for which you have a bit of understanding and knowledge, but you recognize that you need to learn more? Or is it something you don't know at all? We depict these dimensions of "newness" on the horizontal axis of the graph here. The knowledge you do and don't have determines your level of uncertainty. How you choose to best close your knowledge gap depends on the nature of the unknown.

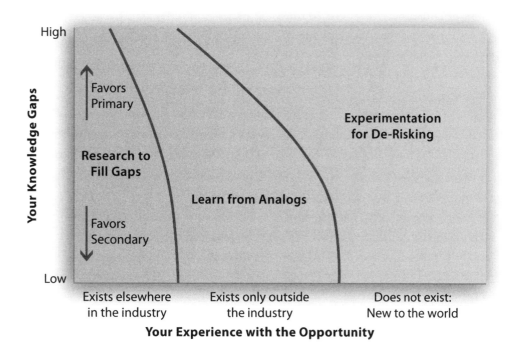

Determining Your Learning Agenda

Primary and secondary research, analogs, and in-market experiments are means by which you increase confidence, thereby managing and mitigating its risk. Let's speak to each of the three techniques in turn.

Learn from Previous, Similar Experience

If there's a history to learn from or a path that customers have already been down that is similar enough to the idea or concept that you are working with, you can research it further by one or more of these means:

+ *Primary market research*—what are the customers' or consumers' reactions to the concept or to the specific questions that you have about the concept?
+ *Secondary research or data* already accrued, which are useful to your concept inquiry.
+ *Historical case examples* you can follow or learn from.

Primary, secondary, or historical research to close your knowledge gap is great if you have access to such information. But breakthrough, innovative concepts are by definition substantially new or different in some way. These techniques are likely to be helpful if you are looking into line extension opportunities, but they will not be as useful if your business concept is new to the industry or new to the world.

Learn Through Analogs

It may be that there are aspects of your concept that have unfolded in another industry. If so, the experience of others from outside your industry may help you increase your understanding of and certainty in regard to one or more of your critical assumptions. Here is a framework:

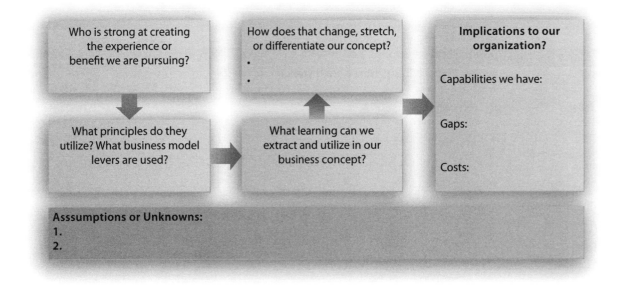

Who is strong at creating the experience or benefit we are pursuing?

What principles do they utilize? What business model levers are used?

How does that change, stretch, or differentiate our concept?
·
·

What learning can we extract and utilize in our business concept?

Implications to our organization?

Capabilities we have:

Gaps:

Costs:

Asssumptions or Unknowns:
1.
2.

As you can see, the framework pushes you to inquire about others' concepts and experiences, so you can then apply selected learning to your concept and adapt it for your context. The type of dialogue implied by the framework should be based on analysis of at least several analogs outside your industry.

Recall that we referred to GE, Siemens, and IBM as companies that successfully evolved and grew base businesses by integrating data and services into the product portfolio. By way of example, if your concept had similar aspects to it, you and your team could look at these companies in terms of the framework to learn and apply best-of learnings to your specific business concept.

● Developing Your Experimentation Agenda

If you believe you concept is compelling—and is one for which there is neither a clear analog nor sufficient relevant experience inside your organization—then you will benefit from iterative experimentation. The technique helps you narrow critical knowledge gaps, and leading practice suggests five important steps to managing and mitigating risk through in-market experimentation:

1. **Identify the key unknowns** about the opportunity that constitute risk. Be specific!

2. **Prioritize the key unknowns**. Ask, "Of all the assumptions supporting our view as to why we will be successful, which is most important? Which assumption is our first priority about which we must learn more through in-market experimentation?"

3. **Design specific experiments that test the priority unknowns**. Again, you should isolate and test only the few critical assumptions that must hold true for you to win.

4. **Test, learn, and apply**. Capture learning from each iteration of an experiment and discuss how the concept should change based on what you just learned.

5. **Repeat! Modify your experiments** on the basis of your new learning, and experiment again with your existing priority assumptions and/or with the "next set" of assumptions that need to be de-risked. Continue until you are sufficiently confident in your assumptions to take the concept to scale.

Let's look at each of these steps in more detail.

Identify the Key, Specific Unknowns That Constitute Risk

Note that we continue to emphasize *specificity*. Too many organizations categorize and assess risk in rather generic terms: "Customer or market risk = high. Operational risk = medium. Financial risk = high." Such general assessments may begin to inform relative types of risk, but each is so vague that it is difficult to do anything with the assessment.

A more useful question is, "Why might the customer risks be high?" For example, you might assess customer risk as high if you believe some or all of the following:

> *Too many organizations categorize and assess risk in generic terms. Specificity matters in terms of risk management and mitigation.*

- Your price point is significantly higher than that offered by current, though inferior, alternatives
- Switching costs are potentially significant
- Your concept's underlying technology is too new and/or is potentially not yet stable
- The "hows" of the route to market for your concept require a significant change in customer purchasing behavior. Will that change in behavior occur?

In practice, it is likely that your concept will have a subset of these elements of customer risk. If you find that each of these customer risk elements is high for your concept, then it is possible that you may have advanced it to this stage of development without sufficiently vetting a few of these areas. Still, as you see from the illustrative list above, by shifting from the general assessment of "high customer risk" to a specific description of the customer risk, you can now focus attention on a specific area. For example, if your greatest uncertainty from the list above were "price point," you could focus on that aspect of your concept and develop a specific in-market learning plan to increase your certainty about it. You would have identified the key issue and now can address it.

Whirlpool Corporation serves as a real-world example. A few years back, the company developed and framed a business concept that we will call "consumer-enabled, custom-built appliances." The innovation team believed that a segment of consumers would place high value on the ability to customize. But the team was very uncertain about the way in which the company could capture economic value. Would the consumer pay a premium for a custom-built appliance, relative to current products available through existing retail partners? Would share-of-market gain be the primary economic driver of the opportunity? Might the proposed concept capture value because consumers will add more features, thereby increasing the total purchase price for the appliance?

Once you've articulated the specific uncertainty at hand, you can actually test it. Whirlpool did so, and learned that the economics of custom-built appliances lay in giving people the opportunity to add all the features they want, because when you do, consumers tend to add more features.[5]

Prioritize the Key Assumptions and Unknowns

Effective experimentation requires that you identify the most central assumptions critical to success. With these assumptions defined, you design and manage a series of iterative test-learn-refine experiments to improve your confidence and understanding. Although it may strike some as paradoxical, taking sufficient time to test and learn more about specific, critical aspects of your concept enables you to move faster and iterate the *overall* concept much more quickly.

To identify the most important assumptions, you should discuss, debate, and decide which assumptions *first and foremost* need to be true for the opportunity to be real, meaningful, and valuable to the organization. The most important assumptions may be in any of the risk categories we mentioned earlier: customer, channel, marketing, operational, competitive, regulatory and legal, financial, or technology. For example, Whirlpool's innovation team had open questions regarding critically important assumptions about their economic model. This *priority unknown* became the basis for a fast and inexpensive set of experiments that allowed them to learn and adjust the business concept accordingly.[6]

The next figure here depicts a simple but useful framework that you and your team can use to agree on the priority of unknowns.

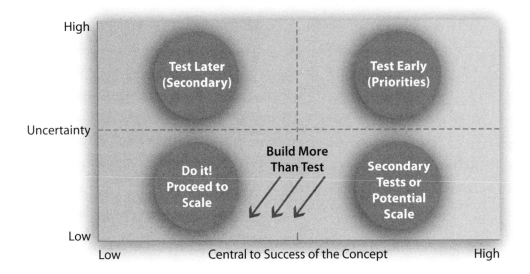

As you can see, the dimensions of level of uncertainty versus the level of importance reflect the two criteria that dictate which assumptions to prioritize. The assumption or assumptions that make it into the northeast corner of the assumptions map should pass the litmus test of "If this is not true, not much else matters." These represent your top-priority assumptions for fast and inexpensive experiment design.

A last note regarding prioritizing key assumptions and unknowns: often you will find that your assumptions fall into four categories:

+ Market and customer affinity
+ Operational viability
+ Technological viability
+ Financial and economic viability

It is sensible that these four tend to be the categories that typically emerge—and that they do so in this priority order. Think of it this way: If customers don't want it, or don't want it as you're offering or positioning it, much of the rest will not matter. If customers want it but you can't deliver on it (operationally), then financials and economics are a moot point. And so on. So although this ordering does not represent a hard-and-fast rule, you can use it as a guide to assist you in prioritizing your assumptions.

Design Experiments to Test the Priority Unknowns

Now that you've established your highest-priority assumptions, how can you test them? Let's first look at some important principles of experiment design. When thinking about designing experiments for business concept learning and de-risking, you should:

+ **Focus on the priority assumptions** necessary to close your knowledge gap. Don't try to test everything about the business concept.
+ **Build for learning, not for earning.** You are not necessarily trying to validate a "mini-me" version of the entire business concept.
+ **Think weeks, not months.**
+ **Think thousands**, not millions of dollars of expense.

+ **Consider experiments on any necessary element of the business concept.** Don't limit experimentation to testing products or offerings only, simply assuming that the rest of the business model elements surrounding the concept will be "as they are in the business today."
+ **Make the learning experiential.** Be there to soak some of it in, firsthand. Don't outsource it to someone else. You'll miss too much rich learning that can be central to the success of the concept and its execution.
+ **Adjust as you go**, even within a given experimentation cycle.

As we've already noted, we encourage "fast and cheap" experimentation. By this we mean small experiments that isolate a single, critical assumption from which you can learn more about "the unknown" and then adjust quickly. As you do so, you will find that you can digest learning from experiments firsthand and quickly. The practice will help you move through successive learning cycles effectively, accelerating your learning.

Figure 6-1 illustrates a framework that can help you and your team think through and design experiments for your concept.

Run "fast and cheap" experiments: small experiments that isolate one or two critical assumptions from which you can quickly learn and iterate.

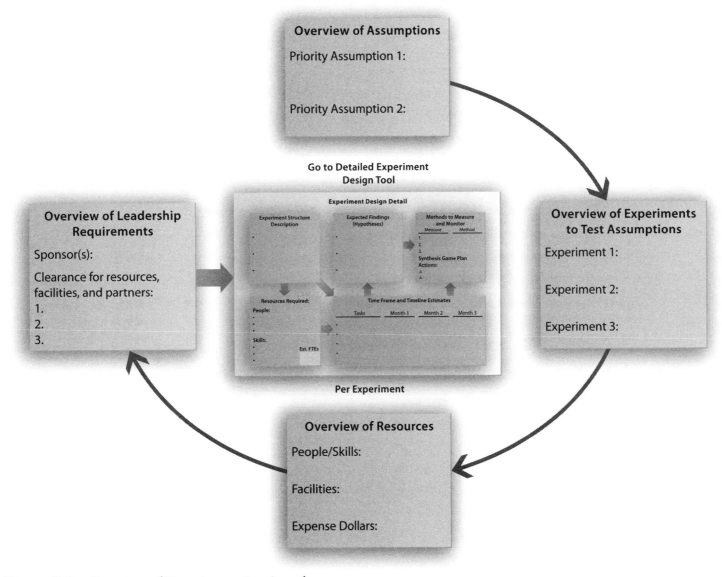

Figure 6-1 Overview of Experimentation Agenda

The framework in Figure 6-1 gets you started on thinking about the potential learning path for the first few critical assumptions that require iterative experimentation. It helps you answer these critical questions:

+ What are the priority assumptions we are looking to learn about?
+ At a macro level: How can we set up the fastest and most inexpensive (but effective) learning path for testing the hypothesis?

+ What are the high-level resources or sponsorships and permissions that we'll need to be able to do this?

Of course, at some point, a more detailed outline of your experiment design will be necessary. Figure 6-2 guides you toward a more detailed outline of any single experiment, including your anticipated resources, timeline, and support.

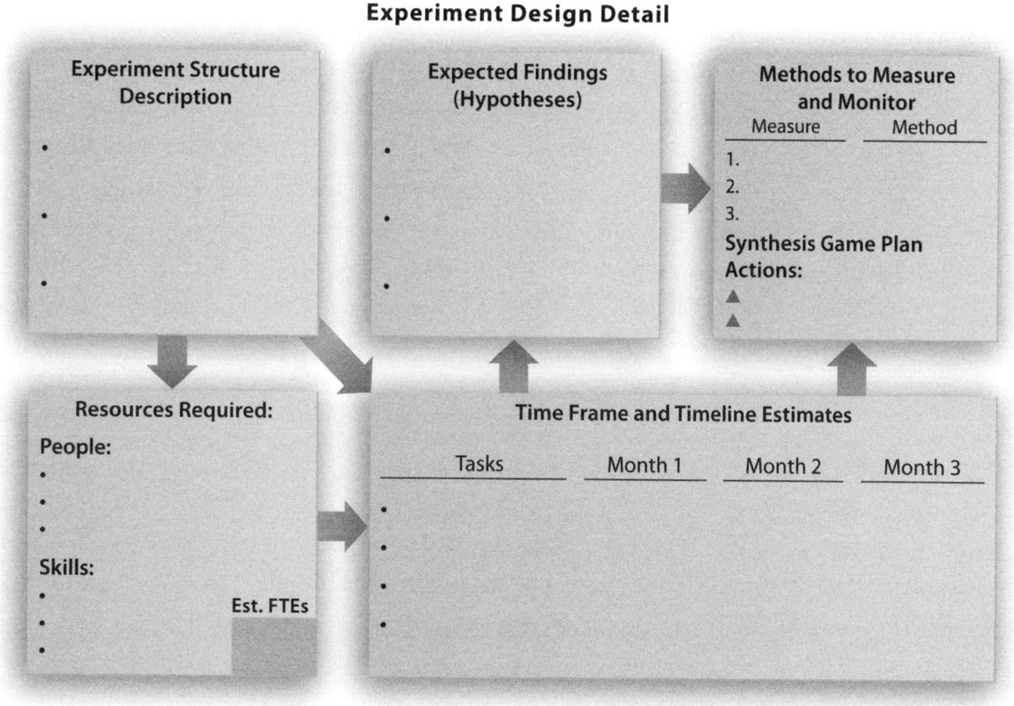

Experiment Design Detail

Experiment Structure Description

Expected Findings (Hypotheses)

Methods to Measure and Monitor

Measure	Method
1.	
2.	
3.	

Synthesis Game Plan Actions:

Resources Required:

People:

Skills:

Est. FTEs

Time Frame and Timeline Estimates

Tasks	Month 1	Month 2	Month 3

Figure 6-2 Detailed Experiment Design

The framework in Figure 6-2 helps you and your team to be disciplined and comprehensive in your thinking by requiring you to detail each experiment. Of course, there may be other questions that you will need to address on a case-by-case basis, but these are some standard questions that typically need to be considered and thought through completely.

Learn, Apply, and Repeat

If your team approaches these frameworks rigorously and thoughtfully, you should at this point have a fully designed experiment. Let's turn now to the next two steps:

+ **Initiate, test, learn, and apply**. How will the concept change based on what we learned?

+ **Repeat!** As we noted early, you should modify your experiment based on your new learning and do it again until you are sufficiently confident in your assumptions to take the concept to scale. Be aware that you will likely be scaling a different concept. This is good! It means you've iterated, improved, and de-risked.

In the following example of iterative experimentation, note the parallel paths of "in-market" and "office" learning activities. Typically, in-market experiences lead to additional questions, some of which can be addressed through offline research and analysis. The time frames are only illustrative, but they are intended to suggest fast iterations through which to build greater confidence regarding your few, critical assumptions.

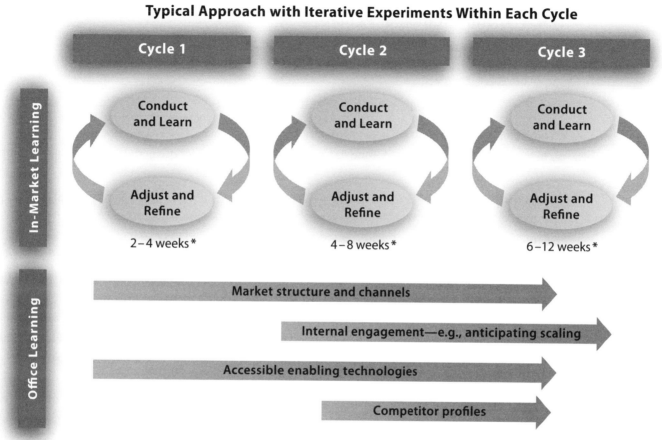

Typical Approach with Iterative Experiments Within Each Cycle

*Time frames are illustrative only and dependent on content-specific factors.

● Experimentation in Action

Let's review some examples that bring these approaches and techniques to life.

Gladiator by Whirlpool Corporation

Gladiator GarageWorks by Whirlpool Corporation is a garage organizing system that includes storage and organization and fit-for-purpose appliances for the garage or basement. It is modular in nature, and hardened for use in the unfinished parts of the home.

As an original idea, Gladiator did not start out looking like its current in-market manifestation. In fact, one could argue that the idea was smaller and certainly quite different from the Gladiator GarageWorks currently marketed and sold in North America. One original germ of an idea was that of a "garage refrigerator." The idea expanded to be that of "garage appliances." After all, appliances were commonly used in the garage, but they were typically "hand-me-down" appliances, such as old refrigerators and freezers, that had been moved out of the house.

Whirlpool's initial idea was framed as "garage appliances made for the garage environment and garage uses." As a team began stretching, elaborating, and iterating the concept, they began to spend more time in the garage to learn. This was a new area of the home to them, as the company's historic focus and attention was the kitchen and laundry room. As they spent time observing garage work and space usage, they learned about a different and relatively unmet need: storage and organization. Garages were a mess, often used as "parking" for everything but cars.

This learning altered the team's view of the concept. Although they stilled viewed it as appliance-centric, their conception began to incorporate other functions: enclosed storage, working space, and hanging storage. They developed a progressive iteration of the concept as a freezer-workbench-storage system, and tested aspects of it in the market.

Although consumer response during this initial test cycle was positive, additional learning surfaced as well. First, the team found that consumers placed much higher importance on storage needs than the team anticipated. In fact, they valued storage at least as much as, and perhaps even a bit more than, the appliance portion of the solution. Second, as they observed consumers building their own workaround solutions, the team realized that do-it-yourself modular solutions were highly sought after. These two observations led them to a revised system that is very close to the current Gladiator GarageWorks solution.

The images here depict the evolution from the original idea to the scaled offering via in-market learning, testing, and iteration.[7]

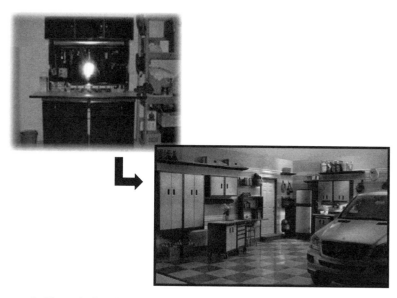

Images provided by Whirlpool Corporation, June 2013.

In this example, iterative in-market learning shifted the emphasis of some key aspects of the nascent business concept[8]:

- ***The product evolved*** from "garage refrigerator" to the full-blown Gladiator GarageWorks System.
- ***The benefits evolved*** from a focus on appliance-like functionality adapted for a garage application to one offering storage for everything from meat or beer to bicycles and sports gear.
- ***The target consumer shifted and expanded***. The product originally started out as an "appliances for men" proposition. But as storage benefits and functionality were integrated within it, the concept began to appeal to Mom. Now it appealed to twice the number of consumers within a given household.
- ***The potential routes to markets broadened*** as storage became a major component of the solution. For existing channels, merchandising options broadened to include store aisles and departments unrelated to appliances. And new channels and formats, such as home store supercenters, also became viable.

The Gladiator example illustrates the importance of several techniques and lessons to guide successful risk management and mitigation:

+ As we've noted in Chapter Four, learning in market and iterating on the business concept are rarely a single-iteration proposition. You must learn and iterate until you are confident in regard to your most important business concept assumptions. Only then should you take the decision to invest in scaling your concept.

+ A single experiment focused on learning more about a single assumption typically leads to learning in that one area—in this case, product configuration. It also brings learning in other unexpected areas, too—in this case, new and additional benefits that appeal to new and additional consumers in the home.

+ In-market learning generally allows you to stretch multiple aspects of the business concept, not just the particular aspect you were testing.

McDonald's and Redbox

Most North American consumers are familiar with Redbox DVD distribution. Fewer are aware that the concept was developed and commercialized by The McDonald's Corporation.

The concept was originally focused on super-convenient, freestanding, automated retail—bigger than a kiosk, much smaller than a convenience store. The notion was that McDonald's would use one of their strongest assets—their large number of premium real estate locations—to grow into retail "beyond burgers." Pairing up new and sophisticated vending technologies with those real estate assets could succeed.[9]

As McDonald's initially considered the concept, questions arose, including, What convenience items might sell best in this kind of format and concept? For answers to this and other questions, there was no existing road map. Instead they would have to test, learn, and adjust based on some in-market experiments.[10]

An early test featured the vending technology, an "unattended convenience store," if you will. It was eighteen feet wide, over six feet high, and held approximately two hundred different items.[11] Through this test, McDonald's quickly learned about which items turned most frequently. Among the top sellers: video rentals. This led McDonald's to reconsider the value proposition as "dinner and a movie," McDonald's style. The team altered the model to focus on unattended DVD sales to accompany fast-food sales—a model that drove traffic and had a much more attractive revenue-to-cost ratio than earlier iterations.[12]

After multiple rounds of testing and iterating, the concept landed on the present Redbox model: top titles only, $1 per day, no late fees. If it costs $20 to purchase the DVD outright and you keep the movie for twenty days or more, it's charged to your credit card and you own it. Rent it for as long as you like, or buy it—your choice.

Redbox installations at scale began at McDonald's locations. But the organization realized that the concept could spread well beyond the restaurants. So they began to install them at all sorts of convenience locations: retail drug chains, grocery stores, shopping malls, and other locations where weekly or more frequent than weekly visits were common. The concept took off.[13]

Redbox now has approximately thirty-four thousand locations throughout the United States and Canada.[14] In 2009, McDonald's sold the growing business model to Coinstar, a leading U.S. vending company, realizing a handsome windfall of around $200 million for the business.[15] (In 2013, Coinstar changed its corporate name to Outerwall.) Redbox continues to innovate, now offering a hybrid of kiosk-based purchases plus streaming video services for a fixed monthly fee. This enables them to compete with the likes of Netflix, innovating their business model as video on demand continues to evolve and grow.[16]

> *Successful innovation feels more like a series of sidebar learnings, iterations, and detours, rather than the clean, neat, "straight-line" path we erroneously think of.*

The Redbox example is a good illustration of the difference between testing for success or failure versus testing for learning and iteration. If McDonald's original "unattended convenience store" concept had been judged on a pass-fail basis, it would have been shelved. The same is likely true for subsequent iterations of the concept. It is through the practice of test-learn-iterate that they landed on the successful Redbox model.

As you can see from the aggregate of our discussion, experimentation, much like the work of innovation in general, is not a "straight-line" path. As you hypothesize, test, learn, and iterate to mitigate risk and optimize the concept, you end up with learnings you never expected to acquire and improvements you would not have otherwise realized. Success feels a bit more like a series of sidebar learnings and conversations, rather than the clea n and neat approach we erroneously think of (or often hear about in retellings of the history of an innovation). You can and should embrace that notion.

Key Take-Aways

- Most organizations conduct risk assessments, but risk is too often defined in a highly general way, making it difficult to identify specific actions for mitigating and managing risk. This is the important difference between "financial risk = high" and "we need to understand whether we'll make money via share gain or margin enhancement or both in this opportunity." The latter is specific enough to allow you to design tests and to learn based on those tests. The former is not and therefore not as helpful.

- Organizations can be much more productive in their risk management if they learn to break the risks down to specifics that they can act on to close their knowledge gaps. Once you identify all the specific and detailed unknowns, you then focus on the few that must hold true for you to win in the market. For these select few, you can then smartly and quickly narrow or close your knowledge gaps.

- You can close your knowledge gap through one or more of three techniques: research, learning through analogs, and in-market experimentation. The newer to the world or to your industry the opportunity is, the more useful it is to experiment as a learning technique and a way to mitigate risk.

- You should design your experiments to be "fast, cheap, and under the radar." The design should help you move quickly so that you can build your understanding by developing new learning on the specific unknowns that you know constitute risk. Avoid the temptation to design experiments to learn about the entirety of your unknowns or to test the entire business model if you are not yet at that stage of commercialization.

- Successful experimentation requires creative design and firsthand involvement from the project team. This will provide visceral learning and enable better iteration of your concept. Keep this axiom in mind: design experiments for learning rather than earning.

- Organizations fear that experimentation will slow them down. Paradoxically, you will move faster and without as many surprises if you take the time to think through design and execute a well-managed experimentation process.

Innovating While in Market

7

We want more innovation and "upside" from our new product/service introductions now that they are in market. How can we innovate and "juice" our in-market business model concept(s)?

I have data that my product or service is not succeeding in the market as planned. Did we sufficiently challenge our go-to-market orthodoxies in launching this product?

We want to innovate both while conceiving a business concept and after it launches. How can we "innovate while flying the plane"?

Most post-launch innovation efforts are initiated by leaders who recognize the substantial imbalance between front-end and postlaunch innovation.

Perhaps you have experienced the euphoria of seeing your new business concept being brought to market after months or years of effort. Now it's time for the returns to roll in. Your innovation work is complete, yes?

Well, maybe. Or maybe there is more upside you can capture. Maybe you can capitalize further on the asset you already have in market, your newly launched concept. The fact is that innovation for a new concept need not stop at launch.

● Innovating While Flying the Plane

Disciplined, postlaunch strategic innovation is feasible and enhances value. Google understands this well. In 2010, for example, Google innovators explored over 13,000 proposed changes to its algorithms. Of these, 8,200 were tested in side-by-side comparisons, 800 were evaluated further in "live traffic," and 516 improvements were made to the search algorithm. That's a 95 percent failure rate—and such failure is a natural act at Google. The process is managed in part through weekly "Search Quality Launch Meetings."[1]

For most other organizations, however, postlaunch innovation does not come naturally. Yet it is a very attractive proposition and one of the underdeveloped frontiers of innovation. A few leading companies are pointing the way by taking select front-end innovation techniques and reapplying them in a fit-for-purpose way to product and service concepts already in market. Think of it as innovating while flying the plane.

Most typically, concerted postlaunch strategic innovation efforts are initiated and enabled through the support of leaders who recognize a substantial imbalance of innovation resources and investment in front-end innovation efforts relative to in-market efforts. Organizations applying these principles, techniques, and approaches improve returns on their innovation investment. To be clear, postlaunch strategic innovation is not limited to poorly performing postlaunch concepts. Rather, in many instances, the efforts are focused on extending and repurposing concepts that are performing just fine, or even unexpectedly well.

We see three general instances in which postlaunch strategic innovation is applied productively to products or services that:

- Produce unexpectedly good results, relative to prelaunch forecast
- Underperform moderately relative to forecast but are not considered obvious failures that should be abandoned
- Are businesses of scale, where even moderate increases in performance will add substantially to bottom-line results

Principles to Guide Postlaunch Innovation

Four principles should guide your efforts.

Apply front-end innovation techniques in a fit-for-purpose way.

Front-end innovation techniques—such as continued learning, insight development, ideation, opportunity elaboration, and experimentation—can and should be applied to concepts postlaunch, whether you have a product that is enjoying higher-than-anticipated success or one that is underperforming, or when you have a keen intuition that there is more upside for a particular concept.

You will need to apply the front-end techniques differently, focusing on the particular objective of improving your in-market performance for a particular concept. Targeted learning postlaunch will guide you to potential changes to your concept and/or may even lead to new, complementary products or services. You know that innovation requires new learning. Continue that new learning to capture the full potential of your newly launched product.

Understand what is fixed and what is malleable for your postlaunch concept.

In practical terms, there are fixed components to an in-market concept that are difficult and expensive to change. Some fixed components, such as base product design or regulatory conformity, may be impossible to change without a complete reconceptualization of a given concept. Yet there are other aspects that can be improved through innovation while in market. These include elements of the marketing mix, such as pricing and promotion, incentives, routes to market, and the channel experience. Focus on what can be productively changed for your particular context. Then apply fit-for-purpose front-end techniques to discover what additional innovations will help you capture more upside.

Use structured pilots for learning.

As we mentioned, the discipline of post-launch strategic innovation is a practitioner's frontier and is likely to be new to many in your organization. You may find it helpful to initiate your postlaunch efforts through a structured pilot. A carefully designed pilot that offers learning by doing is one of the most effective capability-building techniques.

Your pilot should

> *Postlaunch innovation can be productively applied where you are underperforming and/or exceeding expectations. Apply it where you see additional upside to be captured.*

- Include comprehensive coverage of tools and techniques for learning. Try to include as many techniques as is practical and productive, given your objective. This will allow both practitioners and leaders to apply and learn these new techniques in service of capturing more upside for an in-market concept.
- Lean toward simple executions and workstream design for each of the elements of the pilot approach. When you're trying to learn new techniques, approaches, and accompanying behaviors, it is always best to learn to walk before you run.

- Allow for sufficient "space"—people and time availability—to execute your pilot well. It's hard to learn new things when the latest urgent topic is calling your name in a different room, city, or country. Deeper learning that sticks will occur only if you make the space for the development of new capabilities.
- Focus on results, allowing the technique and approach to gain traction within the organization. Focus on real problems that demand real solutions—not just practice runs.

Pick your shots carefully.

Postlaunch strategic innovation requires resources that are different from and additional to your current postlaunch management processes and efforts. Just as you are on the front end of innovation, you will need to be thoughtful and consider your context in choosing the in-market opportunities on which you wish to focus.

Using Front-End Techniques in Postlaunch Activities: Develop New Insights to Enable New Learning

Typically, all or nearly all of your organization's insight work is focused on prelaunch activities within your specific innovation process. Postlaunch, you most likely collect data related to channel sell-in, customer trial, and repurchase. If your launch meets or exceeds projections, pats on the back all around. If your launch falls below expectations, concerns arise: Perhaps our sell-in efforts fell short? Perhaps there is a supply chain fulfillment issue? Perhaps we were wrong about the concept? Perhaps we should pull it back from the market?

Most typically, postlaunch scrutiny focuses on operational root causes, and activity is directed toward addressing shortfalls—sometimes with success and sometimes not. Just as typically, little if any postlaunch scrutiny is focused on developing new insights. So let's take a look at select insight types and see how they may be adapted in a fit-for-purpose way to postlaunch innovation.

+ **Customer insights** with regard to the acquisition cycle, usage, and/or perceived benefits.
+ **Channel insights** relating to in-store sales (for B2C), channel partner activities, and overall channel support.
+ **Online buzz**, which, of course, includes each of the aforementioned insight categories. Your focus here is to authentically monitor, assess, and understand the implications of online conversations and chatter related to your business or concept.
+ **Competitor insights** in regard to the competitive response to your new product or service, with particular emphasis on how this activity informs and, perhaps, may reframe your concept.
+ **Industry orthodoxies** you may challenge, with particular emphasis on each element of the marketing mix.

Customer Insights with Regard to Acquisition in Both the Physical and Virtual Worlds

Here your goal is to understand how your customer is behaving in the acquisition cycle, and you can use observational techniques to do so. You are looking for things that surprise you—both in a general sense and with respect to what you anticipated prior to launch. Ask yourself such questions as

+ What is happening in the physical and virtual prepurchase channel experience, whether B2B or B2C?

- How are customers behaving? Is there anything that surprises us? How does the customer's experience and behavior differ from expectations, and why does it do so?
- Does the behavior suggest an additional customer need or needs that we could meet?

- Might there be a complementary product or service we can offer?
- Do our observations suggest possible alterations to go-to-market elements of the concept?
- What additional enhancements might we provide that innovate on the current concept?

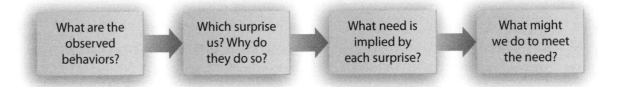

What are the observed behaviors? → Which surprise us? Why do they do so? → What need is implied by each surprise? → What might we do to meet the need?

When your customers enter the store or the relevant section where your product is displayed, what do they do? Do they go to your product first? Or do they take the first product they see? What attracts them to your product and its competitors? If your goal is to get customers to see your product first, to touch it and interact with it, and they are not doing so—what might you do? What changes to the marketing mix and channel support might drive desired changes in behavior? Could you reposition within the format? Could you put up flashing lights that say "come over here"? You might find

small enhancements or revisions that make meaningful differences in the results.

The four broad steps outlined in this figure are helpful for developing customer acquisition insights and for developing customer usage and channel partner insights, described in the next two sections.

Customer/Consumer Insights with Regard to Use

You again apply observational techniques to understand what is enabling or impeding customer usage of your new in-market concept—to understand the delights, the disappointments, and the surprises.

+ What aspects of usage delight and please your customers?
+ What behaviors surprise you? For example, is there a compromise the customer appears to be making? Are they improvising with the product in ways you did not anticipate?
+ Do you sense that there are needs you have not addressed or never anticipated in the original development of the concept?

Of course, you want to be developing usage insights in the real usage environment. For example, in a B2B setting, you may need to observe your customer's product usage in a plant, in the field, or in their research laboratory. In a B2C setting, you may need to observe your consumer's usage in the home, at a restaurant, in a store, or at a NASCAR event.

For customer usage, you will find it helpful to translate the implied needs into specific ideas to improve the in-market concept, such as:

+ An additional feature to include with the product

+ Integration of services to improve the use experience and/or provide additional benefits
+ Changes in packaging
+ Changes to pricing
+ Changes in overall value proposition positioning
+ Changes in other go-to-market practices, such as channel support, merchandising, market communications tactics, and choice of channel

Channel, Sales Associate, and Trade Partner Insights

Your goal here is to understand how activities performed by the channel are enabling or hindering your success. Observe the channel and—when applicable—sales associate behaviors. In many cases, we find that what an organization believes about the activities its channel is performing is not, in fact, actually happening as anticipated. Indeed, when a team goes into the field—to a retailer, distributor, or end user—to observe behavior specific to an in-market concept, they discover "surprises." The surprises emerge from observed unanticipated behaviors, perhaps from a sales associate, a distributor, or an end-use customer, or from online behavior.

When you go into the field, expect and look for surprises by asking yourself questions like these:

+ What activities does each actor in the channel perform? Are these enabling our success, hindering it, or neither?
+ Are there aspects of the entire concept that we can change?
+ Which are related only to the service or product?
+ What changes in channel activities might produce a better result? Does the change also require changes to the product? Which potential changes might require product changes, and which ones do not?

All of your information gathering and observations should be done in the market— in-store or "in-enviro"—wherever that might be. For this type of insight work, it is not helpful to rely on customer interviews or focus groups outside the environment and context about which you are trying to learn.

Observation, inquiry, and data gathering for channel and shopper insights may vary across physical (and digital) environments.

For information gathering in the physical environments, include

+ Observation, and inferences from the observations
+ Customer intercepts and exit interviews
+ Mystery shopping in the form of first-hand learning expeditions
+ Sales associate observations and intercepts
+ Sales and store manager interviews and intercepts

In virtual environments, insight gathering might be a bit tougher. Online insight gathering techniques tend to require a bit more creativity and include

+ Direct access to the online purchasing data—volumes, walk-aways, returns, browses, anything you can get access to—assuming your organization or your organization's channel partners have such data and will provide them.
+ Call center sit-ins. Listen in on a substantial sample of inbound calls: What are the incoming calls and orders about? What are the delights you hear? What are the frustrations? What unmet needs do your findings portend?

+ Netnography—or, in laymen's terms, Web watching. What is the online buzz with regard to your product/offering and its acquisition? What are people saying? What's the chatter? What are the themes and consistent feedback? What of this information can you take away as "needs gaps" that you can leverage to add more juice to the business concept?

Obviously there will be more chatter online about movies and celebrities than there will be about chainsaws or paper towels. Still, if you look, you'll find online chatter of substantial quantity on just about anything. Leverage it.

There are an ever-increasing number of services that monitor customer behavior, preferences, dislikes, and frustrations regarding your competitors, your company, and your products. These services provide a useful and generally inexpensive tool for netnography, enabling you to gather data from an enormously broad number of relevant sources and assisting you in distilling the data down to key insights.

However, we urge you not to outsource *all* of the online chatter monitoring and learning to a third party. There is no substitute for firsthand, experiential learning through which you get the raw, unfiltered input. Give yourself the opportunity to obtain a healthy mix of both casting the net wide through a third-party service and building your own firsthand impressions. One simple way to do this is to Google the topic and read the blogs. As is the case with ethnography, you'll be glad you did. Too much distillation waters down the learning!

Competitive Response Insights

Your goal here is to understand how competitive response to your in-market concept may help you further improve it. Use your competitors' actions as a lens through which to see your concept's strengths and gaps:

+ Do they mimic or copy you, as Samsung has done in following Apple's smartphone and tablet innovations?
+ Do they counter with a poor-man's version of the same innovation or concept or feature?
+ Does their counter get traction? If so, in what ways?

♦ What does the market response to your introduction and/or to your competitors' counter tell you about what the market *really* values? Or what the market *would really* value?

Using in-market research and other desk-based analyses, you then consider what changes might enhance your offering further—either to defend against competitive encroachment or to go on offense. In practice, your opportunity to develop competitor response insights may lag some of the other categories of insights discussed so far. The potential lag is a function of how quickly the competition responds to your in-market innovation.

The framework depicted here reflects the thought process for mining competitor activity for insights that may guide improvements to your in-market concept.

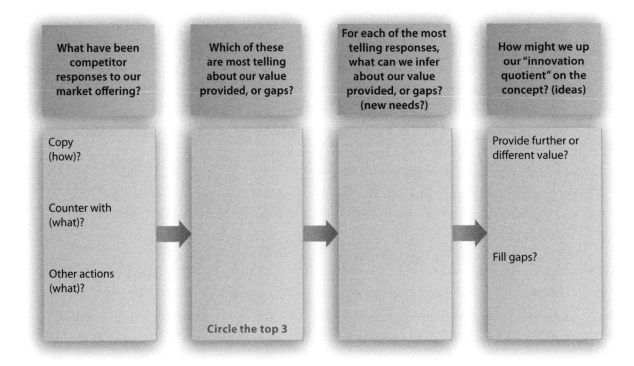

What have been competitor responses to our market offering?	Which of these are most telling about our value provided, or gaps?	For each of the most telling responses, what can we infer about our value provided, or gaps? (new needs?)	How might we up our "innovation quotient" on the concept? (ideas)
Copy (how)?			Provide further or different value?
Counter with (what)?			
Other actions (what)?			Fill gaps?
	Circle the top 3		

New Orthodoxies We Can Challenge

Your goal here is to ensure that in commercializing your concept you did not overlook a profitable opportunity to break with industry convention. Ask yourself: Do the new insights regarding customers and competitors suggest orthodoxies we overlooked? If so, can we profitably challenge them?

Keep in mind that orthodoxies are simply an additional way to frame customer, channel, or competitor insights. But you will often find that framing them in this different manner (in terms of "how we think") can illuminate new innovation possibilities. Applying multiple perspectives in search of new insights is a consistently good principle.

The following is a framework to guide you and your team in converting customer and competitor response insights into new orthodoxy insights.

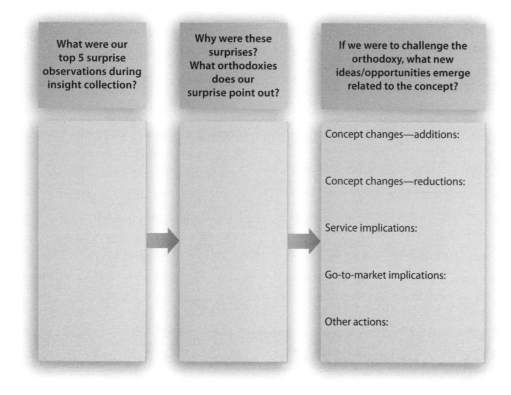

What were our top 5 surprise observations during insight collection?

Why were these surprises? What orthodoxies does our surprise point out?

If we were to challenge the orthodoxy, what new ideas/opportunities emerge related to the concept?

Concept changes—additions:

Concept changes—reductions:

Service implications:

Go-to-market implications:

Other actions:

● Translating Insights into Action

Often we find that as teams gather post-launch insights, improvement ideas regarding promotion, merchandising, and channel support emerge. In some cases, the ideas are sufficiently compelling that the organization either implements them immediately or conducts rapid test-and-learn experiment cycles. As a result, they move quickly to capture more innovation upsides for their concept.

In other instances, organizations take the step of translating their insights into ideas in a more disciplined or deliberate fashion. To do so, they ideate by combining select internal and external insights. Ask yourself: What are the (multiple) new business concept possibilities at the intersection of particular insights we've gained regarding customer behaviors and unmet needs, channel or sales associate behaviors, competitor responses we did not anticipate, or new orthodoxies we've unearthed?

In particular, you should focus on ideas that may help you

- Identify ways by which to target a new "who" with the same concept
- Imagine new positioning possibilities or new ways of catching consumer attention
- Consider new tactics within a channel, additional channels, or both
- Explore the potential of easily added new features

In many cases, these actions could be taken without initiating a massive and impractical redesign of product or platform. You may even be able to develop a progression of ideas to test through experimentation. Figure 7-1 offers a guide for using insight combinations to develop new ideas for and improvements to your postlaunch concept.

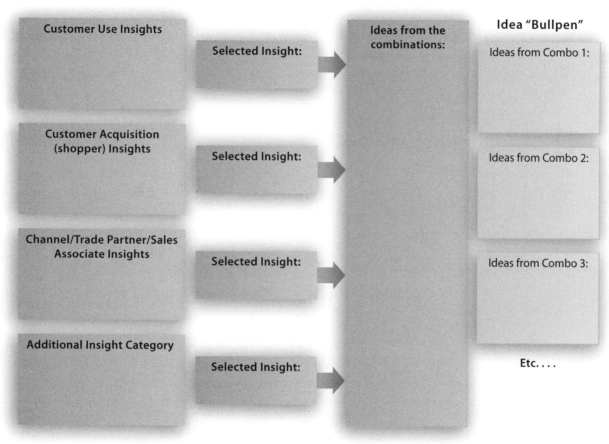

Figure 7-1 Idea Generation from Postlaunch Insights

As you can see, the framework structures your idea generation in ways that have you look at the implications of two or more insights. For example, you may have a channel partner insight and an orthodoxy insight. In the context of the two insights, your team would consider ways in which to meet the particular channel need by breaking with orthodoxy.

As you generate ideas, you may also find it useful to group your ideas into theme-based clusters. For example, you may have a theme related to a particular benefit, an enabling technology, or a set of support activities for one or more of your go-to-market channels. Grouping ideas by themes will allow you to organize your ideas and options in a manner that will enable easier referencing and use, both immediately and in the future.

The following framework depicts two dimensions by which you can position and contrast particular ideas within a given theme. The x-axis represents time to market; the y-axis represents complexity. You will find it helpful to sequence each idea in terms of these two dimensions, allowing you to quickly organize a large number of ideas that you may want to pursue over time. The "further-out" ideas on your timeline represent a reserve of sorts, from which you can pull as the resource allows.

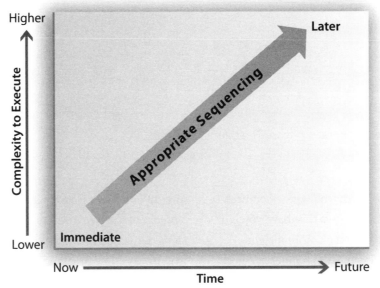

Domain Theme: (Theme or Value That the Aggregation Of These Ideas Drives Toward)

You may find that you have more themes or more ideas within a given theme than you can productively consider or implement all at once. In this instance, you will find it helpful to prioritize them using these criteria:

+ Size of the potential upside
+ Required resources
+ The time required for you to develop new learning and the time required to take action based on the learning
+ Extent of disruption to your current in-market efforts related to the concept

For your particular context, you may wish to add other criteria, such as impact on other concepts in the pipeline or already in market.

Finally, you will need to further frame individual ideas within the domains for execution. Because your concept is already in market, you will want to move fast.

Shown next, an outline of an abbreviated concept elaboration framework will guide you in quickly framing, assessing, and vetting some of these ideas or "business concept add-ons." The point is to think holistically about the idea, its value to customers or other stakeholders, and its impact on you, without bogging down in long exercises in business case writing and analysis paralysis.

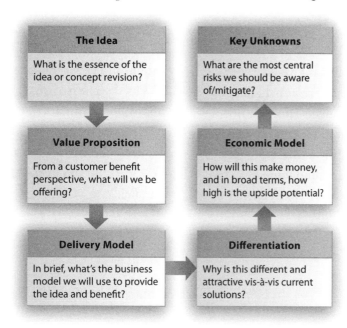

The Idea

What is the essence of the idea or concept revision?

Value Proposition

From a customer benefit perspective, what will we be offering?

Delivery Model

In brief, what's the business model we will use to provide the idea and benefit?

Key Unknowns

What are the most central risks we should be aware of/mitigate?

Economic Model

How will this make money, and in broad terms, how high is the upside potential?

Differentiation

Why is this different and attractive vis-à-vis current solutions?

Continue to Experiment for Postlaunch Learning and Revision

Experimentation and rapid learning and iteration techniques are also likely to be helpful during your postlaunch innovation process. You may have early ideas about additional innovation for the offering or concept that are easily framed but need testing and de-risking.

As Eric Ries describes in *The Lean Startup*, a disciplined approach to rapid experimentation can enable faster time to value for a given concept.[2] We agree and endorse his approach. He suggests applying the discipline prior to full-scale launch. But why should such a high-value technique be fully utilized prelaunch, only to be discarded postlaunch? Through fit-for-purpose experimentation, you can innovate postlaunch, developing and vetting new improvements to surround your in-market concept. You may believe that you can improve your concept by revising promotion, pricing, or support and service to the channel. You may have ideas to improve the product through additional features or even, perhaps, to bring additional complementary products to market. If you are not certain which of these will lead to upside for your in-market concept, you can raise your confidence through postlaunch experimentation.

Postlaunch Innovation: Illustrative Design Approaches

You can think of each of the front-end techniques for gaining new learning—insight development, ideation, opportunity elaboration, and experimentation—as "LEGO blocks" for constructing a specific project approach to in-market, postlaunch innovation that best fits your situation and context. Figure 7-2 illustrates an approach featuring new learning and initial experimentation in parallel.

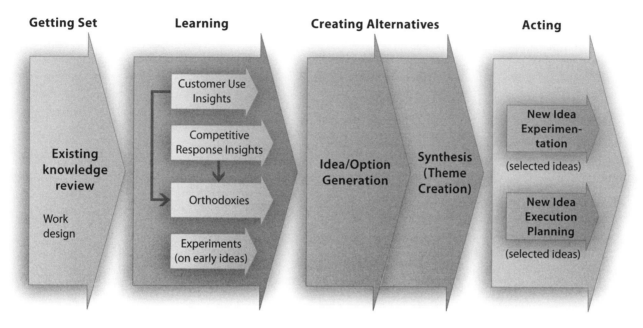

Figure 7-2 Postlaunch Design Example

This approach assumes that you have, right from the start, specific ideas you wish to test in market. You have ideas for which you articulate assumptions—unknowns—that can only be verified through iterative, in-market test-and-learn cycles. The assumptions are within one or more of your four typical priority areas:

1. Market and customer affinity
2. Operational viability
3. Technological viability
4. Financial and economic viability

The approach also assumes that you want to develop additional new learning about your in-market success. For example, perhaps you are having far more success than you and your colleagues ever envisaged. You wonder: Is our success a result of an insightful value proposition well executed? Did we underappreciate the importance of the form factor for the concept? Perhaps our channel support was such that our go-to-market partners were so well incented and supported that volume took off?

As Figure 7-2 depicts, you will run parallel efforts to develop new learning in particular areas while managing a series of iterative experiments that you anticipate will bring greater clarity to a few key unknowns. The effort leads to ideas that you prioritize and then elaborate briefly. Ideally, this then leads to new execution(s) from your experiments and additional experimentation based on the new learning. We deliberately do not suggest specific timing or resources required, as these are wholly dependent on the specific context. Generally speaking, this type of approach requires several weeks or more.

Many successful approaches to postlaunch innovations efforts are variants of the process illustrated in Figure 7-2. You may find, for example, that you could move from insights directly to action, without additional ideation or experimentation.

Your specific approach will vary based on such considerations as

+ **Types of insights you find helpful**. You may have the time and resources to explore many types of insights that can help you develop new learning regarding your in-market concept. Alternatively, you may think that your potential centers wholly on the purchase occasion, and you might therefore focus only there.

+ **Existing ideas and insights developed prelaunch**. Sometimes you can return to prelaunch ideas and insights to identify potential actions you might take to improve your product. In this context, you may be able to "just do it" and take some of those ideas to test or to immediately apply them in market now.

+ **Value and importance of experimentation and the types of experiments**. If you have specific ideas about which you have great certainty, you may skip experimentation. Alternatively, you may want to incorporate it into your work and move through a cycle or two very quickly. The types of experiments you conduct may shorten or extend your timeline. For example, it may take more time to arrange experiments with customers in a B2B setting than it would in a retail environment.

Your starting context necessarily shapes your particular approach to postlaunch innovation. In some instances, you can move through the process with great results in a matter of weeks. You may find that you can use existing ideas and move directly to experimentation. The point here is that you select all or some of the LEGO blocks and configure them in a fit-for-purpose way to your particular in-market circumstance.

● Postlaunch Innovation Pioneers: Select Case Examples

Let's look more closely and holistically at several cases of organizations that have extended the scope of innovation by successfully applying this type of in-market learning.

Whirlpool Corporation

Whirlpool Corporation proactively applied strategic innovation principles to in-market product launches. Through their experience in doing so, the innovation team revamped its end-to-end innovation process to include innovating while in market.[3]

Whirlpool's long-term innovation capability-building efforts are well documented.[4] For a decade, the company focused on the execution and continuous improvement of their front-end innovation process, known internally as the Double Diamond process and approach.[5]

Their high-performing front-end innovation process focuses on insights that lead to ideas that ladder up to domains within which teams develop individual business plans and business concepts that are brought to market. Historically, the approach was quite helpful in generating a comprehensive set of commercialized new ideas and growth paths. Various external sources document that Whirlpool created billions of dollars of new revenue through their work on this front.[6] But they wanted more. Senior leaders and the central innovation team believed that their ten-plus years of experience in creating value through the front end could be extended to postlaunch execution. They *intuitively believed* that there *had to be* upside innovation potential in products recently launched into the market. Simple math instructed them that even small gains on any of their scaled businesses or brands would deliver substantial value to shareholders.

Whirlpool took action consistent with their years of learning, and designed and launched an initial pilot through which they could learn more about the value of postlaunch innovation. The pilot focused on a recent launch in their flagship business: laundry. The choice was made both for the impact that it could have and for the credibility it would help bring to the application of postlaunch innovation techniques. The pilot approach included consumer usage insights, shopper insights, trade partner and sales associate insights, and early experimentation.

Early in the pilot, the team developed about sixty implementable concepts organized into four different "go-to-market" domains. They then extracted ten of the best initial ideas and framed them in more detail, including short and inexpensive experimentation plans. Whirlpool's work resulted in opportunities for innovation on the concept launch that added up to a potential for $50 million in incremental revenues.[7]

This graphic is an overview of the pipeline of postlaunch innovations that Whirlpool created for itself.

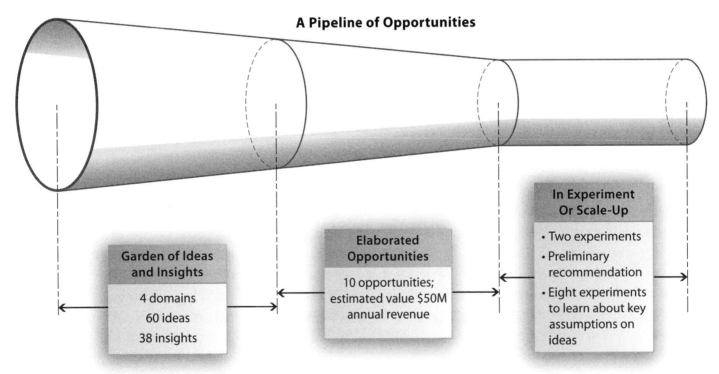

A Pipeline of Opportunities

Garden of Ideas and Insights
4 domains
60 ideas
38 insights

Elaborated Opportunities
10 opportunities; estimated value $50M annual revenue

In Experiment Or Scale-Up
• Two experiments
• Preliminary recommendation
• Eight experiments to learn about key assumptions on ideas

Graphic provided by Whirlpool Corporation.

Whirlpool's innovation in postlaunch activities is made possible by their mastery of their original innovation process. They leveraged strengths and capabilities already built through years of exercising and honing this discipline. They leveraged that capability along with postlaunch design and piloting to further enhance their end-to-end innovation capabilities with proactive pursuit of postlaunch innovation. The company's redesigned "Triple Diamond" innovation process is illustrated here:

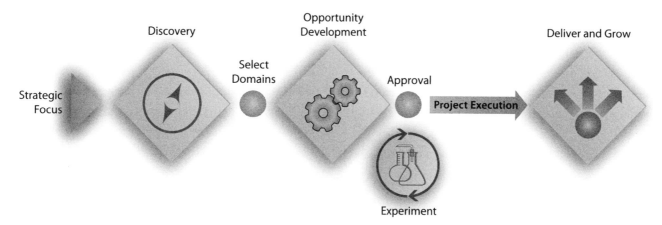

Graphic provided by Whirlpool Corporation.

Reflecting on the effort, Moises Norena, Whirlpool's director of global innovation, notes that many of the insights and potential innovations that Whirlpool developed could be applied across categories—that is, beyond laundry and into refrigeration, cooking, and other new market spaces.[8] Whirlpool's experience is a common outcome of this type of approach.

Moises and the innovation team appropriately view these efforts as a significant management innovation, and at one point termed the change as a shift from a "Launch and Leave" approach to one of "Launch and Love."[9] More recently, as the team promulgates this management process innovation across Whirlpool Corporation, they refer to this stage of the innovation work as "Deliver and Grow."[10]

Herman Miller

Office furniture giant Herman Miller distributes its configurable, modular office furnishing systems through its dealer network. The company's systems can be designed and installed as a fit-for-purpose solution for each customer's needs. Typically the dealer is the channel member who assembles the furniture for the customer at the customer's location(s).

Herman Miller extended its innovation efforts to include in-market activities through an effort dubbed "the Last Mile." The program's initial focus in 2004 was to make "dealers as healthy as possible—and to help them best represent Herman Miller's strengths as a company." For example, Herman Miller teams helped their dealers improve their purchase-order-to-cash cycle, shortening it by fifteen to twenty days.

After several years of success with the Last Mile, the company extended its scope to include postlaunch innovation by specifically focusing on learning more about their customers' frustrations, delights, and unmet needs during the end-to-end delivery and installation process. They learned a lot. For example, although the company had developed a just-in-time delivery system, the parts and modules were being loaded on the trucks at the convenience of the deliverer, rather than that of the receiving customer or of the dealer responsible for assembly at the customer's location. This led to complications and frustrations that the dealer and customer had to cope with, such as

- Having to unload all pieces of a given component of the same type as a group, rather than having the various components consistently matched with other elements of its system. This practice led to longer install times and headaches for both the dealer's installation team and the customer's installation manager.
- Increased storage requirements for the components delivered to the customer that could not yet be installed because one or more of the required complementary elements of the system they formed were not yet delivered.
- Job site clutter arising from the aforementioned mismatches.

The team's new learning and insight led to a completely redesigned delivery process. The changes included loading trucks so that when an order is delivered on-site to a customer, the product is off-loaded according to the dealer's first assembly step. The company also stores finished goods for a particular order until the time at which the order can be shipped completely. The changes save time and money for the dealer and helped the company grow during the last downturn. To enable all this,

Herman Miller developed a laptop-based system to further enhance dealer-to-company communication and coordination on system design and delivery.

These delivery system innovations greatly enhance the company's standing and value to their dealers and customers. Doing business with Herman Miller is now faster and easier than before because of their customer-centric delivery model. This was facilitated by their applying the lens of customer delivery and installation efficiency (and gaps) to their high-quality modular product offering, which had been in market for years.[11]

● Postlaunch Innovation Issues to Anticipate

Because postlaunch innovation work is a new frontier for many practitioners, there are several important issues to consider. Think of each as a "watch out" you should be aware of as you initiate and scale postlaunch innovation within your organization:

Anticipate and prepare for ways through which you can integrate postlaunch innovation techniques into your current commercialization or postlaunch management processes.

Postlaunch innovation will thrive in your organization if and only if it is integrated into other postlaunch processes. Integration provides greater "stickiness" than does conducting these efforts as separate and distinct projects. You know that "special projects" are hard to sustain over time. Therefore, you should anticipate and plan for migration to existing processes and systems. As possible, involve and engage your colleagues actively in your early pilot and subsequent integration of the techniques.

With postlaunch innovation, you will always find yourself playing in someone else's sandbox. Be prepared for push-back, and be proactive about productively addressing it as soon as it surfaces.

Postlaunch in-market innovation ruffles more feathers than innovation that focuses on conceiving and launching brand-new

Postlaunch innovation will thrive in your organization if and only if it is integrated into other postlaunch processes.

Postlaunch innovation is a powerful value-enhancing technique. The upside is there for the taking. Do yourself a favor—don't skip it.

ideas or concepts. Why? Because you have colleagues whose full-time job focuses them on in-market execution and support of the current product portfolio. There are many designers, engineers, marketers, and general managers who have been working on the new product launch for a long time. They are heavily invested, and rightly so. When you begin looking for additional innovations to add to the concept, you are proposing changes in an area that is very near and dear to these folks.

Strong ownership of what's already in place is natural and in many ways quite healthy. Therefore, you must be prepared to engage the relevant constituencies and leadership productively. You can do so by employing a well-thought-through program and a deliberately collaborative and engaging approach, and by engaging a senior sponsor to assist with roadblocks.

Postlaunch innovation must feature experimentation techniques in a big way.

Keep in mind that experimentation means "learn and iterate quickly," not "test and approve" or "test and kill." Continuous reinforcement of this different view of experimentation may be necessary, especially within the community of colleagues accountable for in-market execution.

Productive use of experimentation takes on added importance in the world of postlaunch innovation environment. Why? Because fast, cheap, and focused experimentation is an even more prominent technique in the postlaunch innovation environment. Behaviors often regress to the mean, and your organization may have a history of test-and-approve pilots. If so, it will take much more than one or two conversations or case example experiments to make "learn and iterate quickly" an accepted practice. In short, get yourself ready for an ongoing change management effort on this topic alone.

● ● ●

These are substantial issues to anticipate. And there is no doubt that developing and implementing a sustainable postlaunch innovation capability will be challenging. But when all is said and done, it is a powerful, value-enhancing innovation technique. The upside is there for the taking. Do yourself a favor: try it; don't skip it.

Key Take-Aways

- Postlaunch innovation represents one of innovation's frontiers, and it is a missed opportunity in most organizations. Many front-end techniques and approaches can be reapplied postlaunch in a fit-for-purpose way.

- If postlaunch innovation is a new discipline for your organization, you should approach the effort through a structured, focused pilot. Your organization is likely to have established processes for piloting new initiatives. Learn from them. A deliberately designed pilot structured in a learning-by-doing way is one of the most effective capability-building techniques. There should be change management components to your pilot, as postlaunch innovation represents a change in how the work of innovation is done.

- Experimentation is an important postlaunch innovation technique. Experimentation means "learn and iterate quickly," not "test and approve" or "test and kill." Your success will probably depend in part on your efforts to continually articulate the distinction—particularly if your organization has a history of conducting test-and-approve pilots.

- Anticipate and plan for some issues related to postlaunch innovation, including internal resistance. In particular, others in the organization may feel that you are playing in their sandbox. Proactively collaborate with key stakeholders and leadership to build support for the effort.

Organizing for Innovation

I want my organization to innovate, but the natural tendency of the organization is not to do that. What do I do?

We (the organization's leadership) don't manage our innovation systematically. Thus we don't stick with it over time. What can we do?

We want our leaders . . . our "Top 100" . . . to have capabilities to lead innovation efforts, to design them to get results. What do we do?

How do I integrate innovation concepts and processes into our learning and development programs?

For innovation to take root in an organization, you need to create an environment that is welcoming to your efforts, that reinforces and facilitates your actions. But one of the unspoken truths of innovation is that organizations are built to do exactly what they are already doing. Indeed, the vast majority structure themselves to meet the needs of existing customers with existing product and services, sold through existing go-to-market channels. A few do so with extraordinary success, others disappoint terribly, and the vast majority achieve average results.

> *An unspoken truth of innovation is that organizations are built to do exactly what they are already doing. The vast majority structure themselves to meet the needs of existing customers with existing product and services.*

Of course, organizations are not naturally welcoming of change, nor do they easily adapt and integrate a new direction into their growth efforts. They are wired neither to challenge their own orthodoxies as a matter of course nor to take action that departs from accepted industry convention. Resistance to change is not surprising, but this resistance is generally not acknowledged by companies that desire to build an innovation capability.

If your organization is serious about innovation, you must also be serious about creating an environment in which innovation can flourish. To do so, you will need to ensure that innovation happens through and because of the system—rather than in spite of it. You will need to build innovation muscle and manage innovation as a discipline and capability. How will you do this? By thinking deliberately about the way in which your organizing actions can enable systemic innovation.

A Framework for Organizing the Elements of Innovation

Business school professors, consultants, and perhaps your own organization each have a model or framework to guide organizational design. For example, Whirlpool Corporation's Nancy Tennant first architected and then enabled innovation through a "Wheel of Innovation" framework that helps guide and progress efforts toward the company's goal of driving growth through an embedded innovation competence.[1] The Wheel identifies the critical organizing actions to sustain and extend innovation capabilities over time, including changes to process, augmented metrics, and leadership behaviors.

We find it helpful to think of these actions as a set of "organizing elements" you can use in combination to nurture a culture of innovation in a sustainable and beneficial way. Changes to these organizing elements represent deliberate and disciplined choices for structuring and supporting efforts within your organization to make innovation happen "because of the system." The elements include

+ Your core innovation approach and process
+ Supporting tools and frameworks
+ Skills and skill building
+ Metrics and measures
+ Incentives
+ Surrounding and enabling processes— for example, annual planning, budgeting, and resource allocation
+ Funding mechanisms
+ Organizational communications— internal and external
+ Leadership engagement and decision making (both behaviors and mechanisms or processes)
+ Structural adjustments to facilitate and perpetuate innovation

Figure 8-1 is a visual summary of these organizing elements for innovation. The end game, of course, is to achieve the innovation results you want and need for your organization. You are not organizing for the sake of change. You are organizing to achieve innovation for growth. You may also notice that "culture" is not a separate element. Our view is that the particular combination of the elements listed is what informs and shapes a culture of innovation within any organization.

● Design Principles for Organizing for Innovation

In working with organizations across geographies and industries, we often hear the qualifier, "But things are different here." We agree—differences in innovation ambition, culture, leadership style, and industry structure should lead to distinct and sometimes nuanced actions. For example, Whirlpool Corporation's enabling actions work well within their organization, but if you were to attempt to replicate their actions wholesale within Google, ABB, Shell, or China's Bailian Group, the results would likely disappoint.

Each situation is different, so we caution you against quickly accepting and

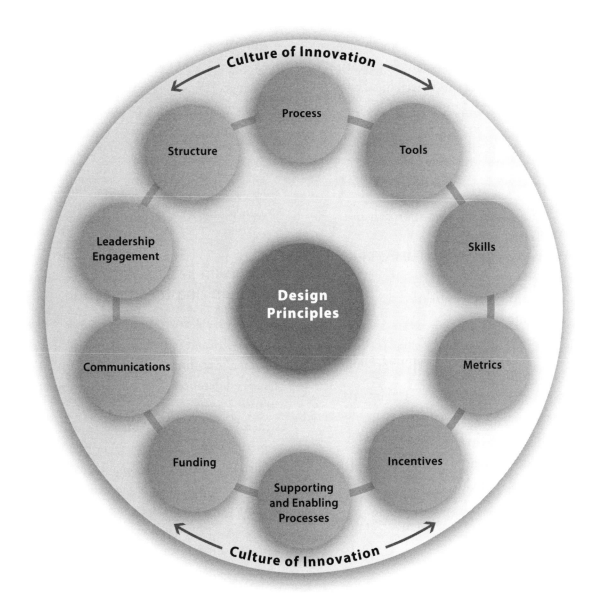

Figure 8-1   Organizing Elements to Enable Innovation

implementing preset approaches. There is no single solution or silver bullet that fits all organizations. There is, however, a set of design principles that are consistently helpful. Use these principles as a guide as you consider which actions may be most helpful to moving your efforts forward. Think of them as a checklist with which you ask yourself whether a given design

+   **Is a comprehensive approach** through which you consider each element as a means by which to enable and sustain your innovation ambition
+   **Reflects a systemic approach** in which several discrete actions reinforce each other, bringing greater coherence and cumulativeness to your efforts
+   **Works with the grain** of the organization's culture, featuring some of the same characteristics prominent in previous successful change efforts
+   **Avoids innovation "islands,"** integrating with key parts of the organization, such as process, leadership, and talent development
+   Enables the organization to **be more open internally** so that it may also be open externally

Think Comprehensively

If you seek to innovate sustainably, you will have to make changes within and across several organizing elements. For example, one organization that embedded its innovation process only within their new product development (NPD) process became frustrated that they were not making sufficient progress on breakthrough innovations. One root cause: although the organization rewired its innovation process well, it did not also make changes to metrics, incentives, and structure, so the measures that align to process objectives for breakthrough were lacking. Also, leadership attention was not sufficiently focused on supporting the objective. The result: an improved NPD process that brought incremental products to market more efficiently, but fell short of delivering breakthrough innovation.

Design Systemically

Any high-performing system has reinforcing mechanisms that work together to accomplish its objective(s). You must design your system the same way. Be careful not to treat design options in an "a la carte" way. In practice you will find that some fit well and

Each situation is different. We caution against quickly accepting and implementing preset approaches for organizing for innovation.

others do not. The system that is "best for you" is one that is guided by your innovation ambition, culture, and marketplace context.

Others in your industry, including direct competitors, may be organizing for innovation at scale. Although it may be helpful to learn and understand the scope of their activities, it would be dangerous to assume that you could take their approach and apply it wholesale to your organization.

> Develop the least traumatic changes to your existing system that get the innovation job done, then get to work learning to manage it. This may sound paradoxical to transformation, *but it's not.*

By way of analogy: Southwest Airlines and Singapore Airlines are both very successful airline companies, each with their own distinct, coherent, and successful business model. If one company were to copy the other's business model and run their operations by it, they would fail. The same is true for your organization: don't copy others' organizational designs wholesale. Instead, design your own. If you do not feel capable of developing a strong systemic design on your own for your organization, pull in some experienced help.

Work with the Grain of the Organization

Develop and execute the least traumatic changes to the existing system that still get the innovation job done for you, then get to work on learning to manage the new system. This may sound paradoxical to the notion of transformation for innovation, but it is not. Any organizational change is difficult to achieve. Innovation has the added challenge of organizing such that the organization can and will do things it has never done before. You don't want to make the transition even more difficult by deliberately targeting big step-change reorganization actions when they're not necessary.

As a starting point, think about significant, deliberate, and successful change(s) within your organization over the last five years. Examples might include a new emphasis on a particular geographic market, an enterprise-wide focus on Six Sigma, or a new business model requiring a different approach to market. You can learn from those involved how they "worked with the grain" to make organizational changes over time that enabled their success. Understand what worked well, what fell short, and what good and bad surprises emerged.

Design a Fit-for-Purpose System

Ask, "What is the primary thing that we need our innovation system to achieve?" For example:

+ Do you need new ideas, such that you need to design a system that favors front-end new thinking and actions, but adoption by the organization is a fait accompli?
+ Do you believe that "ideas are not my problem—getting to action is the problem!" If so, you may want to design a system that first and foremost enables ownership and transition to commercialization as early as possible in the process.

Or perhaps you need to design so as to address both of these problems. What is "best" for you will be different from what is best for other organizations—even those within your own industry. Therefore, you should keep your most important innovation objectives front and center as you structure a fit-for-purpose system. "Fit for purpose" does not dictate that you exclude elements that enable secondary objectives, but the goal is to drive your primary objective(s), with secondary benefits as a welcome bonus.

Avoid Isolated Innovation Islands

You will never achieve innovation at scale in your organization by keeping your activities permanently isolated. Unfortunately, organizations do this far too frequently, declaring that "R&D [or some other named group] should innovate and then we'll pick it up when it's fully vetted and ready."

Most typically, this approach fails because the "isolated island" is rarely able to garner the support and resources needed to move a given innovation forward. Instead, you should design a system that targets driving innovation into the core of the business early and often. It's the best way to avoid "tissue rejection."

Foster Openness and Networks

As we've noted elsewhere in The Guide, Henry Chesbrough recognizes that for an organization to succeed through open innovation—for it to be open externally—it must first be open and aware internally and collaborating across internal organizational boundaries and hierarchy. This is true for the broader discipline of innovation. Innovation works best when individuals, teams, and the entire organization are open to considering new perspectives, ideas, and thinking.

● The Organizing Elements

With the basic design principles top of mind, we can look at the individual organizing elements in Figure 8-1 and discuss how you might consider deploying each to enable innovation.

Innovation Process and Approach

Most organizations have an explicit innovation process in practice or an implicit process through which the work of innovation progresses. There is no one "best" process for innovation, as each organization has unique cultural features that necessarily shape how work gets done. This Guide speaks to building blocks that you can use, and Chapter Ten speaks to alternative designs for various innovation issues and scenarios.

Supporting Tools and Frameworks

Here and throughout The Guide, we share several fit-for-purpose tools and frameworks designed to help you guide dialogue around a specific objective. Tools and supporting training and skill building help you structure, remember, and repeat particular techniques. They help institutionalize a consistent approach.

A caution: too many organizations search for the magical set of tools that they (incorrectly) hope will solve their innovation problem. Don't get caught in that trap. It's not the tools, but rather the work itself and the system that supports the well-executed, end-to-end work of innovation that get results. Tools are just one piece of that equation.

Of course, tools come in all forms: electronic, paper-based, decks of cards, video, and so on. They can even be improvised, "flip-chart-based" tools if you know the materials, techniques, and underlying principles well enough. There are also many software tools available.

As an organization's innovation capability matures, innovators begin tailoring existing tools and creating their own homegrown and customized versions of insight, ideation, and knowledge-capture tools as well. These efforts help weave tools and skills into the fabric of everyday work.

Innovation Skills

Building a critical mass of innovation skills is one of the most important things you can do to create an effective innovation system. To illustrate the point, imagine two different scenarios:

Scenario one: people with innovation skills but no tools or process frameworks
Scenario two: people with innovation tools, but with no skills to use them.

Skills trump tools every time. The good news is that you don't have to trade them off. You can and should use both.

There are, of course, many alternatives for building innovation skills. We find that actions within two broad skill-building categories are most effective:

+ **Skill building through learning interventions.** This includes learning by doing, action learning programs, and conventional training forums.
+ **Skill building through targeted acquisition.** This includes hiring, contracting, open innovation, and alliances and joint ventures.

Learning by Doing

People learn and build skills while making progress on an important innovation issue. Apply a deliberate and structured approach that integrates coaching, facilitation, and mentoring. This approach tends to be superior to pure classroom training or external seminars because it is "the real thing." Many organizations have taken advantage of this technique. Whirlpool Corporation offers an example.

Learning by Doing: Whirlpool Corporation

Whirlpool Corporation has conducted multiple rounds of structured learning-by-doing skill-building efforts over their thirteen-plus years of building and maintaining an innovation system. When senior leadership first initiated efforts to build innovation capability in 1999–2000, innovation teams designed and led regionally focused large-scale efforts that involved scores of people within each region. Leadership supported the efforts through structured, episodic sessions that animated and enabled each of those efforts and shaped an integrated, enterprise-wide agenda. Through these structured work efforts, scores of innovation practitioners became skilled within a year while developing new product concepts that Whirlpool brought to market. Those practitioners then proceeded to drive additional efforts, further extending innovation skills, process, and techniques.[2]

In 2010, Whirlpool sensed that it needed a "booster shot" to revitalize its innovation muscle. Innovation leadership structured and drove a series of projects across each of their regions to turbocharge their innovation pipelines and capabilities, focusing on key product, business model, and service development areas. Over the course of a year, the company rejuvenated and upgraded their innovation skills in each of their regions such that continued use and propagation could occur.[3] Whirlpool's efforts represent leading practice, providing an excellent example of applying the learning-by-doing philosophy to build and maintain innovation muscle.

Action Learning Programs

Action learning techniques also apply learning-by-doing principles through which a team is trained on tools and process. For example, Assurant, a specialty insurance company operating in the United States and select worldwide markets, deploys this technique through their EXCEL*erate* leadership development program. The program helps strengthen and deepen innovation and other key leadership skills of "high potential" managers, thereby boosting capabilities among the future generation of leaders.[4]

The distinction between the action learning approach and the more intense approach Whirlpool Corporation deployed is the extent of engagement and elapsed time required. A typical effective action learning program broadly follows a three-step structure:

1. Design and conduct fit-for-purpose innovation training within the context of a specific, real innovation challenge for which the team must develop a solution that will be commercialized.
2. Apply the training—the approach, techniques, and protocols—to that real innovation challenge over a period of weeks.
3. Return to review and debrief and to learn and apply techniques for the next phase of the work and process.

After three or four rounds, the participants will have completed the whole process, with typically a different level of in-depth learning and experience than that of the "learning by doing" application. The choice between the two options is generally driven by the cost-benefit trade-off scenario that is right for a given organization and situation.

Conventional Training Forums

Although conventional classroom-only training is an option for skill building, we place it last on the list of options. Clearly, classroom training is more beneficial than no structured training, but we find that, by itself, it is the least effective of the alternatives.

If you choose conventional training forums, we urge you to integrate learning-by-doing techniques, such as hands-on exercises, with the frameworks using hypothetical scenarios and process simulations. Although this approach both moves a distance away from the principle of working on real-world challenges and lacks in-the-field learning experiences, it will provide the practitioner with at least a baseline view of the work of innovation.

Skill Acquisition Through Targeted Hiring, Contracting, Open Innovation, and Alliances and Joint Ventures

In many circumstances, you can jump-start your capabilities by bringing in new talent, individuals with deep consumer marketing and human-centered design experience. B2B and B2C companies establishing an internal incubator or an external venture fund will often hire experienced entrepreneurs and, occasionally, those with some experience in venture capital to help them move their efforts forward.

Bringing new talent in to the organization can also enable culture change, and in 2011, the Performance Plastics division of Saint-Gobain did just that. Division president Tom Kinisky had been contemplating ways in which to strengthen innovation. He and his leadership team dedicated significant time to the topic in their leadership meetings and invested resources to develop a long-term strategy to build innovation capabilities to enable organic growth. They developed a shared definition of innovation and a strategy road map to guide the development of their innovation capability; they then looked outside the company for a person to help drive both. Among the hires was Jean Angus, the division's global director of innovation processes. In her first nine months, Jean and her team designed targeted workshops and other interventions through which nearly eight hundred colleagues learned and applied innovation techniques. The efforts resulted in new products, new customer acquisition, and higher employee engagement in their innovation efforts.[5]

Metrics and Measures

Most organizations typically seek to measure innovation efforts with particular and appropriate emphasis on innovation-related revenues. Leaders and practitioners usually seek to understand the current year's anticipated revenue and projections for the following one to three years. This type of focus is appropriate but not sufficient.

We recommend that you expand your thinking beyond an exclusive focus on innovation revenue so as to support a more innovation-friendly system. If you want innovation revenue next year, or the year after, you need activities you can point to *now* that show potential for next year, such as:

+ A measure (or measures) for experiments currently in market or in the pipeline. Of course, not all experiments will lead to new revenue. But over time you will be able to develop ever more accurate estimates for the percentage that do.

+ Qualitative assessments and select quantitative measures for concepts at various stages of development within your pipeline. Some will lead to in-market experiments, and others will move straight to commercial launch.

+ A measure (or measures) of resource and leadership commitment to your overall innovation process and efforts—for example, How many practitioners do you have working on the topic? How much of their time is focused on innovation versus day-to-day work? How many new practitioners are being added to the stable and are available to work on the issue in the future?

The following diagram illustrates how some suggested pipeline metrics can better facilitate results for the organization. It also depicts what we've commonly seen as some reasonable pipeline ratios from one stage of the pipeline to the next.

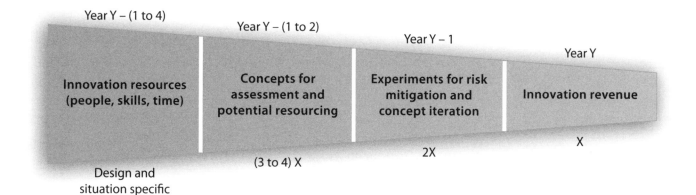

Year Y – (1 to 4)

Year Y – (1 to 2)

Year Y – 1

Year Y

Innovation resources (people, skills, time)

Concepts for assessment and potential resourcing

Experiments for risk mitigation and concept iteration

Innovation revenue

Design and situation specific

(3 to 4) X

2X

X

We find that the initial metrics discussion and the early measuring of innovation activity inevitably lead to internal discussions regarding what "qualifies" as innovation. Here is a practical, short, and simple elaboration of our "an idea successfully commercialized" definition. The idea or concept should

+ Meet an important and unmet need or resolve a significant trade-off or tension
+ Be differentiated from current offerings or solutions
+ Draw strength from capabilities or strategic assets that your organization and, potentially, your partners can bring to bear to help you differentiate and win

+ Provide material impact to your business results

If you can say yes to each of these criteria, you've found an innovation that's attractive to the market and to the organization. Organizations like Whirlpool Corporation, UnitedHealth Group, and Ericsson use variants of this simple, *useable* definition, allowing them to align on a shared definition of innovation against which progress is measured and tracked.

Incentives

An organization's incentive scheme is a delicate element to work with in designing

The old adage that you get what you measure (and pay for) really is true— including with innovation.

and enabling your innovation system. For a variety of reasons, there is often immediate and strong resistance when one raises the topic. We thus always recommend that you initiate any changes to incentive systems only after your innovation ambition is clearly understood, your experience is reasonably deep, and your early results are beginning to validate the organization's initial investment.

Still, if you say you want innovation in the organization and 100 percent of its incentive schemes and rewards are focused elsewhere, you are failing to walk the talk. For those in innovation roles with accountability for a specific innovation outcome, a portion of their incentives should be tied to achieving that outcome. This includes innovators in the businesses, in process and capability support, and in leadership who need to sponsor innovation and drive its results.

As noted above, make incentives one of your later organizing actions to enable innovation, if not your last. Many other elements and actions, such as skills, processes, and goals, must be in place first for incentives to work. Putting incentives in place without a clear point of view on the work to be done, the results you want, or the skills to get there leads to confusion,

frustration, and no results. Get the other critical elements in place first to avoid that kind of train wreck.

In general, we have seen two types of incentives that have helped organizations gain innovation traction. Optimally, you'd like to use a combination of the two.

The Traditional "Performance Management Process" (PMP) Incentive

Often a PMP system will lay out the metrics by which the individual's performance will be measured for the year and detail the percentages of incentive pay available for an award, based on a manager's assessment. It is helpful to your innovation efforts if the incentive system includes an explicit allocation to innovation results, thereby putting teeth into the assertion that innovation is important.

The adage that you get what you measure (and pay for) really is true. We've seen several PMPs that apportion 67 percent of incentive pay to the contribution to achieving financial targets and goals, and 33 percent toward organization building and development, including personal development. Depending on the context, a revision of that formula could apportion 20 percent of incentive pay to innovation results, 60 percent to current-year financials and targets, and 20 percent to organization development. We have also typically seen innovation-focused percentages range from 10 percent for a basic innovation role, and up to 30 percent for a general manager or supporting role to innovation work. We share these ranges as examples; obviously you need to design and deploy a system best matched to your purpose.

Formal Role-Based Designations

Beyond pay-based incentives, you can also leverage the incentive of granting formal innovation or business development responsibilities to those who aspire to them. Rather than being based on a quantitative measure, the incentive is based on the currency of increased organizational esteem. It offers opportunities to innovate as an entrepreneur inside the organization.

This role is highly valued by those with a strong desire to focus on innovation and the development of new business concepts. The attractiveness of the role itself offers a "soft" incentive relative to the "hard" incentive of pay for performance.

Supporting and Enabling Processes

Examples of supporting and enabling processes that surround the work of innovation include

- The annual process that results in the next operating plan and the three- or five-year strategic plan
- The capital budgeting and other resource allocation processes that feed into the annual plans
- Leadership development processes
- Corporate development processes, particularly regarding alliances, joint ventures, technology sourcing, and acquisitions

None of these processes directly addresses "what's next" in terms of new products or services or new routes to market. However, each significantly influences what the organization does and does not do, because each is an internal mechanism through which resources are allocated.

Innovation, like any other significant initiative, places demands on resources on an annual or more frequent basis. Therefore, sustainable innovation systems or processes must be wired into these surrounding processes. Without such enabling action, you will quickly find yourself and your innovation team isolated from the daily rhythms of the organization and its core management processes. You will be on the outside looking in, which, regrettably, is where many innovation efforts sit before they die a premature death.

Experience suggests that if you consider the following questions in the context of your organization and its innovation ambition, you will identify appropriate actions relevant to your situation:

> *Every organization struggles with funding for innovation. It's very tough competing with the "certainty" of the budget needs for the day-to-day business.*

- What are the annual budget and people-resourcing processes and mechanisms within the organization overall? How, specifically, do innovation requests that do not fit the current business or business model integrate into or feed into that system? How might a given innovation resource request compete with other demands on capital, expense, and human resources on a regular basis?

- In what ways might innovation become a part of the annual (or more frequent) strategy *discussions*? How might you make it as prominent as other operational or day-to-day topics?

- Given your innovation focus and ambition, is the way you hook into existing processes appropriate to the opportunities you are generating and considering? What are the alternative ways through which you may achieve better outcomes and desired effects within the organization? For example, are there separate seed funds and a separate conversation that "protect" innovation opportunities and efforts while they are still in their infancy?

- How do current incentives, left unchanged, enable innovation? In what ways might they impede it?

Funding Mechanisms

Every organization struggles with funding for innovation. Remember, organizations are built to do exactly what they are already doing. Therefore, the organization typically has a smoothly running process through which budgets and resources are set for its current core business. Budgeting or setting aside resources for "the road not yet traveled" is not at all easy. Resources are always scarce to start with. When budget-trimming time comes, innovation funding is often an early candidate for cutting. It's very tough competing with the "certainty" of the budget needs for the day-to-day business.

If you are disciplined in your approach, there are ways to secure and protect your innovation funding. We describe some of the most effective mechanisms in the next sections. Of those mechanisms, we favor seed funds for their flexibility and effectiveness, if they are managed with professionalism and resolve. If the organization has evolved to a level of innovation capability where the innovation pipeline is substantial and requiring a more significant percentage of capital and expense, a "capital set-aside" model may also serve you well.

Seed Funds

Seed funds can provide a flexible source of early-stage innovation funding. They typically are budgeted in advance for the entire fiscal year. As a result, funding is available at any time, providing great flexibility in terms of the timing of allocations to a given innovation effort as the need arises. The downside is that seed funds are often treated as something optional, and thus are often the first to be cut come budget-trimming time.

The bottom line with seed funds is that, because of their flexibility, they can be quite effective mechanisms. But if they are not managed with good care and with the same level of rigor and explicit business logic as the day-to-day budgets, they risk being viewed as an illegitimate "fun fund" and will quickly be canceled or withdrawn.

In our experience, the most important action you can take to ensure success in using seed funds is simply to maintain and protect them. If you are able to do so, you should also consider these questions to enable success:

Where should a seed fund reside?
The location of the seed fund depends on the rest of the system you've set up. Broadly speaking, there are two options. Organizations either control and allocate innovation-focused funds from the center, or they do so on a "distributed" basis—out in the business units in some form.

Central control tends to provide a more consistent application of funding criteria and allocation decisions. A distributed approach tends to create better alignment and support for the business units' growth and innovation goals. The decision as to which way to go ought to rest on what the rest of the system looks like and on which approach will most benefit your specific needs and circumstances.

Who should decide how to allocate seed fund monies?

The answer depends in part on your architectural decision regarding central or distributed seed funds. With either choice, it is best if top leadership of the corporate or distributed unit make the allocation decisions, because doing so engages and commits those leaders productively in the work of innovation.

How much should we set aside?

This is a frequently asked question for which many organizations crave a standard answer or metric. Of course it is never that simple in practice. Your response and approach depend on your overall innovation objectives and the way in which a seed fund may help you achieve those objectives.

For example, through your seed fund, do you wish to help support

+ Ideation efforts only? Other aspects of the generalized innovation process, such as experimentation, some level of product development, or early-stage scaling, or combinations thereof? Both?
+ Growth objectives with a specific target? If so, how much you require depends on that target: Are you replacing 10 percent of your existing base? 30 percent? To do so, do you believe that you will need one new opportunity per year in market? Five? Fifty?

Adopting a future-back point-of-view on what *your* business needs, based on the system you've put in place, is a better way to set the budget than to use an external benchmark or study.

A Capital and Expense Set-Aside for Innovation

Some organizations use a "set-aside" in an effort to make innovation more mainstream and to have it be taken seriously more quickly. The advantage to a set-aside is that it focuses mainstream innovation quickly and aggressively by immediately integrating it into the annual budgeting conversation, placing it on par with any other operating budget line item.

The organization cordons off a certain percentage of all capital or capital and expense dollars within its budget, reserving its use only for those work efforts and line items that qualify as innovation as defined earlier in this chapter. Calls on capital or expense can come at any time throughout the budget year—whenever an idea or project emerges and seeks funding. If the organization doesn't use all of the funds, the monies are returned to the bottom line at the end of the year.

The organization may choose to raise the capital or expense (or both) percentages as it improves its innovation capabilities year over year. When Whirlpool Corporation initiated its innovation efforts, it set aside a percentage of all capital for innovation projects and efforts, then looked to raise the percentage over time as the organization built ever stronger innovation muscle.[6]

The advantage of a set-aside is that it helps shift innovation to the organization's mainstream. The disadvantage is that it risks an imbalance between innovation supply and demand and may encourage some to "game the system." Think of it this way:

The amount of the set-aside represents "innovation demand."
The organization's ability to develop budget-worthy innovations represents "innovation supply."

If demand exceeds supply, the size of the innovation set-aside fund will decrease and potentially disappear over time. As organizations begin their concerted innovation efforts, supply rarely outpaces the demand represented by the total set-aside funding. As a result, if there is not a sufficient supply of novel, compelling innovation concepts, some people may reclassify their incremental efforts as being "innovation" or even "breakthrough" in order to capture budget and resources.

Thus your organization might be best served by setting up a flexible but well-managed seed fund to start, then transitioning to a capital/expense set-aside model once you have built the innovation muscle (that is, a sufficient opportunity generation capability) to justify and feed it.

Budgeting Annually for Innovation, a Priori

With this approach, success depends on the ability of the organization to identify its specific innovation needs and budget at the time when annual budgets are set. In practice, this implies forecasting twelve or more months in advance. Unless your organization's innovation efforts are well established, this may be difficult to do.

In general, we've not seen this to be an effective funding method for innovation. Compared to seed funds, this approach is

If you seek to treat innovation as more than a onetime project, you need to make it a part of the organization's dialogue, both internally and externally.

less flexible because you cannot perfectly forecast the specifics of the totality of your innovation needs so far in advance. Annual budgeting thus presents challenges:

+ Innovation tends to require more time and budget flexibility than this approach typically offers. You don't always know when the new idea or project will surface or when it will need to be taken to the next level. By its nature, innovation benefits from time and resource flexibility: it is an iterative learning process; success often requires in-market experimentation that does not always adhere to a corporate calendar.

+ Competing for the exact same dollars within the exact same process tends to put innovation efforts at a disadvantage relative to day-to-day business projects, which, on average, are more certain in their returns and outcomes. As a result, innovation tends to get squeezed down to a level that is not material to the organization.

"Take It on Faith" Budgeting for Innovation

Even less effective than annual budgeting is a "take it on faith" approach by which monies are not explicitly budgeted in any way. Many organizations do this, assuming that when a compelling innovation idea emerges, the project will get funded.

This is usually a bad assumption—not because the players are not acting in good faith (they typically are). Rather, once another portfolio of priorities is agreed on and work begins, one or more initiatives within the portfolio must be killed or delayed for an innovation initiative to be funded. That is a difficult circumstance. People get invested. Efforts gain momentum. Of all the funding structures and techniques discussed here, this is the least preferable.

Organizational Communications

You know that people care about what's being discussed casually and communicated formally by the organization. They especially care about what senior leadership communicates as they speak to enterprise priorities, values, and focus. If you seek to treat innovation as more than a onetime project, you need to make it a part of the organization's dialogue, both internally and externally.

We find that organizations that successfully maintain innovation as a top priority follow the practices listed next.

- Integrate innovation efforts into existing communication channels. If you're already using newsletters, company TV, quarterly town halls, weekly e-updates, intranet postings, or all of these, integrate your innovation updates and conversations into them. If you want to mainstream innovation, use your organization's mainstream communications channels.
- Feature senior leaders in your communication efforts, engaging them in creating and sharing the news. Your colleagues care about what their leaders care about. Get them actively and authentically involved in the conversation. Of course, doing so first requires involving them substantially in the work of innovation. (We discuss this further in Chapter Nine.)
- Establish successes internally before communicating externally. Avoid making promises in advance. For some organizations, announcing ahead of the launch is common practice. This can work for the normal course of business product launches or business activities about which you're fairly certain of timing and results. However, the newer to the world the opportunity or concept is, the less that will be the case. Should you tout your innovation successes? Absolutely

yes. Just make sure you have them before you tout them.

With these practices in mind, communicate through a broad number of vehicles internally, highlighting market successes and the personal stories of colleagues who make them happen. Your regular dialogue is one way to maintain innovation as a priority. Without such actions, your innovation efforts will become a peripheral activity and, even worse, will risk organizational extinction.

Leadership Engagement and Decision Making

Innovation efforts cannot succeed without leadership engagement. We speak at length to this topic in Chapter Nine, but to summarize some of the key points of this important topic, we outline here three specific ways to enable leadership engagement:

- Engage leaders in cocreation.
- Engage leaders as sponsors and decision makers and give them the job of removing roadblocks.
- Prominently feature leadership roles in innovation, thereby highlighting innovation's importance through their visible participation and support.

Remember, innovation equals new learning, for both practitioners and leaders.

Engage Leaders in Cocreation

Structure regular forums and mechanisms within each of your major innovation initiatives. For example, you could involve leaders firsthand in a targeted way in idea generation, opportunity elaboration, or domain-shaping sessions. Ensure that leaders participate in focused ways, shaping the outcomes and experiencing the same new learning as the week-to-week team.

In practice, this approach goes beyond the traditional one of confining leadership involvement to voting yes or no on your efforts. Instead, engage leaders through working sessions in which they participate actively, shaping the opportunities and future innovations. Think of these sessions as a dialogue to advance your efforts while strengthening leadership's understanding of and commitment to the effort.

This approach will engage leaders in cooking in the innovation kitchen, so to speak. They will thus develop a rich understanding of the effort, and you will benefit from their extensive experience, including their past successes and failures. As important, the resulting opportunities and pipeline will be more robust and sticky within the organization, because of the thought involved and the buy-in that you developed from start to finish. Remember, innovation equals new learning, for both practitioners and leaders.

Engage Leaders as Sponsors of Your Efforts

As sponsors, leaders can help you navigate the organization, ensuring that you create preconditions for success, such as by accessing the right talent internally and guiding access externally to customers and external experts.

In one B2B organization, a member of the CEO's team acting as sponsor ensured that the team's initial program charter was structured so that it would be clearly understood and supported by the senior team. During the months-long effort, the sponsor also guided "informal" access to his senior colleagues so that the team could share interim insights and emerging opportunities and direction. The sessions were invaluable to the team, providing important perspective and ensuring that key decision makers understood the foundational learning on which the new concepts were based.

Sponsors also should assume governance and decision-making roles. The structure through which to direct governance is specific to each organization, of course. If innovation efforts are relatively new to your current leadership, it may be appropriate to form an explicit leadership forum such as an Innovation Council or an Innovation Leadership Team to sponsor, guide, and champion innovation.

As innovation integrates into the natural rhythm of the organization's operations, governance typically migrates to existing leadership groups, such as your operating committee, regional leadership team, or business unit leadership team. If innovation efforts are shifted into the mainstream, leaders must be vigilant to ensure that they are not shifted into the background by day-to-day operational decisions and budgeting choices.

Feature Leaders Prominently to Demonstrate the Importance They Place on Innovation

Through the cocreation and sponsorship and governance roles we have described, leaders signal the importance of innovation to the organization. Beyond these roles, there is more that leaders can do to demonstrate innovation's importance even more broadly. For example, UnitedHealth Group's senior team is featured prominently at the company's annual Innovation Day that begins with a private breakfast with select innovators. Beyond this one day, you will often see the CEO and members of his team in the company's innovation center and, occasionally, in the field with an innovation team. They are recognized as prominent internal advocates for innovation: they walk the talk.[7]

Structure

Structure is one of the last organizing elements you should address—if you address it at all. In some cases, organizations do not make or need to make structural changes. Instead they look to build and install robust process, skills, and tools that integrate with existing processes; make sure that measures and incentives are put in place and aligned; and involve existing leadership teams in a productive manner.

In some cases, innovation requires structural revisions around the edges of the organization—for example, the building of a small central or distributed innovation center of excellence (CoE) to assist the rest of the organization and proactively spread tools and skills. But organizations always do well to learn how to do the work first rather than reorganize for innovation without having built that kind of know-how.

Structural Mechanisms

As organizations build and strengthen innovation capabilities, some of the structural mechanisms they may put in place include

Innovation CoE. This comprises a centralized or distributed set of personnel who serve as the organization's innovation experts, or "black belts." The black belts might help fill the pipeline, extend and strengthen innovation capabilities, and/or help extend innovation's reach and impact across the organization.

CoE members, who are typically a mix of full- and part-time employees, should be experienced and knowledgeable in the work of innovation within the context of your organization's innovation ambition, culture, and organization. We find that including some dedicated personnel helps keep innovation capability strong and on the radar. Staffing a CoE with only part-timers increases the risk that the innovation muscle will atrophy quickly.

Targeted reorganization focused on innovation results. For example, once an organization decides to pursue a platform or opportunity, it may create an explicit organization with skilled and dedicated personnel to pursue implementation and commercialization of the innovation agenda it has set for itself.

This type of structural adjustment puts strong emphasis on commercialization to realize market results. It does not, however, necessarily address the issue of further skill building and development of new ideas. We recommend that organizations take both of those needs into consideration as they set up any of their structural or other organizing elements.

Innovation incubator. An incubator is an organizational carve-out designed to concentrate resources and focus in a small group in order to lead and execute innovation activities. Typically the incubator transfers a given initiative to the appropriate business unit or function for further commercialization activity. In some cases, incubators even take on early commercialization activity, and in the extreme, the incubator or a portion of it turns into its own business unit and scales the opportunity.

Which Structural Mechanism(s) to Use?

CoEs and/or targeted reorganizations are well suited to address commercialization, particularly if you assess your organization's capabilities as very strong in generating ideas but poor at execution and commercialization. In practice, this is because both CoEs and targeted reorganization tend to engage the mainstream organization very early on.

Incubators are best suited to circumstances in which your innovation efforts are focused fairly far afield from the core or mainstream businesses. Incubators can nurture and develop opportunities that are so different from the core business that they don't need to be integrated, either early on or possibly ever.

Typically, there are two exit paths for concepts and businesses successfully nurtured in an incubator: a spinoff of the business as a stand-alone entity, or a transfer from the incubator into an existing business within your organization. In either instance, while in the incubator, the concept requires human and financial capital to progress. Therefore, the incubator must be structured a priori to include resource allocation processes and governance. In particular, if the concept is intended to exit to an existing business, success requires careful planning and business unit engagement months or more in advance to eliminate risk of tissue rejection by the receiving unit.

Case Examples: Organizing for Innovation

Let's look at some examples of the systemic application of these elements, highlighting why they represent good fit-for-purpose solutions for the particular organization.

Royal Dutch Shell's GameChanger

Since 1996, Royal Dutch Shell's GameChanger (GC) process[8] has enabled breakthrough innovations such as the following:

- Floating LNG: a novel system for liquefying natural gas for export directly aboard an on-location offshore vessel, thus mitigating costs and impact of subsea pipelines and large onshore facilities
- Swellable elastomers: a new scheme for using elastomers that swell when wet to automatically shut off water inflow into oil wells

Serving as an incubator of sorts, GC is a "simple, flexible and real time innovation process run by an autonomous team." It attracts and screens disruptive ideas and technologies from individuals across and outside Shell. As its leader, Russ Conser, frames it, GC "functions as an angel investor." Its purpose is to provide a conduit for internal or external entrepreneurs to get their idea a hearing and some level of funding and development so as to try to get it to proof-of-concept. Ideas come from colleagues across the organizational hierarchy—quite literally: from anyone, anywhere, at any time, including from outside the organization.

GameChanger resides within the R&D organization. It has about a dozen team members dispersed globally, an internal "GameChanger alumni network," and an annual seed fund budget of roughly 2 percent of all R&D spent—a significant but lean amount. GC leadership believes that doing a lot with a little is key to helping others appreciate the value of breakthrough innovation.

In order for an idea to secure development resources, a proposed idea submitted to GC must be disruptive (that is, game changing) and have the potential for material impact—a high bar, given the size and invested interests of the company. The process is actively managed, with the promise that anyone submitting an idea will receive a response in a week or less. Once an idea is approved and enters the GC process, a supporting GC team member ("sponsor") works with the individual contributor, providing process, tools, coaching, and funding to help the contributor develop the business logic and proof-of-concept for his or her idea.

The GC support comes "free" to the idea "proponent." In return, the original idea proponent commits to work with the GC team on the idea while still maintaining and delivering on the commitments of his or her current job at Shell. This arrangement creates a mutually attractive risk management bridge that can evolve over time as evidence informs changes—more time can be spent in response to positive data.

In some cases, the starting point for an idea may reflect great insight regarding a customer need but may be deficient on an enabling proprietary technology. Or the reverse could be true: strong technology but a poorly articulated CVP.

The time required to move a given idea forward can be anywhere from weeks to more than a year, depending on the nature of the opportunity. The criterion for allowing the opportunity to exit GC and enter into a process of business unit (BU) adoption is that proof-of-concept has been attained in the eyes of GC and a given BU, which commits to take the concept forward through to commercialization.

Of course, there are often bumps in the road, including disagreements as to whether a concept meets the specific criteria of a given gate. Russ and his team monitor the status of all active concepts within the GC portfolio, with particular attention to time within each gate of the GC process. Concepts that lag in a particular gate sometimes receive additional resources to kick-start progress. Beyond attending to a specific opportunity, regular monitoring of the portfolio offers "root cause" assessments of what works and what challenges persist. For example, recently the GC team has been finding that developing channel acceptance—routes to market— is a persistent difficulty for many concepts.

You can think of GC as a "quasi-incubator," as GC's role does not extend to commercialization. These activities are picked up within a Shell BU or outside of Shell in a joint venture or alliance. The GC performs well on the front-end development work, excelling at both concept development and proof-of-concept work. As an incubator, however, GC struggles with some of the symptoms and trade-offs of any incubator system. For example, a GC team and a BU may have differing views in regard to a given concept's commercial readiness.

The GC process and structure is one of the longest running within Shell today. Initially, it began as a decentralized unit within many of the businesses. Since 2010, it has been led and managed globally as a single team. During its lifetime, GC has worked on over three thousand ideas and successfully graduated more than two hundred into ongoing programs for Shell. Like any high-performing system, it is enabled through systemic design of specific organizing elements that complement and reinforce each other, as summarized here:

Systemic Organizing Elements Enabling Shell GameChanger

Element	Description
Process	• Clearly articulated and managed protocols to submit, assess, and carry ideas forward from concept to BU acceptance • Informal but well-accepted paths to engage business units that may be interested in commercializing a given opportunity
Skills	• GC training "on the job," augmented by a "veteran" GameChanger, and an ad hoc set of tools and approaches
Metrics	• Clear definition regarding the type of ideas well suited to GC process • Track elapsed time in process by stage; results used to identify specific concepts that may need additional attention—or shelving
Structure	• A global, focused, and networked team of GC professionals. Some make it a long-term commitment; others move on to other opportunities after shorter tenure • GC "alumni" are used selectively to support a given concept; they also act as a proactive, informal conduit to internal entrepreneurs by encouraging them to submit ideas to GC

Whirlpool Corporation's Thirteen-Year Innovation Embedment Journey

Nancy Tennant and Moises Norena document Whirlpool Corporation's innovation capability-building and embedment journey extensively,[9] and we will not repeat it here. However, we will highlight a few points that illustrate how Whirlpool has effectively used multiple organizing elements in different ways at different times over the course of this journey.

In 2000–2001, Whirlpool built innovation CoEs to support efforts and build and strengthen capability within each of its major regions worldwide: North America, Europe, Latin America, and Asia. Each CoE housed a group of six to twelve practitioners experienced in Whirlpool's Double Diamond innovation process. They were trained and armed with tools and process skills. The practitioners worked with each of Whirlpool's brands, helping them fill their innovation pipeline ("I-Pipe"), which they tracked and managed proactively at both the brand level and at the regional level through a Regional Innovation Council. The Innovation Councils comprised regional leaders with accountability for setting and resourcing priorities overall, including innovation. The councils met monthly, reviewing the innovation pipeline gaps and working on issues of innovation capability or results. Councils worked collaboratively with the relevant BUs and the CoE members involved in a given project or issue.

Over time, Whirlpool migrated innovation to the mainstream by eliminating the regionally organized CoEs and disbursing their innovation experts into the BUs. The goal was to align work more integrally within the BUs and further build innovation efforts into ever-expanding product and concept development work. Innovation Council work was explicitly transitioned to each region's Operating Committee, making innovation an explicit part of the Operating Committee's agenda. These transitions offered the advantage of integration with the business. They also brought a risk that innovation efforts could be overwhelmed by the urgent and comfortably known day-to-day operations.

A few years later, Whirlpool realized that it needed to do a bit of "back to the future" work to maintain the proper level of attention to innovation and to maintain its innovation muscle. It reconstituted small, regionally focused innovation groups (two- to four-member CoEs) led by a regional innovation director and coordinated globally by the global director of innovation, Moises Norena. The innovation leadership decisions and issues remained embedded in the original BU or functional leadership structures.[10]

In 2010, Whirlpool embarked on its most recent phase of innovation capability building. Given a need to turbocharge skill sets, regional innovation pipelines, and even some of the organization's enthusiasm for the topic, Whirlpool launched a next wave of capability-building and pipeline enhancement projects: targeted projects on specific topics using an enhanced and expanded tool set and the internal and external CoE skill sets. In effect, it is a custom-built program to rejuvenate the innovation capability and culture at Whirlpool.

Whirlpool is a very good example of the long-term journey that is true capability building and maintenance for innovation. In that sense, the ability to innovate is no different than any other key competence of the organization. It demands hard work and long-term attention.

This table summarizes Whirlpool's systemic approach to enabling innovation:

Systemic Organizing Elements Enabling Whirlpool Corporation

Element	Description
Process	• A fit-for-purpose process from front end to commercialization • Explicit test-learn-iterate experimentation process
Skills	• Measured, assessed, and characterized by level of mastery
Metrics	• Portfolios tracked by region, including risk-adjusted estimated innovation revenues and number of concepts within each stage, including experimentation
Leadership	• Innovation results and ongoing activity are part of regular reviews, regionally and at the enterprise level • Innovation focus, status, and results discussed annually at senior-level meetings, company-wide
Structure	• A small, central corporate innovation unit with additional resources embedded in the businesses within each major geographic market • Formally defined rolls: regional innovation directors, innovation mentors
Incentives	• Leadership discretionary compensation includes a component tied to innovation performance • Dedicated innovation roles are also compensated based on innovation performance

Crayola and Growth Platforms

Crayola organizes for innovation differently from Shell, Whirlpool Corporation, and many others, by featuring priority domains as a central organizing focus. Within Crayola, a domain is referred to as a "growth platform."

Crayola's growth platforms include detailed migration paths depicting the sequence of opportunities and enabling actions. As the company realized significant success—boosting "top-line growth rates by approximately 50 percent"—they began considering how to sustain and enable their success through specific organizing actions.

After productive internal debate and dialogue, the company elected to organize substantial portions of its marketing department around the growth platforms deemed critical to their future growth. P&L leaders and teams were assigned full-time to each assigned revenue and profit target and tasked with working through a disciplined approach to platform migration.

Systemic Organizing Elements Enabling Crayola

Element	Description
Process	• Explicit front-end of innovation techniques incorporated into Crayola's NPD process and delivery system
Skills	• Platform leaders trained on migration path development and management • Director of innovation as a support structure for innovation skill set and maintenance of growth platform strategy
Metrics	• Portfolios tracked by growth platform
Leadership	• Regular platform and portfolio discussions, with adjustments as appropriate
Structure	• Organize by growth platforms (domains), each with its own financial accountabilities and objectives • Feature integrated business teams within each platform • Director of innovation to enable learning across the organization and to act as innovation process steward and guide

The P&L leaders approached the task holistically, working with an integrated team from finance, operations, and other elements of the delivery supply chain. Crayola's director of innovation acted as a one-person CoE, assisting platform teams in mapping their opportunities, refreshing and elaborating them when appropriate, and advancing the next nascent concept on a given platform into an executable business case, all the while ensuring that its innovative essence remained.

The unique value-creating feature of the system was organizing by platforms, including, making changes to P&L management structure so that it was directly aligned to the platforms brought to market. That change was significant and sent a forceful and unambiguous message to the organization that management was firmly resolved and committed to the success of each platform.[11]

UnitedHealth Group and CoEs

UnitedHealth Group (UHG) deploys enterprise and BU CoEs to enable innovation. BU CoEs are governed by their respective business leadership teams. The enterprise CoE, led by Brandon Rowberry, Meredith Baratz, and Ryan Ambruster, is governed by an Innovation Council comprising senior leaders from each of the businesses and the CoE leadership team.

The Medicare business CoE is led by Jeff Shoemate, and Vidya Raman leads the employer and individual business CoE. Like the enterprise CoE, each business CoE is staffed by a cross-functional innovation team made up of four to twelve individuals. Jeff and Vidya are accountable for developing sustaining and breakthrough opportunities that fit with their respective businesses.

At the enterprise level, Brandon, Meredith, and Ryan are accountable for developing and testing new breakthrough business domains and associated concepts and testing them in market. The Innovation Council directs and governs efforts, including funding decisions from its seed fund.

The enterprise CoE also serves as an audience for concepts that do not naturally fall within one of the businesses. This CoE also cares for the UHG innovation challenge process and enterprise-wide innovation events, including the annual Innovation Day. Finally, the enterprise CoE acts as a steward for innovation, ensuring consistent tools and approaches, training, and broader skill building.

Each CoE is armed with innovation processes and frameworks to support innovation initiatives. Its roles include

- Identifying areas that merit exploration and investigation as potential growth spaces
- Developing business and venture proposals through a front-end process that leads to a specific business plan and resourcing request
- Designing and leading in-market test-learn-iterate experimentation
- Establishing internal and, more recently, external innovation networks as one means by which to enable a culture of innovation
- Designing and leading structured innovation challenges at the BU or corporate level
- Ensuring appropriate governance

The multifaceted charter of each of these CoEs is unique. More commonly, a CoE charter is more limited and focused on a "process only" support role. The BU and enterprise CoEs operate as separate equals, each with a different focus on innovation. The UHG approach works well and is enabled by a strong commitment by UHG senior leadership to systemic innovation and by a strong, experienced, and diverse innovation leadership team.[12]

Systemic Organizing Elements Enabling UnitedHealth Group

Element	Description
Process	• A front-end innovation process that leads to domain-specific business plans and in-market experimentation • Idea management process that focuses on specific innovation challenges
Skills	• Internal training delivered on each innovation project • Innovation frameworks, approaches, and techniques shared across the company with enterprise unit acting as steward
Structure	• Enterprise and BU innovation councils • Annual Innovation Day, featuring success and learning and the "finalists" of an innovation competition

Key Take-Aways

- Enable innovation as a discipline by making changes to the organization over time. Because organizations are built to do exactly what they are already doing, innovation, by definition, requires thinking and acting differently. Doing so sustainably requires changes in how you organize. Changing your organization's culture requires you to change the way work gets done within it.

- Feature innovation design principles as you consider and initiate organizational changes to enable your innovation ambition. Use them as a guide to ensure that you are approaching the challenge effectively while working with the grain of the organization.

- Understand that effective organizational change requires more than simple changes to structure. Think systemically and holistically in initiating changes. Deploy a set of complementary, reinforcing actions to achieve the best results.

- Active leadership involvement from start to finish is critical to success. Feature leaders in cocreation roles. Engage leaders as sponsors and decision makers and give them the job of removing roadblocks.

- Beyond the examples in this Guide and in other innovation books, there are likely to be organizations you know of that are pursuing innovation, and you should learn from them as well.

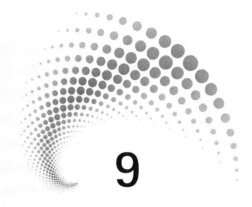

Leading Innovation

9

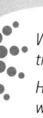

What is the role of leadership in driving, guiding, and catalyzing the work of innovation for the organization?

How do I build an effective leadership agenda for the organization when it comes to leaders' roles and achieving our innovation goals?

How do we develop a shared and aligned view among leadership regarding our innovation "what" and "how"?

How can I (or others) lead on innovation even if I am not in a senior leadership position?

I want to help the organization drive innovation, but conditions are less than "perfect." What can I do?

All of the innovation techniques, processes, metrics, and other organizing elements, perfectly designed, will not enable sustainable innovation if leadership does not understand it, line up behind it, and drive it. If your organization is serious about achieving breakthrough innovation outcomes, leaders will need to play a significant role in getting to action: action on driving the work and on driving results through to meaningful commercial value in market.

Leading innovation successfully takes one of two broad forms. The first (and preferable) is to integrate into your efforts an explicit focus on ensuring a proper role for leadership.

This is not the stereotypical leadership role of "thumbs-up/thumbs-down" votes on recommendations served up on PowerPoint slides in the executive conference room. Rather, leadership's role in innovation is played out through focused, hands-on involvement from start to finish, ensuring a shared and aligned understanding of and commitment to the work of innovation, its objectives, and your approach.

You can think of the second form of leadership as more of a grassroots movement. It requires leadership of a different sort—one that does not carry the positional authority of leaders with budgets, resources, and the ability to make decisions that focus the organization's efforts on innovation.

The grassroots movement works best either when innovation is not high on top leadership's agenda or when there is a gap between the innovation rhetoric and the on-the-ground reality.[1] In these situations, there are productive actions you can take. Some are incremental in nature. But if your actions are focused well, you can benefit cumulatively through a series of well-structured and well-led efforts that over time will make an impact on the organization. It may just be possible that your efforts will advance innovation toward a real enterprise priority over time.

Leading Innovation from the Top

We start with the role of top leadership. As we discussed in Chapter Eight, a leader's role in innovation is to act as

Cocreator. Leadership gets involved in the design of the work and creating and shaping its content. Because innovation produces outcomes that are, by definition, new to the organization, it is difficult if not impossible to play an effective sponsorship and decision-making role in innovation without participating as a cocreator.

Sponsor and decision maker. Leaders initiate the work of innovation and the drive to results. They clearly understand the outcomes of the work. Leaders remove roadblocks and barriers (there will be many!) and help with understanding and breaking down orthodoxies—those mental barriers and impediments in the form of conventional wisdom and things people take as "givens."

A visible advocate for innovation. Beyond a specific innovation project, leaders participate in many other venues, which might include national and regional sales meetings, forums with lead customers and suppliers, and internal communication events. Even a few minutes of a leader's participation in these kinds of forums, in a context relevant to the event, are quite helpful in reminding the organization that innovation remains a top priority.

Develop a Shared, Aligned View

The best way to ensure that leaders perform their innovation roles effectively is to work with them to develop a shared and aligned view on the outcomes you wish to achieve and the optimal approach to bringing about those outcomes. Creating a shared view takes time; it can't be accomplished in a single meeting. Rather, it requires iterative dialogue with the leadership team. As you agree on specific outcomes and an approach, the continuing dialogue will deepen their shared understanding and align their views more closely.

Creating a shared, aligned understanding is critically important for three components:

+ A definition of innovation that is appropriate to your organization
+ The specific outcomes you seek from your innovation efforts
+ The approach through which you will deliver the outcomes

A Definition of Innovation That Is Appropriate to Your Organization

In addition to defining innovation as "an idea successfully commercialized," you should

The role of top leadership includes cocreator, sponsor and decision maker, and visible advocate.

also apply an elaborated definition that helps clarify the work of innovation. As a starting point, you may want to consider the criteria we listed in Chapter Eight:

- Meets an important and unmet need or resolves a significant trade-off or tension
- Is differentiated from today's offerings or solutions
- Draws strength from capabilities or strategic assets that your organization and, potentially, your partners can bring to bear to help you differentiate and win
- Provides material impact to your business results

> Leadership having a shared definition of innovation is central to your success. Without it, efforts quickly derail.

The idea is to establish a few simple criteria that generally describe what "qualifies" as innovation for your organization. In other words, every leader would agree (using the criteria) that a given opportunity does or does not fit with the innovation intent of the organization.

With this shared view, leaders are better positioned to assess the extent to which the organization's innovation efforts are on track or falling short. Metrics will reflect your progress more precisely because you will be measuring the work in terms of the criteria. The criteria also help any given innovation team because they focus the team on the outcome they should target. It helps them shape the opportunity to align with the organization's innovation intent and ambition.

We are repetitive on the definition of innovation because it is so central to your innovation success. We continually encounter many organizations that do not have a shared view of what qualifies as innovation, yet still feature innovation as a top priority for which they invest significantly. They focus on building an innovation pipeline, strengthening skills, and focusing leadership on their efforts without, in practice, having a shared and aligned view about what qualifies as innovation for them. In these instances, innovation is at best slowed considerably; at worst, it is derailed permanently.

The Specific Outcomes You Seek from Your Innovation Efforts

Obviously leaderships' public declarations of innovation's central importance—offered in annual reports, at shareholders' meetings, or in other public forums—rarely speak in any detail to the specific outcomes targeted. But what about your internal discussions?

Do they speak specifically to the distinct innovation outcomes sought? Too often, they do not. It is leadership's role to build shared understanding and alignment to the *specific* outcomes you seek. Do this, and every member of every innovation team in your organization will thank you!

What *specific* outcome (or outcomes) do you seek from innovation? A set of product or service concepts within the core business? adjacent to the core? outside of it? Or perhaps you seek not a single product but to keep your pipeline filled through the use of domains? Or do you want to focus on postlaunch, in-market innovation? Is it organizational capability? If so, what constitutes capability for your organization? Process and tools? Skills? An overall innovation system or architecture?

Or perhaps you seek combinations of the above—or all of the above?

The Approach Through Which You Will Deliver the Outcomes

Any successful project requires thoughtful structure and work planning. Innovation, of course is no different. The leadership team should build a shared understanding of and alignment with the logic and approach of the work, creating confidence that the approach will deliver on the specific outcomes you seek.

By logic, we mean the underlying rationale behind why the work is structured in the way that it is: the rationale regarding your program's scope, leadership's role and involvement, and the timeline and resources required. You must think through your approach in sufficient detail that you have a point of view on the selected design as compared to any other design you might have chosen. If leadership is not lined up behind the approach, you will have a hard time getting to the end game. Leaders will be less likely to do their part to support your ongoing innovation efforts or to remove internal roadblocks that may impede your ability to achieve your targeted outcomes. To put it bluntly, if leaders are halfhearted about the work or its importance, good luck hitting the finish line with outcomes and buy-in.

● ● ●

The best way to ensure that leadership performs their three roles of cocreator, sponsor, and visible advocate is to ensure their shared and aligned understanding of the work of innovation, its outcomes, and your approach. You will succeed in this alignment effort through iterative leadership dialogue—through a leadership engagement agenda pertaining to the organization's innovation work. Leaders are not on point to do the work or to be involved day to day or even week to week. Rather, they will enable your success by guiding and animating the work in their three roles. And the good news for you is that through these roles, leaders will pivot far from their stereotypical "review and approve or kill" mode of work.

Driving Leadership Engagement in Innovation

How do you drive an effective leadership engagement program for innovation efforts? Three core principles should guide you in structuring leadership's actions and roles in efforts that are biased toward more transformative types of innovation efforts:

+ Focused, immersive engagement
+ A shared view through dialogue
+ The rule of thirds

Focused, Immersive Engagement

Engaging leaders in shaping insights, opportunities, experimentation agendas, and other innovation-related content is an excellent way to ensure success. This type of engagement matches directly with the most important of the three roles for leading innovation: cocreation. It offers your best protection against "review and approve or kill" voting.

In fact, as leaders embrace their cocreation role through focused, immersive learning, you will find that you will never limit your reviews of innovation efforts to fully finished outputs. Instead, you will engage leaders in helping to shape the concept's evolution. Say you have a new concept for a target market in which typical pricing is \$3, and you're contemplating a \$15 price point. Bring that topic to the appropriate leadership team and work the logic and conclusions with them. Thinking of going through new channel partners to deliver the differentiated value you want to deliver? Seek a member of the leadership team for inputs on potential candidates, along with their rationale. You see the point: when you have to sort through key elements of the new business concept, engage leadership in the thinking, rather than simply proposing answers and hoping for the thumbs-up.

A Shared View Through Dialogue

Innovation requires new learning and new perspectives: insight regarding customers' unmet needs, frustrations, and unnecessary trade-offs, and an understanding of your core competencies and the way in which each provides unique advantage, are just a few examples. These insights are foundational to shaping your point of view regarding the specific opportunities you might pursue.

Leaders need to participate in shaping these (or other) points of view through regular dialogue and debate. Through leadership dialogue, you will progress to better insights and opportunities. As important, your efforts will have better traction and staying power due to the shared understanding that leadership develops. If you omit the dialogue, you will revert back to the passive "thumbs-up/thumbs-down" voting role that is so very detrimental to innovation. Do so at your own peril.

The Rule of Thirds

In an ideal world, you start with a shared and aligned understanding—about the outcomes, the way to pursue the work, and so on—across the entire leadership team. You live in the real world, however, and you know that organizations almost never have 100 percent alignment behind innovation efforts before they first get started.

The good news is, you don't have to have 100 percent alignment. What you do need is for a third of your leadership to be supportive initially. Even if a second third is agnostic or undecided and the remaining leaders are even opposed to the innovation work efforts or proposed outcomes, you are nevertheless starting from a "good enough" place to get going. More broadly, by structuring a good design, ensuring smart resourcing, and integrating the other two of these principles into your work, you are well positioned for success. But if you "fail" the rule of thirds test, you should proceed cautiously and think about ways to get to at least the threshold level. In these cases, the proper course of action may be to use such techniques as engaging leadership in in-depth co-design of your approach or performing innovation diagnostic work

In an ideal world, you start with full alignment and 100% shared assumptions. In the real world, you start wtih the rule of thirds.

that focuses on establishing shared leadership views on innovation impediments and approaches to overcome them.

●An Example of Innovation Leadership Engagement

Let's look at an example of how robust leadership engagement would manifest itself in a specific innovation approach that targets identifying and acting on new growth concepts. Please keep in mind that any approach is always highly situational, as it is based on the desired outcomes and relative maturity

of your innovation capabilities. Your particular objectives will dictate your particular design and both the overall approach and your specific leadership engagement agenda throughout it.

Figure 9-1 depicts an example of an innovation design that targets developing new product and service concepts through to commercialization, including in-market adjustments for innovation. We assume that some concepts may require experimentation for learning prior to full-on commercialization, whereas others may proceed straight to commercialization in market.

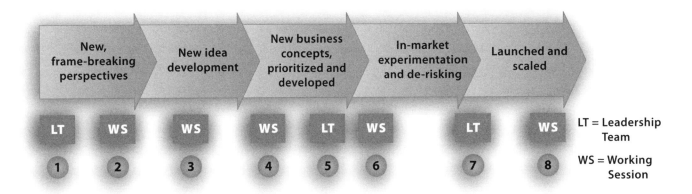

Figure 9-1   Example of an Innovation Work Process with Leadership Engagement

Figure 9-1 also depicts some possible touchpoints with leadership along the way, to engage them as cocreators, sponsors and decision makers, and active advocates for the work. The following table describes a sample engagement agenda (more specifically, what each touchpoint *could* look like). The idea in this example is to provide the structure and a clear conduit for leaders to engage in their three roles, leveraging the principles of leadership engagement discussed earlier. As with the overall design of the work illustrated in Figure 9-1, the leadership engagement agenda we outline here is illustrative only. You need to tailor your design to your specific circumstances.

Example of Leadership Engagement in the Work of Innovation

Mode of Work	Session Objective	Description of the Dialogue
LT **1** Leadership team working session with dialogue and debate, conclusions and revisions	Discuss, refine, and agree on roles, accountabilities, and working-style expectations for leadership.	• Review and discuss targeted outcomes and the underlying rationale to pursue them. • Review, discuss, and finalize the work to get there—our road map—and the time and resource needs. • Review roles and responsibilities for the leadership team and others involved; agree on expectations. • Surface issues to be resolved.
WS **2** Practitioner working session in which leadership joins and works on the issues alongside the team	Share, discuss, and shape emerging insights.	• Understand work in progress on identifying, synthesizing, and prioritizing new, frame-breaking perspectives to inform our thinking about new possible opportunities. • Work with practitioners to add to, synthesize, prioritize, and provide further insight on the perspective-building work.

Continued

Example of Leadership Engagement in the Work of Innovation (Continued)

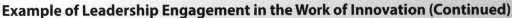

Mode of Work	Session Objective	Description of the Dialogue
WS **3** Practitioner working session in which leadership joins and works on the issues alongside the team	Generate new ideas, actions, and possibilities for the business (a broad set of ideas and options).	• Use new, frame-breaking perspectives and a broad set of new idea development techniques to develop ideas and provide input on areas of focus for going forward with new ideas.
WS **4** Practitioner working session in which leadership joins and works on the issues alongside the team	Select an opportunity (or opportunities) that you would like to progress further.	• Prioritize the highest-potential first opportunities to be worked. • Perform initial framing and stretching of opportunities. • Identify the most attractive and innovative attributes of the opportunities. • Identify the organization's go-forward learning agenda on a per-opportunity basis.
LT **5** Leadership team working session with dialogue and debate, conclusions and revisions	Discuss, refine, shape, and select new growth concept(s).	• Understand current state of assessed and vetted business concepts. • Make choices on revisions or reshaping of opportunities. • Make choices on next steps for resourcing, testing, or other actions.

Mode of Work	Session Objective	Description of the Dialogue
WS **6** Structured working session in which leadership joins and works on the issues alongside practitioners	Develop an approach to manage and mitigate risks related to the concepts.	• Identify central unknowns that represent risks and knowledge gaps to be closed. • Design a fast and inexpensive experimentation plan to close knowledge gaps (de-risk) and enable the organization to iterate on the business concept. • Determine resourcing and make choices on same.
LT **7** Leadership team working session with dialogue and debate, conclusions and revisions	Decide which efforts to take forward to commercialization and/or to continue to refine through experimentation.	• Review work to date (experimentation or other learning agenda conclusions). • Discuss and revise opportunities and decide on action (e.g., continue with experiments, proceed to commercialization, kill the opportunity) • Align on and make choices on resourcing and portfolio implications.
WS **8** Structured working session in which leadership joins and works on the issues alongside practitioners	Agree on postlaunch learning agenda and organizing actions.	• Synthesize learning from postlaunch tracking or postlaunch innovation efforts. • Incorporate into business concept and go-to-market iteration if and as appropriate. • Determine resources and next steps to optimize on the concept's upside and impact.

You see that the approach features two types of work sessions:

+ **"Leadership-centric"** sessions during which leaders review the inputs, shape and synthesize the work, and drive choices and next steps, with the assistance of practitioners or individuals who are working week to week on the effort.
+ **"Practitioner-centric"** working sessions during which the appropriate leaders pull up a chair and get involved in the work at targeted times throughout the work effort.

Each is effective when structured properly, and integrating the two within your specific innovation approach is central to your success. Note how the approach reflects the core design principles of leading innovation. Leaders are immersed in the work in a focused way, acting as cocreators and sponsors.

The approach acknowledges the importance of the rule of thirds through iterative, punctuated leadership dialogue from start to finish. Assuming that efforts begin with one third of leadership supporting the effort, the middle third—those open to acknowledging innovation's potential—often becomes increasingly supportive as they immerse themselves in the effort.

Because you structure the work in a disciplined fashion and feature explicit leadership dialogue, the work and results of innovation tend to sell themselves. This approach is superior to the alternative: an endless set of up-front discussions trying to describe and "sell" the work structure and its outputs a priori. At some point, you need to jump in and make it go.

With experience, you will be able to develop multiple viable designs for a given innovation program and select the one that best fits your particular circumstances. That is why understanding the core principles for leading innovation is so important. The principles serve as your guideposts to effective design of the work of leadership.

● Leading Innovation from the Top: Who's on Point?

Organizations tend to use the word "leadership" quite generally to include the broad group of individuals from senior leaders through to midlevel managers— and sometimes even further down in the organizational hierarchy. For our purposes, optimally the "who" of leadership is the smallest possible leadership team who can marshal the resources and make the decisions necessary to advance new innovation and business opportunities.

The idea here is to have a fast-moving leadership team with the authority to ensure proper resourcing from start to finish, and the accountability to make decisions on scope, objectives, and funding for specific opportunities. This may be the most senior leaders of the organization, especially in the case of searches for breakthrough innovation. If you're looking to shake up the industry, chances are the CEO and the top team are going to have to (and want to!) be involved.

But it also may be the case that the top team within a division, function, business unit, region, or brand is the appropriate team. It all depends on the nature of the organization's setup for decision making, juxtaposed with your program's ambition and the types of decisions and actions implied by that ambition. Let's illustrate with a few examples.

Whirlpool Corporation

When Whirlpool Corporation first initiated its innovation efforts in 2000, the company focused its program regionally with the expectation that specific new concepts would be implemented within a given region. Regional Innovation Leadership Teams (ILTs) were formed; they served in the three roles of cocreator, sponsor, and internal advocate. The regional ILTs comprised the core operating leadership teams for each region. They took on the explicit accountability for the innovation program through distinct meetings and other interactions with the leadership efforts initiated within the region. The structure was effective and necessary to get action and momentum behind innovation at the regional level.[2]

In 2010, when Whirlpool was using brand and functionally based efforts to rejuvenate their innovation capabilities and pipelines, the regional, business, brand, or functional leadership teams took on the role of innovation leadership and were accountable for the outcomes and driving the work. Which leader or leadership team owned the role depended on the particular topic and business that served as the focus of the work. These leadership teams had decision-making authority for the specific innovation program and the support of the office of the CEO, which helped in removing roadblocks when needed.[3]

Shell GameChanger

In the case of the Shell GameChanger (GC) program, the GC team makes nearly all prioritization and resourcing decisions within an approved budget. This is somewhat different than the level of leadership that most organizations would use to manage resourcing of "proof of concepts" for breakthrough innovation efforts, but then again GC is a different kind of system. The team has a sizeable dedicated annual seed fund and the strong backing of senior leadership of Shell R&D as well as Shell corporate. Thus Shell and the GC system adhere to principles and guidelines suggested here, configured in a different and fit-for-purpose way for the Shell R&D organization.[4]

We emphasize who should be engaged (and how) from a leadership standpoint as a response to the frequency with which we see these guidelines ignored. Too often we see organizations delegate innovation down to an innovation team or forum, but the team is held accountable for achieving a particular set of innovation results without being provided with the required authority to resource the effort appropriately or to act on the recommendations and outcomes. This situation is a telltale sign of leadership that is not walking the talk on innovation. They say they want it, but they delegate it away.

● Top Leadership as an Indispensable Element

The "leading innovation" work we've described may sound simple, but it is often the hardest part of getting the job done. We are often asked, "When innovation work efforts fail, why do they do so?" Most often a primary source of failure is the lack of a shared and aligned understanding and commitment to the work of innovation, its objectives, and your specific approach. To ensure success, leaders must embrace the three roles of cocreator, sponsor, and internal advocate. They must be willing to work on the thorny issues for which the answers are not obvious and the trade-offs are difficult.

Leaders often ask—implicitly or explicitly—"Why can't we just go innovate? Why doesn't innovation move forward when we declare it a priority—as it does on other topics like quality and productivity improvements?" You know the answer: organizations are built to do exactly what they are already doing. Innovation is about doing differently.

James Geurts, acquisition executive for the Special Operations Research, Development, and Acquisition Center within the U.S. Special Operations Command, an innovation enthusiast and driver for that organization, told us, "Eisenhower said that 'leadership is infectious, whether it is good or bad,' and I think the same is true of innovation."[5] We couldn't agree more.

Leading from Within: Grassroots–Led Innovation

Grassroots innovation is helpful when there is not yet an enterprise mandate for innovation and you, as leader, do not have the positional authority of a leader with budget, resources, and an ability to make decisions to broadly focus the organization's efforts on innovation. Root causes for the lack of mandate might include

+ Insufficient leadership support and commitment to make innovation one of a few enterprise priorities
+ A lack of shared clarity regarding the work of innovation, its objectives, and the right approach through which to make progress

+ An overreliance on consultants to do the job
+ Misconceptions that success requires the talents of great entrepreneurs like Branson, Brin, or Zuckerberg
+ The pressure of the day-to-day—allowing the urgent to derail the important
+ Past start-and-stop efforts that stalled

Sound familiar? If some of these conditions are similar to those within your organization, it may be that a grassroots approach to leading innovation is the best match for your starting point.

Some Foundational Principles for Grassroots Innovation

The Shell GameChanger (GC) process and innovation system we've discussed follows some foundational principles. GC's Russ Conser believes that these foundational principles are what enabled GC's longevity, success, and migration over time to an enterprise process.[6] GC started with the strong sponsorship of Shell's R&D leadership, then grew to be a corporation-wide

> "Eisenhower said that leadership is infectious whether it is good or bad, and I think the same true of innovation."
>
> —James Geurts, U.S. Special Operations Command

(and very well known) system. We believe that the foundational principles on which GC is built can serve as a strong foundation for initiating and perhaps spreading grassroots innovation as well; these principles include[7]

Grassroots innovation techniques are useful when there is not yet an enterprise mandate for innovation.

- **Openness and transparency.** Anyone inside or outside the organization can submit an idea. The process is clear through each step, including areas of focus, selection criteria, and roles— especially for that of the individual submitting the idea.
- **Collaboration without hierarchy.** From the very beginning, the idea author senses that the process is aligned to help her or him create the clearest and most compelling instantiation of the idea. Russ describes the peer review process as being "like King Arthur's round table. There is no hierarchy . . . If your idea is accepted, you feel good that your peers accepted it . . . If it is rejected, you still feel good that your peers considered it."
- **Resource attraction.** The GC process attracts resources: ideas and talent based on objective assessment and market-based principles. As a result, over time, they have enabled an internal market for each.

- **Learning by doing.** As GC leaders put it, "Although every once in a while an idea comes along that can be analyzed [toward] success, most revolutionary ideas require actually doing something to create a learning opportunity. Only learning by doing floats up hidden assumptions where they can be addressed and assessed. Revolutionary innovation requires one to try many ideas, but also to quickly stop those that aren't going to work."[8]
- **A movement, not a moment.** From the onset of the program, GC's founders had ambitions to elevate the efforts to an enterprise process. Therefore, as the system unfolded, they conceived of their efforts as a movement. Movements attract resources because they have a transcendent purpose. They describe a future world or ambition that is an attractive alternative to today's.

The results are impressive. "Since its inception in 1996, GameChanger has funded three thousand ideas, investing $350 million and resulting in 250 commercial projects," according to Gerald Schotman, executive VP for innovation and R&D and chief technology officer at Shell. Further, about 40 percent of Shell's core exploration and development R&D portfolio has evolved from ideas submitted to GC, and 70 percent of the GC portfolio includes collaboration with people outside Shell.[9]

You can use these same kinds of principles to structure and drive your grassroots efforts and to establish support structures. We describe a few alternative structures for grassroots efforts in the next section.

Some Grassroots Approaches

Some grassroots approaches are helpful in advancing innovation within the organization, sometimes even without support of the top leadership team. These may not all result in industry-changing breakthroughs, but they do provide productive alternatives that allow you to move forward in important ways:

- Business unit or functionally focused projects
- "Frontline innovation" initiatives
- Innovation in smaller bites and shorter bursts

Business Unit or Functionally Focused Projects

These are smaller, focused, yet highly organized and highly targeted innovation efforts.

The effort is aimed at a specific innovation challenge for the business unit (BU) or function. For example, the goal may be to understand how the IT function can enable a step-change improvement in the gathering of consumer insights through broad and efficient monitoring of social media. Or it might be to use innovation to develop specific product or service concepts regarding a specific brand.

For these types of projects, you can organize a small and fast-moving tiger team to structure the approach and attack the problem quickly and effectively, using selected innovation techniques and approaches germane to the issue at hand. Deploy this kind of focused effort to advance innovation within the practical constraints you face and the scope within which you can operate.

The effort requires design and thoughtful scope management such that the team and the appropriately identified players can act on the topic and innovation options developed. You will likely need a functional or lower-level "innovation leadership team" that is properly constructed to be able to do so. By definition, this scenario is one in which you would not have to go all the way to the top of the organization (or even the

BU) if scope, scale, and design are managed properly.

If you choose to pursue this route to accomplishing innovation results, be certain to

+ Scope the work such that you and the designated decision-making team can make the calls and choices on the topic and the options developed.
+ Run a fast and efficient innovation effort. Don't overscope or overengineer it.
+ When you achieve results, advertise them. Show the rest of the organization what is possible.

"Frontline Innovation" Initiatives

Many organizations feature some version of frontline innovation, which they sometimes enable through their own software or through third-party providers like Bright Idea, Spigit, or Exago. In all these versions of frontline innovation software packages and associated processes, small groups get together to ideate and create a wide slate of options about their facility, their job, their function, their favorite charity or cause—you name it. A group ranging from 6 to 160 can organize idea generation sessions using the chosen tools and to address a specific, very focused topic.

Your ability to move with speed and to set clear expectations is critical to achieving success through frontline innovation. This approach is about taking the low-hanging fruit generated from short, quick bursts of structured innovation activity, with the understanding that many of the low-hanging opportunities are going to be "small-i" innovations: small improvements that are quick and easy and that individually might seem insignificant but in the aggregate yield a noticeably better experience or environment.

Our suggestion to spread the word about BU and functionally focused projects applies to frontline innovation as well: when you achieve results, tout them. Success begets more success.

Innovation in Smaller Bites and Shorter Bursts

Bring specific innovation techniques or perspectives to a specific innovation problem. Follow the same pattern of applying specific tools and a clear approach, but in a smaller and more focused fashion than for an end-to-end, top-leadership-led process.

We suggest that you simply bring one tool (two at most) and apply it to "the way we do things here in _____."

For example, suppose you outline your HR unit's or corporate IT's orthodoxies about whom you serve, what you provide, how you provide it, and why you do it that way. What would you find? If you were to overturn or challenge any of those orthodoxies, what new and improved ways might let you better serve the organization, its constituents, or even your organization's external customers?

In many ways, this is a greatly reduced and streamlined version of the frontline innovation technique. It can be organized with very small groups by applying a structured process that can be as brief as a few hours. Voilà—you have near-term improvements to internal functions, processes, and service. With any luck, you may come up with some ideas that apply to your market-facing activities and outside customers or consumers as well.

We recommend you leverage the small-bite, smaller-burst technique by

- Aggregating multiple actions and small-i innovations and getting a critical mass going.
- Communicating your efforts within the organization: tout the successes and the difference the small-i innovations are making.
- Expanding on your ideas by searching for ways to further exploit them: when you find a good idea that can be leveraged elsewhere, spread the word. Let the other facilities, functions, retail outlets, and so on pick it up.

Top-down-supported innovation is great. But not all innovation can be or will be led from the very top. Keep grassroots techniques in your leading innovation arsenal as well. Either way: no leadership, no innovation—full stop.

Whether top-down or grassroots led, if no leadership, then no innovation— full stop.

Key Take-Aways

- Successful leadership learning and engagement is the most important organizing lever you have to ensure that innovation takes hold in your organization. And it is sometimes one of the hardest levers to implement if the prevailing leadership mind-set is that innovation can be delegated downward in its entirety.

- Leadership should be involved in the work of innovation learning, resource allocation, and decision making. The type of leaders you need to involve are those who can make decisions and allocate resources for and sponsor ongoing implementation efforts. Leaders need to act as cocreators, sponsors, and visible advocates.

- The importance of leadership learning is often underestimated or, worse, overlooked. If your ambition is to make innovation sustainable within your organization, you will succeed only if your innovation leaders viscerally understand the approaches and the new learning that led to specific new concepts. Leadership involvement that includes a focus on learning is the best means by which to build understanding and commitment—particularly if your innovation efforts are overturning company and industry orthodoxies.

- An effective leadership engagement agenda can involve the work coming to leaders—for input and shaping—as well as leaders going to where the work is being done—for learning, participation, and further input and shaping as well.

- If conditions for strong top-down sponsorship of innovation efforts and initiatives are less than optimal, consider grassroots techniques to gain traction on your innovation efforts. The techniques can enable incremental innovations that have a cumulative and positive impact on business results and culture. Occasionally, these efforts eventually lead to the development of top-down sponsored efforts and systems.

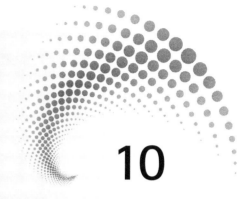

Getting Started

10

I've been asked to lead an innovation program; how do I get started?

What resources do I need? What's the people profile? How do I set objectives?

How do I figure all this out? How do I assess and design for what we need?

> Top leadership has recognized the need for systematic innovation, now you need to figure out how to get started. What to do?

Your boss—the CEO, the chief innovation officer, the COO, you name it—has asked you to come by. He or she says, "We need innovation. We have assembled a road map, and now we need to get an execution plan in place. Have a look and let's talk next week about how we can get started." You do the right thing: you say, "OK, will do," then head back to your office. The whole time you're thinking, *Now what? How do I figure this out?*

What just happened is that top leadership recognized a need for innovation—systematic innovation, not just one-off or serendipitous innovation. But they don't have a point of view on how to get started. So they are delegating the job to you. The "road map" that you are handed doesn't really offer any guidance. Even worse, the tangible objectives that you're being asked to pursue are not clear. The top leaders want innovation, but "innovation" is not really defined. It's still an ideal more than a tangible, defined outcome. So your task will be to take the vague request of "we need innovation" and translate it into a set of focused objectives so that you can shape a disciplined, well-conceived approach to the particular innovation challenge.

Designing from Outcomes Back

Start by thinking about outcomes or objectives before considering any particular approach. It sounds obvious to say that you should be thoughtful about what it is you are trying to accomplish before you set out to do it. Unfortunately, we too often see individuals and teams react in knee-jerk fashion and reach immediately for a consulting firm or B-school guru who will *tell them what to do*.

Our advice: avoid being suckered into the "I have a problem, and this expert has a way to get it done" approach. It's not that external expertise isn't helpful—it is. Rather, the issue is that without thoroughly understanding the specific outcomes you seek, you can't possibly know which internal or external expert you might turn to. As the saying goes, if you don't know where you are going, any road will take you there. Starting with this approach will result in wasted work with no good outcomes. Instead, focus first on what you are looking to achieve.

Answer these kinds of questions to define the specific outcomes you'd like to achieve and the constraints within which you need to work:

- What are our overall *specific and tangible objectives* for our innovation efforts? Which are longer term? shorter term?
- What are the realistic boundaries and practical constraints within which we are operating? Which people and skills can we apply to the effort? For what percentage of their time? For how long? What kind of budget will they have? Can they travel? What are they/we constrained from doing?
- In addition to people and skills, what other resources will we need?
- What innovation approach can we use to achieve the objectives within the constraints? Can they be reconciled? If not, can one or another change?
- What are the start-up steps?

As the next graphic suggests, you need to apply an iterative thinking process to develop a specific approach and program design. As you iterate, you will sometimes conclude that the initial objectives cannot be achieved, given the practical constraints. For example, you may set an initial objective of enabling an enterprise-wide capability, but you learn that leadership is not able to commit to the necessary roles of cocreator, sponsor, and visible advocate. In this instance, you

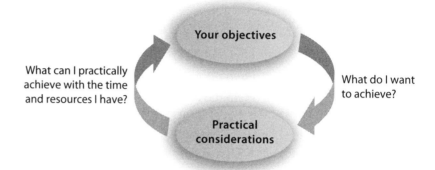

would need either to rethink the objectives or make your case to senior leadership for their commitment, ensuring that all key stakeholders understand the necessary trade-offs you may need to make in selecting a particular approach.

● Different Types of Innovation Outcomes

We observe at least six broad types of innovation objectives or outcomes for which program leaders design an approach:

> *Starting with approach rather than outcomes in your design leads to wasted effort—if you don't know where you're going, any road will take you there.*

1. **Give me more ideas I can act on**. "We don't have enough ideas—we need more and better ideas.

Help me develop new product or service concepts that I can commercialize in the next twelve to thirty-six months."

"Help me get innovation fast."

"Help me improve colleague engagement while efficiently capturing their improvement and innovation ideas—generally or for a specific challenge."

2. **Help me with the ideas I already have.**

"Help me take the ideas I already have to market."

"Ideas are not our problem—we have plenty of ideas. How do I know which we should take to market?

3. **Make my innovation efforts more strategic.**

"We need more coherent innovation. Right now, it's all one-offs."

"Help me fill my pipeline for the next three to five years in a strategically sensible way."

"Help me understand the linkage between 'strategy' and 'innovation'— I feel that they should be linked and integrated, but don't know how I can do it."

"We need new growth platforms to drive our innovation agenda."

4. **Help me manage risk smartly.**

"I have a new, promising, but uncertain idea. How do I sensibly proceed?"

"Our organization won't pursue big and promising ideas because they are perceived to be too risky. What can we do?"

5. **Help me innovate postlaunch.**

"All my innovation thinking and work is up until launch. Why don't I keep innovating postlaunch?"

"How can I innovate postlaunch without derailing existing in-market executions?

6. **Strengthen our innovation capabilities.**

"Help me strengthen some basic innovation skills."

"Help me create enough innovation black belts across the organization."

"Help me build leadership's capabilities in leading innovation."

"Help me redesign our process(es) to better enable innovation."

"Help me enable a culture of innovation to achieve our growth goals."

"Help me redesign _____ process(es) to better enable innovation" (for example, open innovation processes, stage-gate processes, supply chain management processes)

The first critical step in developing an approach that is fit for your particular purpose and circumstance is to get specific—to unpack the general "we need" statement to come up with the specific outcomes that you want and need. Using these six broad categories as a starting point, you can ask yourself, your team, and leadership why you and/or they want more innovation. Is it in order to

1. Give us more ideas?
2. Bring existing but nascent ideas to market?
3. Ensure that our innovation efforts are linked to strategy? That there is strategic coherence?
4. Help us manage risk smartly?
5. Innovate postlaunch?
6. Strengthen innovation capabilities in a specific way to achieve a specific outcome?

In the next section, we will look at an illustrative approach designed to deliver results for the one or more of the outcomes expressed in each of these six categories. You will see that we do not repeat approaches we have referenced elsewhere in The Guide, such as open innovation, innovation fast, innovation accelerators, and "innovating in market."

Keep in mind that the "right" approach should be based on your innovation ambition and the practical considerations of your starting point.

High-Level Designs for Frequently Desired Outcomes

The fact is that there are several designs you can use to approach any given innovation challenge. With experience, skills, knowledge, and an appreciation of your organization's culture, you and your colleagues should be able to design the right approach.

Let's look at specific problems, and examples of some possible designs to address them.

Outcome 1: Give Me More Ideas I Can Commercialize and Scale

"We don't have enough ideas—we need more and better ideas. Help me develop new product or service concepts that I can commercialize in the next twelve to thirty-six months."

"Help me get innovation fast."

"Help me improve colleague engagement while efficiently capturing their improvement and innovation ideas—generally or for a specific challenge."

If your need is for "more ideas," we advocate that you take an insight-driven approach. Doing so will best position you to develop the new, frame-breaking perspectives on market, industry, and your organization that are particularly useful for generating compelling ideas. Figure 10-1 illustrates an approach to generating new ideas.

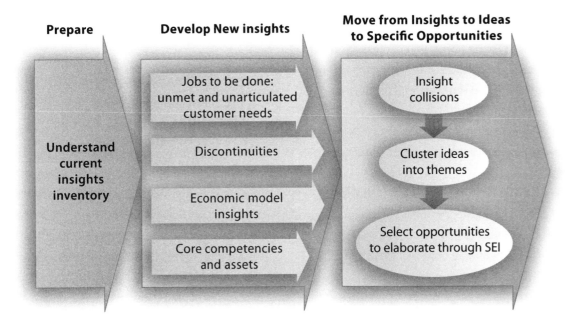

Figure 10-1 New Perspectives to Generate New Ideas

Notice that you begin this approach by understanding your current insight foundation. You can and should use and build on your existing customer, market, and organization insights to develop frame-breaking perspectives. You can then close gaps and develop new perspectives using the types of "insight collisions" that you find most helpful.

In the last phase of work, you use the collision of insights to generate ideas. As you do so, you may find it helpful to cluster the ideas into specific themes related to a particular customer benefit, thereby helping you view a particular broad theme from several different perspectives. There may also be ideas that stand on their own.

After reviewing the set of ideas and theme-based clusters, select the most interesting few and then apply SEI techniques to stretch, elaborate, and refine them further. The elapsed time for each phase and the resources required to do the work vary significantly based on circumstances. Please also note that the approach depicted in Figure 10-1—and those we subsequently detail in this chapter—do not speak to specific milestone meetings, leadership engagement sessions, or other specific working sessions. Those should be incorporated into

your design thinking as well and the specifics and timing will vary based on circumstances.

Outcome 2: Help Me with the Ideas I Already Have

"Help me take the ideas I already have to market."

"Ideas are not our problem—we have plenty of ideas. How do I know which we should take to market?"

In some circumstances, there is an existing pipeline of ideas, but, for a variety of reasons, the ideas are "stuck." The organization cannot get them converted from idea to actionable concept. Or, as a variant, the organization lacks a sufficient stable of up-front ideas *and* it cannot drive them through to execution.

In cases where your central objective is to move ideas from the "nascent" state to a more actionable and executable stage, an approach like that illustrated in Figure 10-2 is helpful.

This approach integrates many of the elaboration techniques described elsewhere in The Guide, and assumes that you will apply several rounds of elaboration and iteration based on your learning and on identifying critical assumptions and unknowns. This type of design can act as a stand-alone design

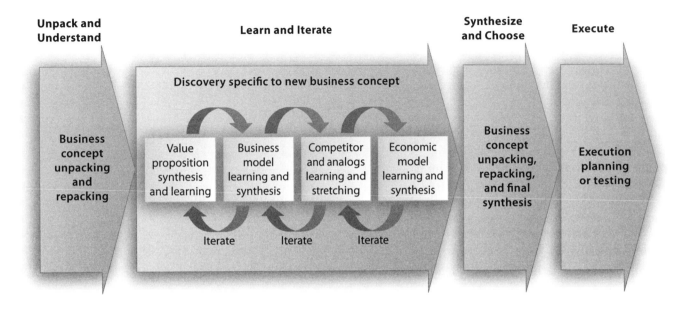

Figure 10-2 Getting to Action on a Synthesized Business Concept

if the organization already has nascent ideas. It can also act as the "back end" to a "front-end" process that generates new (nascent) ideas, as shown in Figure 10-1.

Outcome 3: Make My Innovation Efforts More Strategic

"We need more coherent innovation. Right now, it's all one-offs."

"Help me fill my pipeline for the next three to five years in a strategically sensible way."

"Help me understand the linkage between 'strategy' and 'innovation'—I feel that they should be linked and integrated, but don't know how I can do it."

"We need new growth platforms to drive our innovation agenda."

Such statements as "We need more coherent innovation" and "We need new growth platforms to drive our innovation agenda"—which we hear from leaders across industries—represent a desire for strategic innovation. These expressions may also be pointing to a desire for an innovation strategy—a framework that recommends "where to play" in your markets and identifies the basis on which the company will compete and win sustainably.

We will not speak to specific approaches to crafting corporate strategy here. Rather we will share an illustrative approach that helps you shift from "one-off" product innovation to a domaining discipline that will fill your pipeline for several years.

The illustrative approach shown in Figure 10-1 focuses on developing specific

concepts. Note that the approach does not feature the notion of building and elaborating strategic domains or growth spaces. If you want to bring greater strategic coherence and logic to your efforts, you can apply the domaining technique described in Chapter Three. Figure 10-3 illustrates a simple approach for shifting away from one-off product innovation and bringing greater strategic coherence and logic to your efforts by building and elaborating strategic domains or growth spaces.

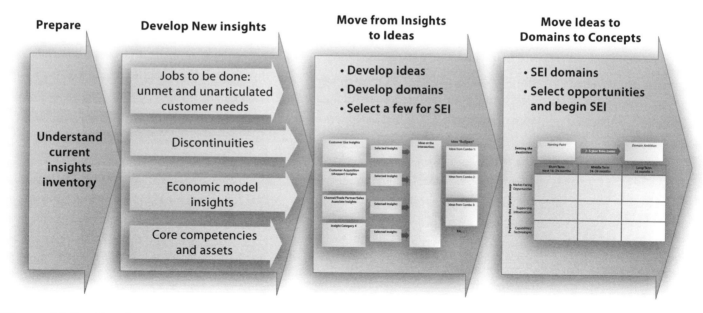

Figure 10-3   Developing Innovation Domains

Note that the first two steps are essentially the same as the approach illustrated in Figure 10-1. Step three (which incorporates use of the framework shown in Figure 7-1) focuses on generating a large set of ideas in order to identify bigger growth spaces—domains—that you could pursue. In step four, you use the framework shown in Figure 3-1 to elaborate, assess, and prioritize the strategic growth spaces—domains. That work may typically include

+ Developing a detailed migration map.
+ Mapping current initiatives (if there are any) to each priority domain. Doing so will help you bring greater coherence and strategic clarity to existing efforts.
+ Deepening your understanding of a given domain through additional insight work.

The overarching idea of this approach is to identify a strategically coherent growth agenda. You do so by creating and selecting a domain with many promising concepts, each of which delivers the same broad value proposition. This technique enables you to shift from one-off efforts by filling your pipeline with a portfolio of strategically related opportunities. Of course there is much work that follows in order to bring concepts to market successfully.

Outcome 4: Help Me Manage Risk Smartly

"I have a new, promising, but uncertain idea. How do I sensibly proceed?"
"Our organization won't pursue big and promising ideas because they are perceived to be too risky. What can we do?"

Let's say you have a fully developed business concept—on paper—and you have identified critical assumptions and unknowns that must hold true for you to succeed. Your team and leadership see risk because of the unknowns regarding your concept. As a result, your efforts may be stalled or stuck.

You know from Chapter Six that you can get unstuck by managing and mitigating risk related to your unknowns through experimentation and other techniques for closing knowledge gaps. Figure 10-4 illustrates one example of how you can do so through experimentation efforts featuring several iterations of in-market learning.

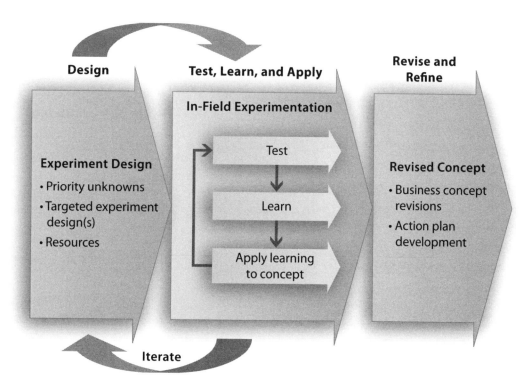

Figure 10-4 Experimentation and Business Concept Iteration

Smartly designed market-based experiments should be used to close knowledge gap(s) on specific unknowns. These experiments provide fast, low-cost, under-the-radar methods for managing and mitigating risk. Often the approach features several learning cycles through which you refine and de-risk the opportunity, positioning you to launch with confidence and ensuring that you have the right amount of resources.

This type of design may be used in stand-alone fashion for concepts that are fully vetted, or you can add it to other phases of idea and concept development.

Outcome 5: Help Me Innovate Postlaunch

"All my innovation thinking and work is up until launch. Why don't I keep innovating postlaunch?"

"How can I innovate postlaunch without derailing existing in-market executions?

As we've noted, postlaunch innovation is the innovation practitioner's frontier. In Chapter Seven, we speak in great detail about specific approaches you can use to innovate postlaunch. For our purposes here, we summarize four important design principles that should guide you in any postlaunch innovation approach:

+ **Apply front-end innovation techniques in a fit-for-purpose way.** For example, consider such techniques as continued learning, insight development, ideation, opportunity elaboration, and experimentation. Focus on the particular objective of improving your in-market performance for a particular concept. We've established that innovation requires new learning. Continue that new learning

postlaunch to capture the full potential of your newly launched product or service.

+ **Understand what is fixed and what is malleable for your postlaunch concept.** In practical terms, there are fixed components to an in-market concept that are difficult and expensive to change. Some fixed components, such as base product design or regulatory conformity, may be impossible to change without a complete reconceptualization of a given concept. Yet there are other aspects that can be improved through innovation while in market. These include elements of the marketing mix, such as pricing and promotion, incentives, routes to market, and the channel experience. Focus on what can be productively changed for your particular context. Then apply fit-for-purpose front-end techniques to discover what additional innovations will help you capture more upside.

+ **Use structured pilots for learning.** The discipline of postlaunch strategic innovation is likely to be new to many in your organization. If so, you will find it helpful to initiate your postlaunch efforts through a structured pilot. As you do, include comprehensive coverage of tools and techniques for learning, to allow both practitioners and leaders to apply and learn these new techniques in service of capturing more upside for an in-market concept.

+ **Pick your shots carefully**. Postlaunch strategic innovation requires resources that are different from and additional to your current postlaunch management processes and efforts. You will need to be thoughtful in the in-market opportunities on which you wish to focus and apply those resources.

Outcome 6: Strengthen Our Innovation Capabilities

We share two distinctly different approaches in this section. The first is designed to strengthen some basic skills; the second is designed to enable a culture of innovation through capability building within a more comprehensive end-to-end innovation process.

Strengthen Basic Innovation Skills

"Help me strengthen some basic innovation skills."

"Help me create enough innovation black belts across the organization."

Several leading universities, such as Stanford, IMD, and Babson, offer various types of innovation training for business executives. But you don't need to go to an executive learning class to strengthen basic innovation skills. You can build your own curricula drawing from many sources, including those aspects of your internal innovation efforts that have worked well for you.

Ideally you should structure the skill building in a way that applies a given concept to a specific challenge that your training cohort may face. For example, if you wish to strengthen skills in risk management and mitigation, you could design a one-day session to focus on current concepts for which the techniques are relevant, or you could choose to focus on a historical example from your organization or the industry.

You may, for example, choose to focus your training on one or more insight techniques, as depicted here:

Objectives and brief overview of innovation in our organization	• Share objectives and set training in context of overall innovation efforts for the organization
Surfacing Unmet Needs	• Learn and apply techniques such as end-to-end experience mapping and surfacing tensions
Reframing Jobs to Be Done	• Understand how looking at jobs to be done is helpful in reframing our view of served market—and surfacing potential disruptions to it
Identifying and Using Orthodoxies	• Identify industry orthodoxies that may unnecessarily prevent us from seeing or pursuing opportunities
Identifying Potential Dimensions of Competition—Exploring White Space	• Explore the dimension of competition—ours and others'—to identify potential white space opportunities
Discussion and shared learning	• Share reflections and discuss specific ways one might apply the learning from today's session

Working Sessions   **Discussion/Plenary Sessions**

As you can see, this session focuses exclusively on learning and applying select insight techniques, and the majority of the session is structured as applied learning for each concept using smaller teams. Typically you would construct a working-session format in which a given group applies the new technique in a hands-on manner. You could choose to structure working sessions as facilitated or self-directed sessions, depending on your objectives.

The specific time required for each session should be based on your desired outcome. If you want deeper skills and mastery, you may need more than a day to meet your objective. By contrast, you could decide that you wish to focus only on a single insight area, in which case your session would be shorter. Whatever your innovation training needs, just be sure to stay focused on the outcome(s) you seek as you structure the session.

Building Innovation Capabilities and Enabling Mind-Set Shifts at Saint-Gobain Performance Plastics

Saint-Gobain Performance Plastics operates seven business units across fifty plants in Asia, Europe, and North America. It is a business in which "80% of sales are from a business model based on engineer to customer interaction and greater than 35% of sales are from products less than 5 years old," suggesting both success in innovation and an imperative to continue innovating.[1] As president Tom Kinisky notes, "Every company wants to have growth and everybody wants to be part of a dynamic, growing organization . . . The fun of launching new products, the idea that new processes are coming to our factory floor . . . everybody wants that. With growth is the opportunity for more experiences, for career development and enhanced job satisfaction. [Therefore we seek] not just innovation [but] sustainable innovation. We want it to be part of the fabric of who we are every single day."[2]

To develop capabilities and shift mind-sets, Tom asked Jean Angus, director of innovation processes, to create a fit-for-purpose innovation program that could be rolled out to every part of the organization. Tom and Jean were very clear that the training should lead to a business result, including strengthening existing customer relationships, establishing new customer relationships, and, over time, driving continued profitable growth. The diagram depicts their high-level approach[3]:

Assess	**Design**	**Pilot**	**Scale**
Assess current core innovation approach and processes	Develop training curriculum and long-term plan	Conduct; learn; refine approach	Roll out training enterprise wide and begin certification
• Interviews with business leadership • Employee surveys • Assessment of current supporting and enabling processes and gaps	• Develop internal branding for the effort, linking it to business strategy • Design and select tools (customized and off the shelf) and supporting materials • Set governance and process to move from training to ideas to in-market actions	• Develop BU-specific insights — e.g., core competencies, disruptive trends, and customer insights • Hold collaborative sessions; debrief and revise as appropriate	• Design and agree on skill level mastery — components and assessment criteria • Integrate training efforts with appropriate HR processes • Develop pool of internal trainers, facilitators, and coaches to enable "train the trainers" approach

As you can see, developing the training required significant effort, starting first with an assessment of what was working well inside the company and what was limiting it from realizing its full innovation potential. From there, Jean and her team developed the specific training curriculum for individuals and teams and quickly rolled it out across the organization. Individuals practiced using basic innovation tools and processes. Some learned to facilitate insights and step-change or breakthrough solutions. Others progressed further to facilitate and coach business teams on strategic innovation. Full scaling of the program was to begin in 2013, with the goal of more than fifteen hundred colleagues trained by the end of that year. Ongoing efforts to certify internal innovators at various levels of mastery continues, as this table depicts[4]:

Saint-Gobain Performance Plastics Innovation Training Program Platforms:						
Platform	**People**		**Solutions**		**Strategy**	
Role	Creativity and Innovation Practitioner		Creativity and Innovation Facilitator		Creativity and Innovation Coach	
Level	Level 1	Level 2	Level 3	Level 4	Level 5	Level 6
Course name	Basic Innovative Thinking	Practicing Creativity and Innovation	Facilitating Creativity and Innovation	Designing for Outcomes	Coaching for Creativity and Innovation	Master Innovation Trainer, Facilitator, and Coach
Percent trained	100% of organization	20–25% of organization	15% of organization	10% of organization	3–5% of organization	1% of organization
Course focus	Saint-Gobain Performance Plastics Innovation Training Program Platforms: **Everyone** in organization gaining awareness of innovation program, processes and tools	People learn and practice more tools while solving personal and business challenges with innovation coach. Any person completing level 1 course can volunteer for this course	People learn skill of creative facilitation, art of improvisation, and more tools. Any person demonstrating competence in applying level 2 tools and having certain facilitator attributes can be selected for course	People learn skill of facilitating team insights, designing for step-change solutions, and coaching level 3 facilitators. Any person demonstrating competence in facilitating level 3 tools can be selected for course	People learn skill of facilitating business team strategic insights, designing for breakthrough solutions, and coaching teams on customer engagement immersion process. Any person demonstrating competence in facilitating level 4 tools can be selected for course	People learn to coach business teams and leaders on all innovation platforms, execute all innovation training programs, and design for sessions for business team strategic insights and business model solutions. Any person demonstrating competence in facilitating and coaching level 4 tools can be selected for course
Competencies and outcomes	Generates many creative, incremental solutions Sets tone for enabling innovative culture	Designs for incremental solutions and generates step-change solutions	Facilitates step-change solutions and action plans in teams	Facilitates insights and breakthrough solutions with action plans in teams Coaches and designs for level 3 facilitators	Facilitates and coaches business insights and strategic direction in business teams Coaches and designs for levels 3 and 4 facilitators	Deep understanding of Performance Plastics Innovation program Trains, coaches, facilitates, and designs for all innovation levels

Saint-Gobain offers a detailed example of a well-designed and well-executed innovation training regimen, one that is thoroughly thought through with regard to

+ Outcomes desired (for example, specifically defined levels of innovation mastery across a specified cross-section of the organization)
+ The design to achieve those outcomes

You will want to achieve this level of outcomes-back thinking and design for your own training program. Of course, you will need to take your organization's desired outcomes, inputs, and constraints into account.

Enable a Culture of Innovation to Achieve Growth

"Help me build leadership's capabilities in leading innovation."
"Help me redesign our process(es) to better enable innovation."

"Help me enable a culture of innovation to achieve our growth goals."
"Help me redesign _____ process(es) to better enable innovation."

The approach we discuss here is the most complex and, if executed well, capable of yielding the highest impact because it encompasses the innovation needs across each of the first four categories and adds a fifth: fostering a culture of innovation to achieve your growth goals.

The objectives of this approach, which demands a highly structured leadership agenda, include filling the pipeline, enabling innovation-friendly processes, building skills, and shifting mind-sets. At its broadest level, the approach seeks systemic change so that the organization innovates *because of* its processes and systems rather than in spite of those systems.

These objectives represent a big challenge, so the approach comprises the most variables and alternatives. It is therefore nearly impossible to peg a standard design or template that addresses a standard circumstance, because when you peel the onion back a layer or two, there *is* no standard circumstance. In that context, let's have a look at a very high-level illustrative approach (Figure 10-5).

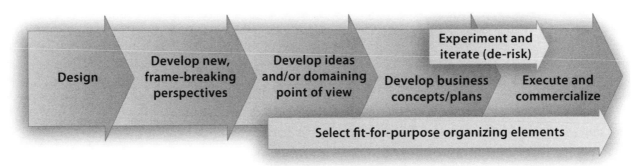

Figure 10-5   Innovation Capability-Building and Embedment Work

This example assumes that the innovation capabilities the organization would like to build or strengthen cover each phase of the end-to-end innovation process. Comprehensive capability is achieved through learning by doing, because the approach assumes that both a leadership team and a working team are engaged throughout. The working team will learn the end-to-end set of skills and tools as it applies them in each phase. Leadership will engage in their part of that transformation agenda and may pursue a structured leadership agenda that features them in their roles as cocreators, sponsors, and visible advocates. By so doing, leadership will understand and participate in organization design efforts and dialogue at the back end of the work effort.

Getting Started: Assembling the Team

We are often asked for guidance regarding how to form an innovation team: what the ideal team profile is, how it might vary by person and role, and how many members to have.

We argue that you serve yourself well to think in terms of overall team composition rather than individual profiles. Given the nature of innovation work, you need many attributes to enable successful innovation work—more attributes than is realistic to try to find in any one individual. For example, at times you will need all or some of the following:

- Divergent and convergent tendencies
- Creative thinking
- Business concept development capabilities calling for high levels of business acumen
- Some new-to-the-business and new-to-the-industry thinking and, at times, some long-in-the-tooth experience in both the industry and in business model development and vetting
- Some experience from those who make the product, and some from those who market or sell it

The list of attributes is too long to expect to find in one human being, no matter how talented he or she may be. So we recommend that you think "team" rather than individual. Not only that, you're looking at a big workload! You will be well served to get yourself a generous number of arms and legs to help carry it.

The mapping tool in Figure 10-6 guides you in thinking through and structuring the most effective group or team to drive your innovation work. It helps you assemble a cross-section of individuals, regardless of team size, ensuring a good mix of backgrounds, perspectives, and experiences.

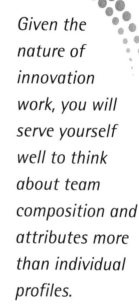

Given the nature of innovation work, you will serve yourself well to think about team composition and attributes more than individual profiles.

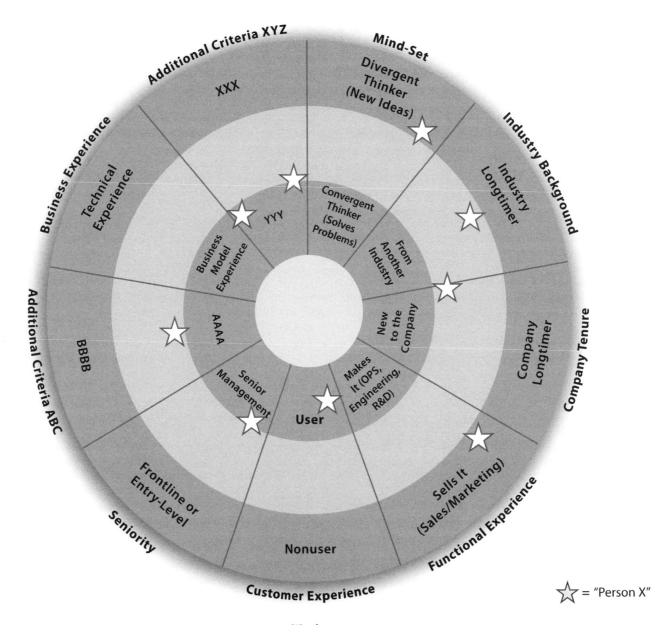

Figure 10-6 Team Cross-Section Mapping Tool

Our example is populated with one hypothetical individual, Person X, to give you a sense of how to fill out the map. The stars indicate where Person X falls on each dimension. You can map all of the names of individuals you are considering on each of the dimensions on this single framework. After you map the 3, 5, 12, 20, or 200 individuals whom you are considering for the work, you should look for spread and gaps:

+ *Spread:* Have you covered the dimensions as best you can, given the size of group you are planning to staff?
+ *Gaps:* Where are the big gaps and soft spots in the staffing of the work? What can you do to shore up the soft spots? Can you find other alternatives or additions? Can you augment those gaps in skills or perspectives in some other fashion, such as through part-time participation of others, or leadership interventions?

You should develop and strengthen your team's skill sets to shape and design innovation work efforts as much as possible over time. Highly developed design skills come with "flight hours" of doing the work—understanding the underlying principles that undergird the work and gaining experience with the techniques in general.

These skills allow the organization to become increasingly proficient at addressing innovation challenges in real time without having to go to outside help or counsel. This is not to say that you will never want to go to outside organizations for data or outside perspectives and input. Rather, it is to say that you should develop self-sufficiency in designing innovation work by building this skill internally. Even if you work with an outside partner to get started in learning the work of innovation and creating your own internal design skills, developing these skills internally over time is probably one of the most valuable things you can do for your organization's innovation capability-building efforts.

● Assessing Issues and Approach: Innovation Assessment and Design

"How do I know I am starting at the right place with my innovation efforts?"

"We don't know if we have good ideas or not. How can we assess whether we have good ideas or bad ideas—or no 'real' ideas at all?"

"We need more innovation, but we're not getting it. And we don't know why. Help us understand what we're doing wrong and what to do to fix it."

In many instances, an organization is not able to identify the specific outcomes and corresponding approach it seeks. Leadership or team views may vary as to which outcome should be a near-term priority or which root causes impede innovation within the organization. In such circumstances, it is helpful to conduct an innovation assessment both to diagnose root-cause inhibitors and to surface and sequence the particular innovation outcomes you wish to achieve.

Figure 10-7 depicts a high-level example of an assessment and design structure.

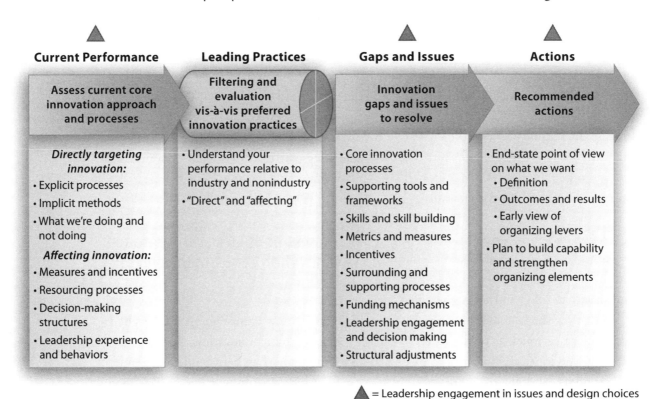

Figure 10-7   Example of an Assessment and Design Process

This approach helps you (1) assess what is currently in place that directly supports and enables innovation and (2) identify the organizational systems and processes that indirectly impede the work of innovation in material ways. As you develop your findings regarding actions or processes that support or impede innovation, you can begin to discuss what to do to improve your situation. As you consider potential actions, assess your situation against leading innovation principles and practices to develop specific recommendations.

The next sections take a closer look at each major work element depicted in Figure 10-7.

Develop an As-Is View of Innovation and New Product Development Processes and Outcomes

What does the organization do to enable innovation and new product development work?

+ What are the explicit, documented work processes and plans for innovation and new product development? What is supposed to happen through these processes and plans?

+ In practice, what actually happens? In what ways does the actual work of innovation deviate from the "documented" process? Are there workarounds? Improvisations? If so, are these harmful or helpful? What are the current pipeline and portfolio outcomes?

+ What are the gaps? Where are shortfalls vis-à-vis the organization's innovation and growth needs and goals?

Develop an As-Is View of Resource Allocation and Other Indirect Work Processes That Affect Innovation and Growth Work Efforts

What does the organization do today with regard to resource allocation and related processes and decision-making forums?

+ What do capital and expense allocations currently look like, and how do they work—or not work—in conjunction with innovation?

+ How does personnel allocation work and not work vis-à-vis innovation needs and processes?

+ How does annual planning and resource allocation work intersect (or not) with the work of innovation? Is there a formal intersection?

+ How does human resource and talent management take innovation needs and work into account?

You must assess each of these elements with complete objectivity. Your assessment should produce a grounded-in-reality analysis of what is actually happening vis-à-vis innovation needs. Think of it as the current-day picture of innovation—good and bad. It is a look in the mirror, and it needs to be an honest one.

Identify Leading Innovation Principles and Practices

Juxtapose the as-is picture onto the "ideal" as represented by the leading principles and practices described throughout The Guide. They collectively articulate a clear point of view on what, ideally, would be happening, both at the level of principle and at the level of action.

Identify Priority Gaps and Capability-Building/Enhancement Areas

Identify specific need areas and prioritize them.

+ Where are the gaps? What are we not doing? What should we be doing differently?

+ What are the *priority* gaps? Where should we focus first on shoring up capability, and why?

+ What are the options for gap-filling actions? (There are usually several.) What are the trade-offs related to the options we are considering?

Recommend Organizational Changes

Develop an actionable point of view to address the gaps by making changes to specific organizing elements.

+ For each capability-building area, which priority action will we take onboard, and why?

+ What are the resources required to do that?

+ What are the realistic resources we can put against the priority action(s)? Are the resources we are committing sufficient to accomplish our objectives?

+ If we take all of our gap-filling actions and recommendations in aggregate, do they work with one another? Is it a comprehensive approach through which we consider each element as a means by which to enable and sustain our innovation ambition? Does it reflect a systemic approach in which several discrete actions reinforce each other, bringing greater coherence and cumulativeness to our efforts?

+ Do we have an implementation game plan that articulates a sequence of activities with target dates for completion and checkpoints along the way?

Innovation Assessment at Crayola

When Crayola began seeking more innovation in 2004, they started by applying an innovation assessment and design technique.[5] One of their motivations was based on an unsuccessful foray into adult writing instruments a few years earlier. Although that concept was well regarded prior to launch, the effort was not successful because the "attempt stretched too far from Crayola's core [competencies, and it] lacked the brand equity to attract and retain this new customer segment."[6] Crayola had many more ideas they could commercialize, but wanted to know which were the most promising. They also wanted to know if there were alterations they could make overall to their innovation system and capability (including but not limited to their existing stage-gate process).[7]

In working through an assessment and design exercise, Crayola concluded the following[8]:

- In order to know which ideas are best to pursue, develop a point of view about which customer problems to solve and which industry rules are most advantageous to challenge. Consumer insights and industry paradigms to challenge are a necessary foundation to having a point of view on best ideas to pursue through to commercialization.
- Learn and apply these and other innovation techniques first, before redesigning your internal processes. Learn to do the work of innovation, building skills and understanding as the important first step in efforts to strengthen innovation capabilities. In other words, skills before process (or other redesign of organizing elements).
- Initiate changes to specific organizing elements, such as process and structure, after you establish a shared and aligned understanding of where to play and how to win. Over time, these changes at Crayola included:
  - *The "No Limits" platform:* This is one example of a point of view regarding the specific actions—products and enabling organizing actions—the company took to fulfill consumers' unmet needs.[9]

- *A redesigned stage-gate process:* The innovation team integrated some new innovation techniques into their existing stage-gate process, including building new perspectives and developing and prioritizing platforms.[10]
- *Structural changes:* Leadership reorganized their marketing department by focusing centrally around growth platform (domain) propositions such as No Limits. They put P&L leaders in charge of driving No Limits as well as other platforms. Clearly leadership held a strong conviction that if a platform (domain) represented a significant source of future value for the company, they were going to align to those propositions organizationally.[11]

Skills trump tools. Don't get caught up in "tools myopia."

The beginning of Crayola's innovation capability-building efforts and journey are documented extensively in the 2008 Corporate Executive Board study focusing on innovating the business model while sustaining core performance.[12]

One other point on assessment and design work: if you need outside help, get it! That advice may be true in general, but we emphasize it here in particular. Even if you have already established a comprehensive point of view on innovation, gaining an objective perspective from qualified and trustworthy third parties on what your organization is doing and not doing can be quite valuable.

● Before You Begin: Some Additional Tips

As you are getting started on your innovation and capability-building journey, keep these points in mind:

- Skills trump frameworks. Frameworks are scaffolding to build, teach, and maintain skills and process. Skills for developing internal and external insights, ideas, business concepts, and experimentation are more central and crucial than a given framework. Don't lose sight of that or get caught up in "tools myopia."

- You will build your strongest innovation skills through learning by doing. It requires a lot of "flight hours." Innovation is a learned skill rather than a rote task. It is much more akin to learning to be a good brand manager or general manager than it is to learning your math tables. Tools are of great use, but the process is not nearly as formulaic as some would have you believe (or hope that it would be!).

- Innovation is not a rigid process as much as it is a wide-ranging set of tools and approaches that you can and should piece together optimally *for you*. Everyone's situation varies on specifics that matter a great deal. There is no standard set play that works for everyone.

+ The skills for design of each of your innovation approaches are critical! Build them over time and supplement them periodically with outside assistance.

Building and having access to skills in the areas of diagnosing and designing the work of innovation will be of high value right from the start.

We hope that these tips and design examples are of assistance as you begin. You are off on your quest to build a better innovation system. Good luck!

Key Take-Aways

- Getting started on an innovation effort should be an outcomes-driven design exercise. Identify specific outcomes before selecting the approach—always. Designing an approach to achieve those outcomes then entails a discussion of "trade-offs" so that you very clearly understand what you can practically achieve given your situation.

- Across organizations of different size, geographies, and structure, there are several broad types of innovation objectives or outcomes for which program leaders commonly design an approach. These categories reflect the majority (but not all) of the ways in which the "innovation problem" is expressed as a team converges on a specific approach for their organization. The six we speak to in this chapter are

  1. More ideas

  2. Unsticking existing ideas

  3. Strategic coherence in concept development efforts and a need to link strategy with innovation

  4. Managing and mitigating risks

  5. Innovating postlaunch

  6. Building innovation capability

- When staffing the work of innovation, it is best to think about the portfolio of skills and characteristics you want in a team. Think about a given team's cross-section and characteristics as a whole, rather than considering characteristics purely on an individual-by-individual basis. Avoid the "hero model" and think about the team of people who can assist you in achieving your specific innovation objectives.

- If you are having trouble clearly articulating innovation objectives or a design to achieve them, and/or establishing a shared leadership view about them, then adopting a structured approach to assessment and design might be your best path forward. Don't circle around the topics; use assessment and design as a way to move forward productively.

- Getting started and developing designs are areas where experience helps the most. If you are short on experience and uncertain or confused about how to get started, a little bit of experienced help (from inside or outside) will go a long way.

Conclusion and Looking Ahead 11

You know that innovation is difficult. As you've seen throughout The Guide, it is difficult because organizations are structured and managed to execute their current model, and innovation—particularly breakthrough innovation—focuses on creating the new. You seek to create new concepts for the core business, for adjacencies, and for outside the core. There are healthy tensions between a focus on the new and the critically important need to manage and execute today's business. Each is important, and each requires continuous learning.

Your innovation efforts require new learning and frame-breaking perspectives, as well as ongoing learning and iterative exploration. That is why a critical first step is the proactive development of new perspectives as inputs for creating new ideas and opportunities. It is why you should "just say no" to initiating ideation until you've had the chance to develop new perspectives on the market, your industry, and even your own organization to add to your existing perspectives. Give yourself the right to productively ideate by doing that work first.

You also know that although innovation is difficult, it is not impossible. Nor is its mastery limited to those unique individuals who are naturally gifted with creativity, foresight, and imagination. That is a myth. Through the example of the many organizations we feature, you know that you and your organization can develop sustaining innovation capabilities as a means by which to grow. You can make innovation a pervasive capability, if that is your ambition. Or you can improve existing efforts through a disciplined application of specific innovation tools, frameworks, and approaches.

Whatever your ambition, success demands that you think and act differently—not just about insights but also about each aspect of innovation. For example, one of our preferred idea development techniques—insight collision—is an approach different from traditional brainstorming and gives you a better chance to get to breakthrough innovation concepts and spaces. Domaining is a departure from the one-off, single-point-in-time innovation efforts prevalent in many organizations today.

You know that commercializing and scaling distinctive concepts demand that innovation remain inherent within your nascent concept and through to the back-end innovation process. They require much more than just taking the concept and executing it. You must stretch, elaborate, and iterate (SEI) the concept through a disciplined and structured thought process, bringing continued new learning on the "what, who, and how" of the business concept. You now have a set of frameworks and approaches to help you do so. Take full advantage of these techniques—these are business concept development tools you can use continually as you work idea after idea into an innovative, fully described concept that you can bring to the marketplace successfully.

You understand that you can do "innovation fast" in appropriate circumstances through techniques for framing short-form approaches to addressing targeted innovation challenges. The approaches vary, and they should be fit-for-purpose designs that explicitly acknowledge the trade-offs between your objectives and your constraints.

You also understand that in later stages of innovation, you can manage and mitigate risk smartly by focusing on the few, critical assumptions about which you have insufficient knowledge. You can de-risk promising but uncertain opportunities through a variety of techniques—most important, in-market experimentation. In so doing, you shift from merely assessing risk to managing it. And you can carry that practice forward into an innovator's emerging frontier: postlaunch in-market experimentation, whereby you continue to garner and apply new learning for fast-cycle concept iteration and optimization once you are in market.

You appreciate that there are ways in which you can create a surrounding environment that is welcoming to your innovation efforts, reinforcing and enabling your actions and thereby making it more likely that innovation will take root as a discipline and capability, if that is your ambition. With the support of leadership, you can make changes to the organization over time by thinking systemically and holistically. And you can initiate changes through a set of complementary, reinforcing actions to achieve the best results.

You know that it is important to ensure a shared and aligned understanding of leaders' three critical roles: that of cocreator, sponsor, and visible advocate. Leadership is critical to innovation's success and can take several forms depending on your objectives and the current circumstances of your organization.

You appreciate even more deeply the importance of designing your innovation work in an "outcomes-back" way and describing those outcomes as specifically as possible. Specificity helps you ensure that your designed approach will deliver the outcomes you desire.

Flexible, Reconfigurable Techniques for Addressing Innovation Challenges

Throughout The Guide, we share a menu of approaches, frameworks, and techniques for specific innovation challenges. As we've mentioned elsewhere, you should think of these as LEGO blocks of sorts, which can be configured in ways that are best matched to your desired outcome and starting circumstances. For example, you can apply front-end techniques to postlaunch, in-market innovation, and draw on the SEI techniques for initial concept development and later-stage refinement. These techniques are not rigid processes. In practice, not every one of your innovation efforts will run across the end-to-end innovation process. Consider the techniques in The Guide

> *Consider the techniques in The Guide as a flexible and reconfigurable portfolio of elements that can be used individually or in combinations that are fit-for-purpose for your particular innovation challenge(s).*

as constituting a flexible and reconfigurable portfolio of elements that can be used individually or in a combination fit for your purpose for a given innovation challenge. It is difficult to overstate the importance of viewing the material in this manner.

Because the techniques are flexible, developing the skills to design an innovation approach is critical. This type of skill is built through experience—you and your colleagues need flight hours. Find ways to log those flight hours. In an organization where innovation roles rotate in and out of the CoEs and the businesses, make sure you retain at least a small cadre of individuals with deep innovation experience. This way you can proactively transfer capabilities to the next generation of innovation leaders within the company.

In this context, we believe that you should have at least one person dedicated to enabling innovation in a full-time role. This person may rotate to other responsibilities over time, but the role should be maintained on a full-time basis. Avoid the mistake of short-lived innovation rotations and roles. It takes several years to develop mastery.

• • •

The imperative for innovation in your organization will not go away: the external environment is changing too rapidly. In this respect, the work of innovation is never done. The mechanisms for attaining and incorporating new learning into your innovation "system" or work efforts must be ongoing. If you stop, innovation will stop.

You are never fully "done" with your organizational capability-building efforts. Colleagues transition to other roles or leave the organization, and market and competitive forces shift quickly. There will always be capability gaps to close, problems and issues to address, and elements of your innovation system to refine or augment.

You will also never be fully done developing your individual innovation skills, because there are always new innovation frontiers for innovation practitioners to master. Just consider some of the practices and techniques that are highly prevalent today but were innovation frontiers not so long ago. For example, open innovation, which Henry Chesbrough advocated for at least a decade, has been largely embraced across a majority of organizations globally. By contrast, as we've noted in The Guide, postlaunch innovation is a frontier that we believe presents enormous upside potential for those organizations willing to try new approaches and techniques to explore it. Other frontiers include architecting networked and reinforcing ecosystems, as Apple has done so magnificently, and reconceiving the fundamental organizational structure of the industrial organization, as Gary Hamel advocates doing through what he calls Management Innovation.[1]

So you are never "fully done." You'll never "arrive." Don't ever expect to operate on autopilot. If innovation equals attaining new learning and then converting that new learning into new-to-the-industry actions (and in many cases "unnatural acts" for the organization), then how could you possibly put that kind of system on autopilot? It defies logic that you would.

● Be Alert for Common Pitfalls

As you strengthen your innovation capabilities, be mindful of some of the commonly held misbeliefs that we have flagged throughout The Guide:

+ **"Innovation is about tools and process only."** It's not about the tools; it's about the new learning. Tools and process are simply codified and organized scaffolding to help you get to that learning. At the end of the day, it's the new learning—process-enabled or not—that allows you to innovate. Think "skills more than tools."

+ **"Innovation is about technology only."** It's not about the technology but, rather, about the job the customer hires the technology to do. Technology may help and may even provide some advantage, but it is the business model design, particularly the customer value proposition, that helps you deliver on "jobs to be done."

+ **"Innovation is about ideas or creativity only."** If innovation equals a new idea successfully commercialized, then there is a lot more to innovation than just ideation or creativity. If your innovation work efforts and your innovation system do not take this into account, then you've severely hamstrung your chances for high-impact innovation.

+ **"Commercialization is about execution, not innovation."** Too often we hear a person say, "Once we get the new ideas, we know how to do the

You are never "fully done." You'll never "arrive." Don't ever expect to operate on autopilot.

commercialization." That statement assumes a lot—namely, that the new idea requires a commercialization model that is identical to that of existing offerings. This then begs the question, exactly how "new" is it? This misbelief implicitly assumes that there is little or no value in challenging the many elements of the prospective business concept and leaves a lot of innovation potential on the table.

The "we got it" view comports with a product- or technology-centric view of innovation. But that view tends to ignore many other elements of the business model, such as pricing, channel, and in-market support. You must think through and challenge all elements of the business concept, including its go-to-market aspects and actions. That's the way to widen the innovation aperture and enhance your chances of high-impact commercialization.

• **"Innovation can be delegated down,"** and leadership can be apprised once you have a good concept developed (or even commercialized). But trying to create breakthrough innovation without leadership engagement or involvement is a mistake. You may survive the mistake and succeed—but only infrequently. As we've stated throughout The Guide, leadership should be engaged in creating the points of view on both content (innovations) and the innovation system and process (capability). When they do that, the process gains traction. When they don't, you're doing it the hard way. Sustaining that mode of work is improbable if not impossible.

• **The work of innovation stops at launch.** Leading-edge innovators know better and do it differently. Google, Whirlpool Corporation, and others make proactive efforts and deploy mechanisms to perpetuate postlaunch learning and iteration to capture "upside" on opportunities already in market. This is where such innovators are leading in systematic and systemic capability. You should do so also.

● ● ●

We close with thanks to you, our reader. Too often, innovation happens despite the system, rather than because of it. We appreciate that your innovation work is difficult and at times frustratingly so. Although it is hard work, it can be exceptionally rewarding. You may be tasked with this work for a brief period, or you may decide to focus your career on it. In any case, your efforts are critical to keeping your organization vital and prospering. You can shape its future because you can create the future through innovation.

We hope that your work to drive the discipline of systematic and systemic innovation is as rewarding for you as ours has been for us. Enjoy the journey.

You may drive innovation work for brief periods, or you may focus your career on it. In any case, your efforts are critical to your organization's vitality and continued success

Notes

Chapter 1

1. The authors are grateful to Holly Green, who first introduced us to the notion of innovation IQ. See her article "Test Your Innovation IQ" in *Forbes*, December 6, 2011, http://www.forbes.com/sites/work-in-progress/2011/12/06/test-your-innovation-iq/.

2. Peter Skarzynski and Rowan Gibson, *Innovation to the Core: A Blueprint for Transforming the Way Your Company Innovates* (Boston: Harvard Business School Publishing, 2008).

3. "Henry Chesbrough's Top Tips on Applying Open Innovation," IdeaConnection (blog), December 14, 2012, http://www.ideaconnection.com/blog/2012/12/henry-chesbroughs-top-tips-on-applying-open-innovation/.

Chapter 2

1. Walter Isaacson, *Steve Jobs* (New York: Simon & Schuster, 2011).

2. Paul M. Johnson, *Creators: From Chaucer and Dürer to Picasso and Disney* (New York: HarperCollins, 2006).

3. "Why Is a Good Insight Like a Refrigerator?" WPP (2004), http://www.wpp.com/wpp/marketing/marketresearch/why-is-a-good-insight-like-a-refrigerator.htm.

4. Gary Hamel, *What Matters Now: How to Win in a World of Relentless Change, Ferocious Competition, and Unstoppable Innovation* (San Francisco: Jossey-Bass, 2012).

5. Yogi Berra with Dave Kaplan, *You Observe a Lot by Watching: What I've Learned About Teamwork from the Yankees and Life* (Hoboken, NJ: Wiley, 2009).

6. The sentiment is variously attributed to Body Shop founder Anita Roddick, Xerox PARC founder John Seeley Brown, and automotive innovator Robert Lutz (among others). See, for example, Geoff Ficke, "Great Businesses Are Built on Instinct and Vision, Not Focus Groups," EzineArticles.com, http://ezinearticles.com/?Great-Businesses-Are-Built-on-Instinct-and-Vision,-Not-Focus-Groups&id=2303106.

7. Jim Lovel, "The Story Behind Fridge Pack," *Atlanta Business Chronicle*, August 5, 2002, http://www.bizjournals.com/atlanta/stories/2002/08/05/story5.html?page=all.

8. Interviews with Crayola innovation leaders, June through August 2013; "Directed Innovation Mapping," in Business Leadership Forum, *Innovating the Business Model While Sustaining Core Performance* (Arlington, VA: Corporate Executive Board, 2008), 65–98.

9. Interviews with Crayola innovation leaders, June through August 2013.

10. Ibid.

11. Ibid.

12. In addition to the sources cited in note 8, please see Bruce Horowitz, "Crayola Draws on New Ideas as Crayons Make Room for 'Mess-Less' Toys," *USA Today*, December 6, 2006, http://usatoday30.usatoday.com/money/industries/retail/2006-12-06-crayola-revamp_x.htm.

13. Authors' interviews with Praxair Corporation innovation leaders, May through August 2013.

14. "Praxair Announces Launch of All-in-One Portable Medical Oxygen System," December 13, 1999, http://www.praxair.com/news/1999/praxair-announces-launch-of-allinone-portable-medical-oxygen-system.

15. Although the term *ecosystem* is a bit of a mouthful, the concept receives excellent treatment by these Forrester Research authors: Harley Manning and Kerry Bodine, *Outside In: The Power of Putting Customers at the Center of Your Business* (New York: Houghton Mifflin Harcourt, 2012).

16. Clayton M. Christensen, Scott Cook, and Taddy Hall, "What Customers Want from Your Products," Working Knowledge Series, Harvard Business School, January 16, 2006, http://hbswk.hbs.edu/item/5170.html.

17. Ibid.

18. Bennett Brenton, "Increasing Customer Empathy to Drive Growth and Innovation," presentation shared at the PDMA, Chicago Chapter Innovation Day Conference, Schaumburg, IL, September 27, 2013.

19. Interviews with Saint-Gobain Performance Plastics innovation and business leadership, May through July 2013.

20. Ibid.

21. Jean Angus, "Hack: Building Innovation Competencies Through Fit for Purpose Training," M-Prize, January 7, 2013, http://www.mixprize.org/hack/don%E2%80%99t-use-your-new-innovation-project-change-your-business-model-%E2%80%93-build-what-you-do-well-and-e.

22. Richard V. Kozinets, "On Netnography: Initial Reflections on Consumer Investigations of Cyberculture," in *Advances in Consumer Research*, ed. J. Alba and W. Hutchinson (Provo, UT: Association for Consumer Research, 1998), 25: 366–371.

23. Richard V. Kozinets, *Netnography: Doing Ethnographic Research Online* (London: SAGE, 2010), 10.

24. Doc Searls, *The Intention Economy: When Customers Take Charge* (Boston: Harvard Business Review Press, 2012).

Notes

25. Peter Drucker, *Innovation and Entrepreneurship* (New York: HarperBusiness, 1993), 35.

26. "An Interview with Gary Hamel," *Strategy and Business*, October 1, 1997, http://www.strategy-business.com/article/13304?gko=732a5.

27. Peter Drucker first applied this concept to business. Peter F. Drucker, *The Age of Discontinuity: Guidelines to Our Changing Society* (New York: Harper & Row, 1969).

28. Gary Hamel, *What Matters Now*.

29. Adapted from Gary Hamel, *Leading the Revolution* (Boston: Harvard Business School Publishing, 2000), 121–134. See also Peter Skarzynski and Rowan Gibson, *Innovation to the Core: A Blueprint for Transforming the Way Your Company Innovates* (Boston: Harvard Business School Publishing, 2008), 55–61.

30. C. K. Prahalad and Gary Hamel, "The Core Competence of the Corporation," *Harvard Business Review*, May-June 1990, 79–90. See also Gary Hamel and Aimé Heene (eds.), *Competence-Based Competition* (West Sussex: Wiley, 1994).

31. Drucker, *Innovation and Entrepreneurship*.

32. Gary Hamel and Peter Skarzynski, "Innovation: The New Route to New Wealth," *Leader to Leader*, Winter 2001. Retrieved from http://www.journalofaccountancy.com/Issues/2001/Nov/InnovationTheNewRouteToWealth.htm.

33. Ibid.

34. Gary Hamel, "The Concept of Core Competence," in *Competence Based Competition*, ed. Gary Hamel and Aime Heené (West Sussex: Wiley, 1994), 11–33.

35. Ibid.

36. Ibid.

37. Interviews with Saint-Gobain innovation leadership, May through August 2013.

38. Alexander Osterwalder and Yves Pigneur, *Business Model Generation* (Hoboken, NJ: Wiley, 2010), 14.

39. Ibid., 16–46.

40. The endowment figure cited is for 2013. Harvard Business School, "Supplemental Financial Information," *Annual Report 2011*, http://www.hbs.edu/annualreport/2011/financials/supplemental-information/; "Cost Summary," http://www.hbs.edu/mba/financial-aid/Pages/cost-summary.aspx.

41. Apollo Group, Credit Suisse 2013 Global Services Conference [presentation], March 2013, http://investors.apollo.edu/phoenix.zhtml?c=79624&p=irol-presentations.

42. GE Capital, http://www.gecapital.com/en/.

Chapter 3

1. For more information on innovation architecture, see Peter Skarzynski and Rowan Gibson, *Innovation to the Core* (Boston: Harvard Business School Publishing, 2008), 137–158.

2. Interviews with Ericsson innovation leaders, March through August 2013. See also "The Company," Ericsson, http://www.ericsson.com/thecompany.

3. See, for example, their strategy and innovation services group, accessed here, June 2013, http://www.ericsson.com/ourportfolio/services/business-strategy-and-planning.

4. Interviews with Shell GameChanger Group innovation leaders, October 2012 and August 2013. Also adapted from Rafael Ramirez, Leo Roodhart, and Willem Manders, "How Shell's Domains Link Innovation and Strategy," *Long Range Planning*, January 1, 2011. (Article can be viewed at http://www.sbs.ox.ac.uk/ideas-impact/insights-research/strategy-innovation/how-shell-links-innovation-and-strategy.)

5. Interviews with UnitedHealth Group innovation leaders, February through August 2013.

6. Interviews with Crayola innovation leaders, June through August 2013; "Directed Innovation Mapping," in Business Leadership Forum, *Innovating the Business Model While Sustaining Core Performance* (Arlington, VA: Corporate Executive Board, 2008), 65–98.

7. Ibid.

8. Ibid.

9. Skarzynski and Gibson, *Innovation to the Core*.

10. Adapted from Gary Hamel and C. K. Prahalad, *Competing for the Future* (Boston: Harvard Business Press, 1994), 107–122.

11. Horace Dediu, "Measuring the I-Tunes Video Store," asymco (June 19, 2013), http://www.asymco.com/2013/06/19/measuring-the-itunes-video-store/.

12. Horace Dediu, "Escaping PCs," asymco.com (April 16, 2013), http://www.asymco.com/2013/04/16/escaping-pcs/.

13. "Apple Dominates Mobile Phone Makers with 72% Profit Share Worldwide in Q412," *MAC Daily News*, February 7, 2013, http://macdailynews.com/2013/02/06/apple-dominates-mobile-phone-makers-with-72-profit-share-worldwide-in-q412/.

14. Horace Dediu, "What's an Apple User Worth?" asymco.com (June 14, 2013), http://www.asymco.com/2013/06/14/whats-an-apple-user-worth/.

15. Eric Mack, "iTunes Claims 25B Total Downloads, 15B Since 2010," CNET, February 6, 2013, http://news.cnet.com/8301-13579_3-57567928-37/itunes-claims-25b-total-downloads-15b-since-2010/.

16. The authors are grateful to colleague and friend Anthony Campbell for suggesting this example and providing detailed research and an initial draft illustrating it.

Chapter 4

1. Interviews with Ericsson Corporation innovation leadership, March through August 2013.

2. Interviews with Crayola LLC innovation leadership; "Directed Innovation Mapping," in Business Leadership Forum, *Innovating the Business Model While Sustaining Core Performance* (Arlington, VA: Corporate Executive Board, 2008), 65–98.

3. Ibid.

Chapter 5

1. Karsten Horn, "The Product Life Cycle Is in Decline," Digital Supply Chain (November 1, 2012), http://www.supplychaindigital.com/procurement/the-product-life-cycle-is-in-decline.

2. Yankee Group, "Apple's New Record: The Fastest Product to Ramp to $1 Billion," *Wireless Week*, May 5, 2010, http://www.wirelessweek.com/news/2010/05/apple%E2%80%99s-new-record-fastest-product-ramp-1-billion.

3. *CEO Succession Practices: 2012 Edition*, The Conference Board, April 2012. Available at http://www.conference-board.org/publications/publicationdetail.cfm?publicationid=2168.

4. "Average CEO Tenure Down, Turnover Expected," *NACD Directorship*, May 16, 2012, http://www.directorship.com/average-tenure-of-ceos-down-more-turnover-expected/.

5. Interviews with SORDAC innovation leaders, June 2013; internal documents.

6. Bill Shephard, "Science and Technology in Irregular Warfare," U.S. Special Operations Command (August 11, 2010), http://www.dtic.mil/ndia/2010specialmissions/2_Shepherdmod.pdf.

7. USSOC internal presentation reviewed by authors.

8. Osvald M. Bjelland and Robert Chapman Wood, "An Inside View of IBM's IdeaJam," *Sloan Review*, October 2008, http://sloanreview.mit.edu/article/an-inside-view-of-ibms-innovation-jam/.

9. Interviews with innovation leadership, UnitedHealth Group, February through August 2013, and internal UHG documents.

10. Ibid.

11. "PT and Innovation," Portugal Telecom technology & INNOVATION conference (October 29–30, 2012), http://innovation.telecom.pt/pt-and-innovation/innovationpt.

12. "Every Employee Is an Innovator: Royal Dutch Shell CEO," YouTube (May 18, 2012), http://www.youtube.com/watch?v=aULgVi4ESAw.

13. Interviews with innovation leadership, Ericsson Corporation, March through August 2013; Magnus Karlsson and George Kakhadze, "Everyone Innovates Everyday—Collaborative Idea Management at Ericsson," Management Innovation eXchange, July 15, 2011, http://www.managementexchange.com/story/everyone-innovates-everyday-collaborative-idea-management-ericsson.

14. Mondelēz International Inc. is the new name for a $36 billion portfolio of snack businesses formerly within Kraft Foods Inc. The remaining businesses of Kraft Foods Inc. continue to operate under the Kraft name.

15. Rae Ann Fera, "How Mondelēz International Innovates on the Fly in 8 (Sort Of) Easy Steps, *Fast Company*, February 7, 2013, http://www.fastcocreate.com/1682100/how-mondelez-international-innovates-on-the-fly-in-8-sort-of-easy-steps#1.

16. Henry Chesbrough, *Open Innovation* (Boston: Harvard Press, 2003).

17. "Open Innovation: What's Behind the Buzzword?" Accenture (February 3, 2012), http://www.accenture.com/us-en/Pages/insight-open-innovation.aspx.

18. Interviews with Mondelēz innovation leaders, May through August 2013.

19. Olive Keough, "Building from the Outside In," *Irish Times*, August 27, 2012,

http://www.irishtimes.com/business/sectors/technology/building-from-the-outside-in-1.543486.

20. Mike Hanlon, "Tassimo's New Micro Brewing Architecture," *Gizmag* (September 4, 2005), http://www.gizmag.com/go/4529/.

21. "Choosing the Right Partner: Kraft Foods and Bosch and Siemens Home Appliance Group Brew the Right Mix with Tassimo," Management Roundtable, http://www.roundtable.com/membership/quick-insights/QI_Kraft.

22. Keough, "Building."

23. Interviews with innovation leadership, Avery Dennison Corporation, February through August 2013.

Chapter 6

1. Stefan H. Thomke, *Experimentation Matters* (Boston: Harvard Business Review Press, 2003).

2. Eric Ries, *The Lean Startup: How Today's Entrepreneurs Use Continuous Innovation to Create Radically Successful Businesses* (New York: Crown Business, 2011).

3. Ted Greenwald, "Upstart Eric Ries Has the Stage and the Crowd Is Going Wild," *Wired*, May 18, 2012, http://www.wired.com/business/2012/05/ff_gururies/.

4. Ibid.

5. Interviews with Whirlpool Corporation innovation leaders, March through August 2013.

6. Ibid.

7. Moises Norena, "Whirlpool's Innovation Journey: An On-Going Quest for a Rock-Solid and Inescapable Innovation Capability," M-PRIZE (Management Innovation eXchange), January 23, 2013, http://www.mixprize.org/story/whirlpools-innovation-journey; interviews with Whirlpool Corporation innovation leaders.

8. Ibid.

9. Davis Freeburg, "A Virtual Happy Meal: McDonald's Redbox a Smashing Success," *Seeking Alpha*, December 1, 2006, http://seekingalpha.com/article/21558-a-virtual-happy-meal-mcdonalds-redbox-a-smashing-success; interviews with McDonald's Corporation innovation leaders, May through August 2013.

10. "The History of Redbox," Redbox, http://www.redbox.com/timeline; interviews with McDonald's Corporation innovation leaders.

11. "McDonald's Closing Vending Machines," *Washington Post*, November 14, 2003, accessed at http://www.synthstuff.com/mt/archives/individual/2003/11/mcdonalds_closing_vending_machines.html; Freeburg, "A Virtual Happy Meal"; "History of Redbox."

12. "Meal and a Movie Made Easy with Redbox and McDonald's USA," *Business Wire*, November 30, 2006, http://www.businesswire.com/news/home/20061130005105/en/Meal-Movie-Easy-Redbox-TM-McDonalds-USA; interviews with McDonald's Corporation innovation leaders.

13. "Redbox," http://redboxpressroom.com/factsheets/TheHistoryofRedbox.pdf; "History of Redbox"; interviews with McDonald's Corporation innovation leaders.

14. "Redbox," Wikipedia, http://en.wikipedia.org/wiki/Redbox.

15. Coinstar purchased 47.3% of Redbox in 2005. In 2009, McDonald's Corporation sold its remaining interest for what was publicly acknowledged to be $156–$180 million. Details on the 2005 transaction can be found at "Coinstar and McDonald's Ventures to Deliver Market-Leading DVD Rental Kiosks; Coinstar to Enter High Growth DVD Market with $20 Million Redbox Investment," *Business Wire*, November 17, 2005, http://www.businesswire.com/news/home/20051117005832/en/Coinstar-McDonalds-Ventures-Deliver-Market-Leading-DVD-Rental; and Amy Martinex, "Coinstar to Buy Remaining Stake in Redbox," *Seattle Times*, February 13, 2009, http://seattletimes.com/html/businesstechnology/2008738567_coinstar13.html.

16. Ryan Faughnder, "Netflix Rival Redbox Instant to Be Available on Roku This Summer," *Los Angeles Times*, June 6, 2013, http://articles.latimes.com/2013/jun/06/entertainment/la-et-ct-netflix-redbox-instant-roku-20130606.

Chapter 7

1. "About Search," Google, http://www.google.com/competition/howgooglesearchworks.html; Steven Levy, "Exclusive: How Google's Algorithm Rules the Web," *Wired Magazine*, February 22, 2010, http://www.wired.com/magazine/2010/02/ff_google_algorithm/all/1.

2. Eric Ries, *The Lean Startup: How Today's Entrepreneurs Use Continuous Innovation to Create Radically Successful Businesses* (New York: Crown Business, 2011).

3. Whirlpool Corporation's Moises Norena writes of a short-form opportunity framing tool that is similar in spirit in his article "Closing Whirlpool's Innovation Process with a Bow," Management Innovation eXchange, October 10, 2012, http://www.managementexchange.com/story/closing-whirlpool%E2%80%99s-innovation-process-bow.

4. Moises Norena, "Whirlpool's Innovation Story: An On-Going Quest for a Rock-Solid and Inescapable Innovation Capability," M-PRIZE (Management Innovation eXchange), January 23, 2013, http://www.mixprize.org/story/whirlpools-innovation-journey; Nancy Tennant Snyder and Deborah L. Duarte, *Strategic Innovation: Embedding Innovation as a Core Competency in Your Organization* (San Francisco: Jossey-Bass, 2003); Nancy Tennant Snyder and Deborah L. Duarte, *Unleashing Innovation: How Whirlpool Transformed an Industry* (San Francisco: Jossey-Bass, 2008).

5. J. D. Rapp, "Inside Whirlpool's Innovation Machine," Management Innovation eXchange, January 23, 2013, http://www.managementexchange.com/story/inside-whirlpools-innovation-machine.

6. Jessie Scanlon, "How Whirlpool Puts New Ideas Through the Wringer," *Bloomberg Businessweek*, August 3, 2009, http://www.businessweek.com/innovate/content/aug2009/id2009083_452757.htm; Tennant Snyder and Duarte, *Unleashing Innovation*.

7. Norena, "Closing Whirlpool's Innovation Process," interviews with Whirlpool Corporation innovation leaders, March through August 2013.

8. Ibid.

9. Ibid.

10. Moises Norena, "Whirlpool's Innovation Story: An On-Going Quest for a Rock-Solid and Inescapable Innovation Capability," M-PRIZE (Management Innovation eXchange), January 23, 2013, http://www.mixprize.org/story/whirlpools-innovation-journey; interviews with Whirlpool Corporation innovation leaders, March through August 2013.

11. Bill Brichard, "Herman Miller Designs for Growth," *Strategy + Business*, Summer 2010, http://m.strategy-business.com/article/10206?gko=9695a.

Chapter 8

1. Nancy Tennant Snyder and Deborah L. Duarte, *Strategic Innovation: Building Innovation as a Core Competency at the Whirlpool Corporation* (San Francisco: Jossey-Bass, 2003).

2. Ibid.

3. Interviews with Whirlpool Corporation innovation leaders, March through August 2013; Moises Norena, "Whirlpool's Innovation Story: An On-going Quest for a Rock-Solid and Inescapable Innovation Capability," January 23, 2013, M-PRIZE (Management Innovation eXchange), http://www.mixprize.org/story/whirlpools-innovation-journey.

4. Interviews with Assurant HR leadership, June 2013.

5. Interviews with Saint-Gobain Performance Plastics innovation and business leadership, May through July 2013.

6. Robert C. Wolcott and Michael J. Lippitz, "Whirlpool: Building an Innovation Culture (WHR)" (October 13, 2010), http://www.benzinga.com/life/movers-shakers/10/10/522393/whirlpool-building-an-innovation-culture-whr; interviews with Whirlpool Corporation innovation leaders, March through August 2013.

7. Interviews with UnitedHealth Group innovation leaders, February through August 2013.

8. Information and quotations in the Shell GameChanger case description and summary graphic are derived from interviews with Shell GameChanger Group innovation leaders, October 2012 and August 2013.

9. Tennant Snyder and Duarte, *Strategic Innovation*; Nancy Tennant Snyder and Deborah L. Duarte, *Unleashing Innovation: How Whirlpool Transformed an Industry* (San Francisco: Jossey-Bass, 2008); Norena, "Whirlpool's Innovation Story."

10. The following are sources for the Whirlpool Corporation case description and summary graphic: Tennant Snyder and Duarte, *Strategic Innovation*; Tennant Snyder and Duarte, *Unleashing Innovation*; Jan Rivkin, Dorothy Leonard, and Gary Hamel, "Change at Whirlpool Corporation (A), (B), and (C)"

(case studies) (Boston: Harvard Business Press, March 6, 2006); Norena, "Whirlpool's Innovation Story"; Moises Norena, "Closing Whirlpool's Innovation Process with a Bow," Management Innovation eXchange, October 10, 2012, http://www.managementexchange .com/story/closing-whirlpool%E2%80%99s-innovation-process-bow; and interviews with Whirlpool Corporation innovation leaders.

11. The following are sources for the Crayola case description and summary graphic: "Directed Innovation Mapping," in Business Leadership Forum, *Innovating the Business Model While Sustaining Core Performance* (Arlington, VA: Corporate Executive Board, 2008), 65–98; interviews with Crayola LLC leadership, May 2013 and July 2013.

12. The UnitedHealth Group case description and summary graphic are based on interviews with Innovation Leadership, UnitedHealth Group innovation leaders, February through August 2013.

Chapter 9

1. The authors are grateful to Gary Hamel, who years back first framed the challenges of an innovation "rhetoric reality gap" inside large organizations. "Interview with Gary Hamel," Emerald Management First, http://managers .emeraldinsight.com/change_management/ interviews/pdf/hamel.pdf. See also Peter Skarzynski and Rowan Gibson, *Innovation*

to the Core (Boston: Harvard Business School Publishing, 2008).

2. Nancy Tennant Snyder and Deborah L. Duarte, *Strategic Innovation: Building Innovation as a Core Competency at the Whirlpool Corporation* (San Francisco: Jossey-Bass, 2003); Jan Rivkin, Dorothy Leonard, and Gary Hamel, "Change at Whirlpool Corporation (A), (B), and (C)" (case studies) (Boston: Harvard Business Press, March 6, 2006).

3. Moises Norena, "Whirlpool's Innovation Story: An On-Going Quest for a Rock-Solid and Inescapable Innovation Capability," M-PRIZE (Management Innovation eXchange), January 23, 2013, http://www. mixprize.org/story/whirlpools-innovation-journey; interviews with Whirlpool Corporation innovation leaders, March through August 2013.

4. Interviews with Shell GameChanger Group innovation leaders, October 2012 and August 2013; Russell Conser, "Space to Free the Mind," *Strategy & Innovation* 6, no. 4 (July-August 2008); article can be accessed at http://www.innosight.com/innovation-resources/loader.cfm?csModule=security/ getfile&pageid=2520.

5. Interviews with leaders at United States Special Operations Command, Special Operations Research, Development, and Acquisition Center (SORDAC), June 2013.

6. Interviews with Shell GameChanger Group innovation leaders.

7. Ibid.

8. Russ Conser, Hans Haringa, Henk Mooiweer, and Wim Schinkel, "Shell GameChanger—a Safe Place to Get Crazy Ideas Started," Management Innovation eXchange, January 7, 2013, http://www.managementexchange.com/story/shell-game-changer.

9. Interviews with Shell GameChanger Group innovation leaders; Andrea Meyer, "Open Innovation Through Angel Investing," Working Knowledge, January 12, 2013, http://www.workingknowledge.com/blog/gamechanger-open-innovation-through-angel-investing/.

Chapter 10

1. Jean Angus, "Building Innovation Competencies Through Fit for Purpose Training," M-PRIZE (Management Innovation eXchange), January 7, 2013, http://www.mixprize.org/hack/don%E2%80%99t-use-your-new-innovation-project-change-your-business-model-%E2%80%93-build-what-you-do-well-and-e.

2. Quoted in Angus, "Building Innovation Capabilities."

3. Interviews with Saint-Gobain Performance Plastics innovation leaders, May through August 2013.

4. Ibid.

5. Interviews with Crayola LLC innovation leaders, June through August 2013.

6. "Directed Innovation Mapping," in Business Leadership Forum, *Innovating the Business Model While Sustaining Core Performance* (Arlington, VA: Corporate Executive Board, 2008), 65.

7. Interviews with Crayola LLC innovation leaders.

8. Ibid.

9. "Directed Innovation Mapping," 71.

10. Ibid., 85.

11. Ibid., 89.

12. "Directed Innovation Mapping."

Chapter 11

1. Gary Hamel with Bill Breen, *The Future of Management* (Boston: Harvard Business School Press, 2007); Gary Hamel, *What Matters Now* (San Francisco: Jossey-Bass, 2012).

Acknowledgments

In 1995, Gary Hamel first introduced us to the notion that innovation was a discipline that could be taught, learned, and applied. Since then, his thinking and writing profoundly shaped our approach to strategy and strategic innovation. We thank him and acknowledge his influence on our approaches to systematic innovation.

Other thought leaders pioneered concepts we discuss in The Guide. In particular we thank Professors Clayton Christensen and Henry Chesbrough for their contributions to innovation practices globally, and for their influences on the thought processes offered in The Guide. Stefan Thomke's early work led us to think more holistically about mitigating risk through experimentation; more recently, Eric Ries extended this thinking further with, among other frameworks, the Minimal Viable Product (MVP). We are grateful to Alex Osterwalder and his colleagues for making business model innovation tools and frameworks accessible to practitioners beyond academia.

We are particularly grateful to Nancy Tennant for her early encouragement to write The Guide and her many suggestions to make it practical and focused on the most critical innovation challenges. Thanks too for connecting us with innovation practitioners within Whirlpool so that we could learn and share their stories accurately.

In addition to Nancy, many colleagues and friends provided helpful feedback on our writing from beginning to end, including David Ankaert, Anthony Campbell, Ariella Gastel, Susan Goode, Carl Hamilton, Chris Jones, Jorge Latre, Pierre Loewe, Toby Nord, and Robert Vipperman.

The Guide is filled with details from several companies that illustrate examples of leading practice in a given area. Moises Norena, Nancy Tennant, Alloyd Blackmon,

Acknowledgments

and Barbara Rand were especially helpful in providing information and insight into Whirlpool Corporation's past, as well as ongoing innovation efforts. We also appreciate the willingness of Whirlpool Corporation to allow us to speak to their story.

Shell Gamechanger's Russ Conser will have retired by the time The Guide is published. We wish him well, thank him for his help, and compliment him for his multiyear leadership of Shell's exceptional innovation process. Thanks too to his colleagues who shared specifics on techniques and results that contributed to The Guide: Mathias Appel, Mandar Apte, Alison Falendar, Liz Fleming, Lorna Ortiz-Soto, Henk Mooiweer, Corey Radtke, Mike Reynolds, and Mark Verschuren.

Many innovation leaders from UnitedHealth Group (UHG) invested their time to help us make this book a reality. First and foremost, Brandon Rowberry shared ideas for The Guide and detailed specifics regarding UHG's innovation efforts. Brandon connected us with other UHG innovators who also helped us with the book including Ryan Armbruster, David Berglund, Meredith Baratz, Jason Goux,

Ben Kehl, Justin Ley, Todd Nielsen, Marty Nyman, Vidya Raman, and Jeff Shoemate.

We've known Ericsson's Magnus Karlsson for nearly two decades and are delighted to include aspects of his organization's innovation approach and success in The Guide. In addition, Magnus' read of portions of the materials early on was quite helpful in bringing greater clarity to our messages and descriptions.

Tom Kinisky and Jean Angus patiently shared detailed descriptions of innovation efforts within Saint-Gobain's Performance Plastics Division and, more broadly, shared their perspective regarding potential "new frontiers" for innovation within large global enterprises.

Mr. James "Hondo" Geurts was generous with his time and passionate about the urgency for and success of innovation with The United States Special Operations Command (USSOC). We thank him and his team in the Special Operations Research, Development, & Acquisition Center (SORDAC) for guiding us in sharing a few select examples of "innovation fast" within SORDAC.

The Crayola organization has an impressive history of innovation, and their most recent efforts offer compelling examples of disciplined innovation approaches and organizing actions. We hope we adequately describe their organization's impressive achievements. We thank Mike Perry and Sharon Difelice in particular for offering their perspectives and sharing the organization's story in The Guide.

Our thanks to Avery Dennison's Jay Gouliard, Bassam Hallak, and Judy Abelman for providing access to global innovation efforts within their organization, particularly their Brandfire techniques that enable "fast innovation."

Cathy Feierstein was kind enough to share some of their story of leadership development approaches and how innovation plays a role in those efforts within Assurant, Inc.

Praxair positively disrupted the medical gas industry through its Grab 'n Go® medical oxygen delivery system. Our thanks to Praxair, Inc., for sharing their history and impact.

Thanks to McDonald's CFO, Pete Bensen, for allowing us to share the Redbox® story and its genesis within the McDonald's® Corporation. McDonald's® former Strategy and Corporate Venture EVP Mats Lederhausen was especially helpful in ensuring that our description of Redbox® reflects accurately that concept's evolution from Post-it note to its current manifestation across more than 36,000 locations. Thanks too to Chris Catalano, former Chief Investment Officer for McDonald's® Ventures. Chris and Mats steered Redbox® from concept to its sale to Coinstar, and are currently scaling quite interesting businesses in Sterling Partners and BeCause, LLC.

We are grateful for advice and support of the publishing team at Jossey Bass/ Wiley: Susan Williams, Janis Fisher Chan, Kathleen Dolan Davies, Rob Brandt, Mark Karmendy, and Michele Jones. This team was enormously helpful in clarifying principles, techniques, and approaches throughout the book and keeping us focused relentlessly on ensuring that The Guide was practical.

Finally, our thanks to our families for their support and patience as we embarked on and completed this project—especially to Caren Skarzynski and Betsy Crosswhite for their input throughout. And as always, with great love for and thanks to our kids: Meghan, Luke, Mack, Jake, Sophie, and Greta (Skarzynski), and Wesley, Shane, and Jenna (Crosswhite).

About the Authors

Peter Skarzynski advises global organizations and their leadership on strategy, innovation, and organizational change. A frequent corporate and conference speaker, he is lead author of the global bestselling *Innovation to the Core* and author of numerous other articles on topics described in The Guide.

David Crosswhite is a senior advisor to CEO-level leadership within large organizations regarding their most significant growth strategy challenges. For over twenty years he has guided Global 1000 companies in structuring and implementing their transformation efforts in service of growth and innovation. He writes and speaks regularly on the topic. David resides in the Chicago area with his wife and three children.

Continue the journey: www.innovatorsfieldguide.com

Index